Evil in Mind

Evil in Mind

The Psychology of Harming Others

CHRISTOPHER T. BURRIS

OXFORD UNIVERSITY PRESS

OXFORD
UNIVERSITY PRESS

Oxford University Press is a department of the University of Oxford. It furthers the University's objective of excellence in research, scholarship, and education by publishing worldwide. Oxford is a registered trade mark of Oxford University Press in the UK and certain other countries.

Published in the United States of America by Oxford University Press
198 Madison Avenue, New York, NY 10016, United States of America.

Library of Congress Cataloging-in-Publication Data
Names: Burris, Christopher T., author.
Title: Evil in mind : the psychology of harming others / Christopher T. Burris.
Description: New York, NY : Oxford University Press, [2022] |
Includes bibliographical references and index.
Identifiers: LCCN 2021052610 (print) | LCCN 2021052611 (ebook) |
ISBN 9780197637180 (hardback) | ISBN 9780197637203 (epub) |
ISBN 9780197637210
Subjects: LCSH: Aggressiveness. | Cruelty—Psychological aspects. | Good and evil.
Classification: LCC BF575.A3 B79 2022 (print) | LCC BF575.A3 (ebook) |
DDC 155.2/32—dc23/eng/20220105
LC record available at https://lccn.loc.gov/2021052610
LC ebook record available at https://lccn.loc.gov/2021052611

DOI: 10.1093/oso/9780197637180.001.0001

1 3 5 7 9 8 6 4 2

Printed by Integrated Books International, United States of America

Contents

Preface

It's been over 20 years since I first created and taught a course called *Psychology of Evil.* As a quite new faculty member of the Department of Psychology at St. Jerome's University (part of the University of Waterloo, Canada), the course seemed like an odd-but-logical fusion of my research interests in the psychology of religion and my clinical interviewing experiences in a maximum-security prison. It was a happy coincidence that my course planning coincided with the release of Roy Baumeister's thought-provoking *Evil: Inside Human Violence and Cruelty.* That book has had a lasting impact on my thinking—and as the adopted course textbook, on literally thousands of my students.

With two more decades of human history behind us, the topic of evil seems no less relevant. But because there's been more thinking and (a lot!) more relevant research undertaken in that span, now seems like as good a time as any to revisit the topic from a psychological perspective. Before we launch into that, however, it makes sense to give you some idea of what to expect—and what not to expect—in this book.

The four chapters in Part 1 introduce what I suggest are the core principles necessary for understanding evil from a psychological perspective. In Chapter 1, I argue that people "diagnose" evil whenever they perceive that a person's behavior matches up with certain key features (sit tight—we'll get to them soon!). Chapter 2 explains why the mental jump from "evil" behavior to "evil" people is often a small one, and it also unpacks the assumptions people make about evildoers—for example, that evildoers are beyond reason or redemption. Given that our most negative reactions are typically reserved for those whom we judge to be "evil," we shouldn't be surprised that people often try to deflect that label if possible, so Chapter 3 delves into why being labeled "evil" can feel so uncomfortable. It also presents the menu of typical deflection strategies. Of course, trying to weasel out from under the "evil" label would be a lot less necessary if people weren't motivated to pursue a course of action despite its harmful consequences for others. Chapter 4 aims to offer you some insight regarding the mindset behind such choices.

Having made a case for the core psychological principles of evil in Part 1, I shift to a topical approach in Part 2. Each of those four chapters focuses on a specific phenomenon that many people might expect a book about evil to address—that is, hate, sadism, serial killers, and "organized evil" such as corporate corruption and genocide. My main goal is to show how Part 1's core principles play out in each of these specific contexts.

The brief Epilogue (otherwise known as Chapter 9) summarizes the main ideas presented in Parts 1 and 2. I also try to anticipate and address at least some of the nagging questions that may pop into your head as you read. By the time you're done, I hope you'll have begun to develop your own answers to the two biggest questions that reading any book of this sort should provoke: "So what?" and "Now what?"

Having laid out where you and I are headed in broad terms, there are a few more things that ought to be addressed. For example, one of my big challenges was to settle on the "right" writing style so that a broad swath of readers—psychology students, fellow academics, indulgent friends and relatives, and interested laypeople—would find this book both accessible and informative. As I hope you can see already, I've opted for a somewhat informal, conversational style when I can. Having said that, because this book takes a psychological—versus, say, a philosophical or theological—approach to evil, I've also tried to link the ideas I present to existing research when it seems relevant. That means that the writing will get a little technical sometimes. My hope is that unpacking how certain studies were conducted will help you better understand and appreciate whatever implications for the psychology of evil we might be trying to draw from them.

Because every research study has its limitations, it also has its critics. Some are quick to dismiss a study's findings based on some methodological detail or because the study's participants were "too ________" (few, similar to each other, etc.). For others, the dismissal seems more personal: "Well, that's not *my* experience." It's true that no single study—or set of studies—can give a once-for-all-time-and-all-people declaration of truth. But, by documenting trends and tendencies, research *can* tell us what certain people are more likely to do, and under what circumstances. And when trying to understand evil, I'd argue that that's *way* better than nothing.

At the same time, I'd certainly agree that it's beneficial whenever researchers can gather information from different parts of the world when trying to understand a specific phenomenon. That's why, throughout this book, I've made a point to identify the countries in which the research I discuss was conducted, and/or from which the authors hail. Unless the context makes it clear, you'll see those countries listed alphabetically in brackets wherever the work is first cited in a chapter. (Note that I use [international] when more than two countries are involved.) Although I limited my search to English-language sources and did not attempt to be exhaustive, especially when there's a ton of work on a particular topic, I'm pleased that I could include evil-relevant research from six continents in this book. Sorry for the snub, Antarctica.

I also included a few stories. Of course, the biggest downside of specific examples is that any one is likely to contain so many peculiarities that it's hard to generalize beyond it. In this respect, anecdotes are certainly of more limited value compared to the studies to which I've just alluded. Nevertheless, I know that a well-chosen real-world example can grab your attention . . . *and* engage your emotions. This is particularly important in a book about the psychology of evil. To be blunt, I need to make you feel at least somewhat uncomfortable. Otherwise, whatever I'm writing about will probably not seem "evil" enough. At the same time, I've made a conscious choice to present only the details necessary for you to get the point of a specific example. Beyond that is sensationalism, voyeurism, and ghoulishness—none of which, I would argue, helps you *understand* evil from a psychological perspective.

Before we launch in, I want to offer a big thanks to St. Jerome's University (in the University of Waterloo, Canada): Without the ridiculous privilege of a year-long sabbatical courtesy of SJU, this book never would have happened. Thanks also to John Rempel and Geoff Navara—both colleagues and dear friends—for the evil-related research collaborations and discussions over the years. Thanks to Ray Paloutzian for his unfailingly warm mentorship and encouragement. Thanks to Roy Baumeister for his 1997 book, and for feedback on early drafts of some of Part 1's chapters. Thanks to Nadina Persaud, Katie Pratt, and everyone else at Oxford University Press who made it possible for you to read this sentence right now. Thanks to my many undergraduate research assistants—most recently Tansyn Hood and Marina Vrebac—who have helped with collecting data and digging into relevant literature, and to those Psychology of Evil students whose interest and enthusiasm inspires me to keep on trying to figure this stuff out. Lastly, thanks to those who have loved me enough to encourage me to walk through the world with more mindful, thoughtful steps—if this book does any good for you as a reader, please thank them in your own mind as well.

One word of caution as we get started: The label "evil" is often reserved for people and acts that we experience as the most abhorrent and objectionable. Very rarely do we apply it to loved ones or to ourselves. Clearly, "evil" is a loaded term. As you read, it's therefore quite possible that you'll find yourself feeling smug and self-righteous when you agree with my interpretations, and indignant and outraged when you don't. When you find yourself experiencing reactions like this, I encourage you not to ignore them. Instead, *try to learn from them*. The very fact that people often have different understandings of, and reactions to, evil is one of the reasons why this book was written. We deal with this issue head-on in Chapter 1.

PART 1
CORE PRINCIPLES

1
What Is "Evil"?

"Why is there evil?"

That's a big question. And a very human one.

It's the ultimate intellectual puzzle for some, and pondering it can seem like an occupational requirement for theologians and philosophers (see Cenkner, 1997 [international]). For others—perhaps most of us—the question is more of an *emotional* puzzle (cf. Alford, 1997 [USA]). It is a reaction to observed suffering, be it others' or one's own. "Evil" can also enter the conversation when reacting to the observed suffering of non-human creatures, be it in the form of cruelty inflicted upon individual animals (e.g., Lockwood, 2004 [USA]) or acts that directly or indirectly hasten the extinction of a species (e.g., Biello, 2014 [USA]). Understood as an emotional puzzle, the "Why?" question can be quite accurately rephrased as: "Why did *this specific event*—as well as *all events that have made me feel the same way*—happen?"

Whether in its original or revised form, the question is honest, heartfelt, and legitimate. I get it.

But it's also premature.

First Things First

Before asking why there is evil, it is vital that we come to a common understanding concerning *what evil is*, psychologically speaking. To do so, we need to look behind the assertion that "I know evil when I see it" and ask *why* people think that they know evil when they see it. The answer is not as self-evident as you might think. Let's consider some possibilities.

Does "evil" = suffering?

The simplest, most straightforward possibility is that seeing "evil" is a response to *perceived suffering*. This may seem to work quite well when

Evil in Mind. Christopher T. Burris, Oxford University Press. © Oxford University Press 2022.
DOI: 10.1093/oso/9780197637180.003.0001

perceived suffering can be traced to the actions of a perpetrator. What if perceived suffering is the result of a genetic anomaly that makes a person abnormally sensitive to pain, or an accident spawned by an unforeseeable combination of bad timing and the laws of physics, however (cf. Schilling, 2021 [UK])? The suffering is no less real. And it is both lamentable and extremely unfortunate. But is it "*evil*"?

Does "evil" = inflicted suffering?

Consider another example: For many, the thought of watching a dog convulse after ingesting inadvertently spilled antifreeze is horrific. But contrast this with the case of an American woman who fatally stabbed her boyfriend's dog after months of forcing drain cleaner and bleach down the dog's throat. And who journaled about how pleasurable this course of action was (*Daily Mail* Reporter, 2012). Invoking the term "evil" seems much more fitting when coming to terms with the second versus the first example. Why? Because, in the latter case, the dog's suffering was the result of intentional behavior.

This seems to get us a step closer to understanding what evil is. That is, perhaps perceived suffering isn't enough. Rather, we also need to take into account how that suffering came to be, so perhaps evil should be understood as (the perception of) *intentionally inflicted suffering*. This was foreshadowed by the subtitle of the book you're reading, and it's congruent with Gray et al.'s (2012 [USA]) assertion that all moral violations can be seen as variations on the theme of *perceived intentional harm*.

Keep in mind that harm and suffering can be *non-physical* as well as *physical*. Thus, although death, pain, and disfigurement are obvious "evil" candidates when perceived as intentionally inflicted, so too are psychosocial scars resulting from intimidation, reputational damage, strategic economic disadvantage, and the like.

"Evil's" missing piece

But we've still not quite arrived at a clear understanding of what evil is, psychologically speaking. As Baumeister (1997 [USA], p. 8) put it: "Defining evil as intentional interpersonal harm leaves many gray areas." There is an inescapably subjective element when people apply the term "evil" to an act in question. Perpetrators, victims, their respective allies, and detached observers all have different agendas and different perspectives. Thus, even when intentions are clear and harm is severe, people's willingness to identify an act as "evil" can differ dramatically. Let's work through a simple example.

Ms. X killed two men.

Was this an "evil" act? Taking it to the next level, is Ms. X "evil"?

Although you may have made snap judgments, it's also possible that you feel reluctant to answer either question without more information. So let's see what more information does. Suppose that Ms. X believed that the two men she killed were attempting to take her young daughter away from her. I suspect that you would be less likely to label either Ms. X or her actions as "evil" under those circumstances. You might even think that she is a hero. In contrast, suppose that the two men had designated her as beneficiary of their ample life insurance policies. Under those circumstances, you would probably be much more likely to see Ms. X and her actions as "evil."

Now imagine that the two men in the first scenario were attempting to carry out a custody order after a court designated Ms. X to be an unfit caregiver based on a mound of evidence. Imagine that the two men in the second scenario were estranged family members who had subjected Ms. X to years of abuse. What happens to your "evil" appraisals then?

The important thing to observe here is that your appraisals probably bounced around depending on the specific backstory you were given. Critically, this may have happened despite the fact that *the same actor performed the same intentional act that resulted in severe harm.*

As a final layer of complexity, think about how your opinions concerning whether Ms. X and her actions should be regarded as evil might shift if you were Ms. X or one of the dead men's loved ones rather than a detached reader reflecting on a hypothetical situation. Is there a common principle that applies across the various contexts and perceivers that can help make sense of differing conclusions concerning whether Ms. X's behavior (and, ultimately, Ms. X herself) should be considered "evil"?

Yes.

Ms. X's behavior will likely be regarded as "evil" *to the extent that it is perceived to be unjustifiable* under the circumstances. People harm each other—often intentionally, and sometimes severely. "Evil" is relevant only when the reasons perceived to be driving such actions are judged to be unacceptable—which is itself often driven by gut reactions. Indeed, as Haidt (2013 [USA], p. 287) put it: "Moral reasoning is something we engage in after an automatic process (passion, emotion or, more generally, intuition) has already pointed us toward a judgment or conclusion. We engage in moral reasoning not to figure out what is really true, but to prepare for social interactions in which we might be called upon to justify our judgments to others." Chapter 3 presents a menu of basic strategies that people use to come to terms with their own harmful acts as well as sway others' perceptions of them. When those strategies fall flat—when no reason offered seems sufficient to offset the suffering experienced or observed—*there* is "evil."

With all of this as a backdrop, we're finally in a position to offer a psychological answer to the "what is 'evil'?" question.

"Evil" Is a Label

You may have noticed that I have consistently used phrases like "'evil' judgments" or "perceived as 'evil,'" and that the word *evil* often appears in quotation marks. These are deliberate choices intended to drive home the point that "evil" is a *label* assigned to behaviors rather than an inherent quality of those behaviors. That is, applying the "evil" label is a subjective process. "Subjective" does *not* mean "random," however. Rather, people are most likely to judge a behavior to be evil when they perceive three prototypic features. Specifically, the behavior in question is seen as (1) *intentionally* producing (2) *harm* that is (3) judged to be *unjustifiable* (see Burris & Rempel, 2008 [Canada]; cf. Gray et al., 2012, who similarly advocate a prototype approach when making sense of judgments of immorality).

Taking away any one of these three features decreases the perceived applicability of the "evil" label. Thus, if a person is convinced that the harm resulting from a behavior is relatively minor and/or unintentional, then the behavior is less likely to be labeled "evil." Likewise, if the reasons presented for the behavior are seen as "good enough," then the behavior is less likely to be labeled "evil." Rarely, if ever, will there be 100% consensus. At minimum, perpetrators themselves are often extremely reluctant to accept the "evil" label (you'll see why in Chapter 3). In particular, because harm severity and, to a lesser extent, intention are comparatively easy to establish, it is the *justifiability* of a behavior that most often generates vigorous disagreement.

This three-feature model of evil behavior formalizes what a number of other scholars have intuited, particularly with respect to the pivotal role of justifiability. For example, Winter (2006 [UK], p. 153, brackets inserted) observed that when "this label ['evil'] is applied to an act or its perpetrator, it is often also stated that the act is incomprehensible." McKeown and Stowell-Smith (2006 [UK], p. 110) poetically expressed the same idea, suggesting that the label's "most powerful significance is in exposing the hollowness of comprehension carved out by the acts in question. Thus, the marking out of behavior as evil indicates nothing less than our powerlessness to adequately explain: evil becomes shorthand for incomprehension." Dubnick and Justice (2006 [UK/USA], p. 237) equated evil with that which is morally inexplicable. Anderson (2006 [USA], p. 723) argued that evil is a fail-safe concept that people invoke to help explain (harmful) behavior that otherwise "doesn't make sense." Finally, Ruffles (2004 [Australia], pp. 115–116, emphasis added) suggested that "the concept of evil is much more likely to be evoked when confronted with an individual who understands the difference between right and wrong, yet proceeds to commit a heinously wrongful act without any clear motivation and which, therefore, *defies rational explanation*."

Govrin (2018 [Israel]) questioned the adequacy of the three-feature model. Armed with a series of thought experiments, he proposed instead that people detect "evil" when there is an "asymmetric" relationship between perpetrator and victim (that is, when there is a power differential) and when, with an "inaccessible" mind, the perpetrator adopts a derisive attitude toward a vulnerable victim and remains steadfastly remorseless for any suffering that the victim endures. Examined closely, Govrin's proposal overlaps the three-feature model substantially, however. For example, the "perpetrator" and "victim" labels respectively imply *intentionality* and *harm*, and a power differential—even if fleeting and situation-specific—simply allows harm to be inflicted. Moreover, "inaccessible" is Govrin's shorthand for judging a perpetrator's motives to be incomprehensible, or *unjustifiable*. The leftover bits (attitude toward victim and lack of remorse) concern the perpetrator: They are therefore more germane to understanding how people respond to perceived "evildoers" (see Chapter 2) than to understanding "evil" behavior per se.

Pertinent research is scarce but seems to support the three-feature model. For example, Mason et al. (2002) conducted interviews with forensic psychiatric staff in the UK concerning their attitudes toward the hospitalized offenders with whom they worked. Mason et al. noted that a shift from understanding patients' behavior in psychiatric terms to "evil" was signified by staff's use of terms "such as 'beyond', 'too far', 'incomprehensible', 'inexplicable' and 'beggars belief'" (p. 84). Alford (1997) asked a diverse group of

American interviewees—including retirees and incarcerated offenders—whether Nazi war criminal Adolf Eichmann was evil. Strikingly, Alford reported that almost two-thirds of his sample said that Eichmann wasn't. Non-offenders who maintained this position "used the 'just a cog in the war machine' argument: he didn't have any choice, he was just doing his job, if he didn't do it someone else would have, and he would have gotten himself killed for no reason at all" (p. 9). Offenders' justifications were less bureaucratic and even more cynical: *All of life* is a "war," and so everyone must kill or be killed.

Complementing these two interview-based studies is a questionnaire-based one by Quiles et al. (2010 [Belgium/Spain]). Over 300 Spanish university participants were presented with a variety of behaviors and asked to rate (among other things) how evil they thought each behavior was. Intentionality and potential or actual harm (that is, two of the three features of "evil") were arguably present in all behaviors. Most notably, *"evil" ratings went down as the perceived justifiability of the behavior increased*, even when the harm that resulted was comparably severe. For example, "Killing just for pleasure" averaged near the top of the "evil" rating scale, whereas "Killing another person to defend oneself" averaged near the bottom. Moreover, consistent with my earlier suggestion that perceived "evil" can be based on non-physical as well as physical harm, "Making a child anxious" and "Lying to obtain something at the cost of others" were both rated well above the midpoint on the "evil" rating scale.

Some Implications of the Three-Feature Model of "Evil"

In this chapter, I've made the case that "evil" is a label that people can apply to *any* behavior that they perceive to be *harmful*, *intentional*, and *unjustifiable*. This simple idea has a number of important implications. Let's look at some.

First, *harm severity does not guarantee consensus of "evil" judgments*. Because perceived intent and justifiability also have an impact on people's judgments, there's a fair bit of wiggle room. Take genocide, for example: It's probably at or near the top of many people's list of instances of extreme evil (which is why a chunk of Chapter 8 is devoted to examining it). Many of those who orchestrate and perpetrate genocide don't see it that way, however. To them, genocide is not evil, but good (or at least necessary). Why? The enormity of the task—intentionally inflicting harm on an entire group of people—requires not only much planning but also much justification.

Second, *it is legitimate to look for evil in everyday contexts.* That is, although stories of torture chambers and killing fields may shock and anger the world, perceptions of evil are not restricted to such contexts. For example, the television talk show circuit is strewn with disgruntled exes and estranged family members who describe the target of their animosity as "evil." Indeed, statements such as "they're selfish and hateful and they ruined my life!" point to a perceived match between the target's behavior and the three features of "evil."

Third, *the subjective nature of "evil" judgments creates tension.* For example, victims of especially cruel acts, along with their sympathizers, may feel that their suffering is trivialized when others use the term "evil" in more everyday contexts. After all, how can a domestic dispute possibly compare to surviving a massacre by hiding under a pile of bodies (cf. Miller, 2019 [USA])? On the other hand, those who feel exploited and victimized amidst difficult family circumstances may feel that such a comparison delegitimizes their own experience, and that they are entirely justified when invoking the "evil" label. In turn, individuals affected by both types of experience may look at some of my later claims—that many pranks are sadistically motivated and match the prototypic features of "evil," for example (see Chapter 6)—with skepticism, if not outright mockery: "Are you serious?! That's not *really* 'evil'!"

Clearly, the severity of harm resulting from intentional acts has a huge impact on people's judgments, and "evil" is most likely on the lips of victims. That doesn't undercut the three-feature model of "evil," however. Instead, it's entirely consistent with the model. I encourage you to keep this in mind as you read and react to the events and experiences described throughout the remainder of this book.

Looking Ahead

Although this chapter is brief, it is absolutely foundational for where we're headed next. Why are certain people, as well as certain non-human entities such as demons, labeled "evil"? They are seen as engaging in "evil" behavior—that is, behavior that conforms to the three-feature model (see Chapter 2). How do people try to avoid appearing "evil" to themselves and others? They employ deflection strategies that are mostly designed to portray their behavior as being inconsistent with the three-feature model (see Chapter 3). Chapter 4 lays out the general principles that help decode why people engage in "evil" behavior. Chapters 5 through 8 show how all of the above plays out even when the harm under consideration is extreme.

So now let's consider what it means to *be* "evil."

References

Alford, C. F. (1997). The political psychology of evil. *Political Psychology*, *18*(1), 1–17. doi:10.1111/0162-895X.00042

Anderson, J. F. (2006). The rhetorical impact of evil on public policy. *Administration and Society*, *37*(6), 719–730. doi:10.1177/0095399705282880

Baumeister, R. F. (1997). *Evil: Inside human cruelty and violence*. W. H. Freeman.

Biello, D. (2014, June 27). 3 billion to zero: What happened to the Passenger Pigeon? https://www.scientificamerican.com/article/3-billion-to-zero-what-happened-to-the-passenger-pigeon/

Burris, C. T., & Rempel, J. K. (2008). The devil you think you know: A psychology of evil. In N. Billias (Ed.), *Territories of evil* (pp. 13–28). Rodopi.

Cenkner, W. (1997). *Evil and the response of world religion*. Paragon House.

Daily Mail Reporter (2012, November 5). Woman "tortured boyfriend's dog for months by forcing it to drink bleach before slitting its throat." http://www.dailymail.co.uk/news/article-2227892/Sean-Janas-tortured-boyfriends-dog-forcing-drink-bleach-slitting-throat.html

Dubnick, M. J., & Justice, J. B. (2006). Accountability and the evil of administrative ethics. *Administration and Society*, *38*(2), 236–267. doi:10.1177/0095399705285999

Govrin, A. (2018). The cognition of severe moral failure: A novel approach to the perception of evil. *Frontiers in Psychology*, *9*, 557. doi:10.3389/fpsyg.2018.00557

Gray, K., Waytz, A., & Young, L. (2012) The moral dyad: A fundamental template unifying moral judgment. *Psychological Inquiry*, *23*(2), 206–215. doi:10.1080/1047840X.2012.686247

Haidt, J. (2013). Moral psychology for the twenty-first century. *Journal of Moral Education*, *42*(3), 281–297. doi:10.1080/03057240.2013.817327

Lockwood, R. (2004). Foreword. In L. Merz-Perez & K. M. Heide (Eds.), *Animal cruelty: Pathways to violence against people* (pp. ix–xii). AltaMira Press.

Mason, T., Richman, J., & Mercer, D. (2002). The influence of evil on forensic clinical practice. *International Journal of Mental Health Nursing*, *11*(2), 80–93. doi:10.1046/j.1440-0979.2002.00231.x

McKeown, M., & Stowell-Smith, M. (2006). The comforts of evil: Dangerous personalities in high-security hospitals and the horror film. In T. Mason (Ed.), *Forensic psychiatry: Influences of evil* (pp. 109–134). Humana Press.

Miller, E. D. (2019). Codifying gradients of evil in select YouTube comment postings. *Human Behavior and Emerging Technologies*, *1*(3), 216–222. doi:10.1002/hbe2.155

Quiles, M. N., Morera, M. D., Correa, A. D., & Leyens, J. P. (2010). What do people mean when speaking of evilness? *Spanish Journal of Psychology*, *13*(2), 788–797. doi:10.1017/S1138741600002444

Ruffles, J. (2004) Diagnosing evil in Australian courts. *Psychiatry, Psychology and Law, 11*(1), 113–121. doi:10.1375/pplt.2004.11.1.113

Schilling, M. (2021). A virocentric perspective on evil. *Zygon, 56*(1), 19–33. doi:10.1111/zygo.12669

Winter, D. A. (2006). Destruction as a constructive choice. In T. Mason (Ed.), *Forensic psychiatry: Influences of evil* (pp. 153–178). Humana Press.

2
"Evildoers": Who (or What) Earns the Title?

Are some people just plain evil? How do you know?

From a psychological standpoint, "knowing" starts with observation and ends with an inference. In the language of Chapter 1's three-feature model, whenever *unjustifiable harm* is seen to be the result of the *intentions* of an agent, then that agent is likely to be labeled "evil." Simply put, "evil" deeds are done by "evildoers."

At first glance, this may seem like an obvious, uninteresting statement requiring no more effort to deduce than looking in a dictionary. But there's more to it than that. Specifically, there's a pull toward the "evildoer" label that is built into the prototypic features of "evil" behavior. How so? People often try to justify their own failures and misdeeds—to themselves and to others—by pointing to situational factors. That is, they make what psychologists call "external attributions" when pressed to account for some undesirable outcome.

If "evil" behavior is unjustifiable behavior, then—by definition—it cannot be excused or explained away by pointing to the situation. But if people's behavior cannot be explained in terms of the situation, then what's the alternative? It must be something about *them*, in which case "they did what they did *because they're evil*" sounds like a good-enough explanation (cf. Ellard et al., 2002 [Canada]; van Prooijen & van de Veer, 2010 [Netherlands]). This is not a trivial matter, for labeling someone an "evildoer" (or, simply, "evil") activates a number of consequential assumptions and expectations about that person that we shall examine shortly.

Invisible "Evildoers"

Before doing so, however, let's consider "evil" spirits, because I'd suggest that some people's understandings of them follow the same pattern that was

Evil in Mind. Christopher T. Burris, Oxford University Press. © Oxford University Press 2022.
DOI: 10.1093/oso/9780197637180.003.0002

just described for human agents of harm. In other words, the three-feature model still applies. Now to be clear, the focus here is on how *some* people make sense of *certain* events. As a reader, you may or may not be able to relate—you could be coming from the perspective of an established faith, your own individual beliefs, or no faith at all. That shouldn't matter here as long as you remember that we'll be looking at *human understandings*, not metaphysical facts.

So when is a human perceiver most likely to conclude that unseen "evildoers"—that is, evil spirits—are operating in the world? Based on the three-feature model, three conditions must be met.

First, an event resulting in a negative outcome—that is, *harm*—must be perceived. Compared to those involving positive outcomes, negative events are more likely to grab our attention and beg for explanation (see Baumeister et al., 2001 [Netherlands/USA]). This makes perfect sense from a survival standpoint: The next good event won't destroy us, but the next bad one might. If we can understand why negative events happen, we might be able to keep them from happening, or at least minimize their impact, in the future.

Second, naturalistic causes *known to the perceiver*—for example, humans, animals, or environmental forces—must be seen as insufficient explanations for the harm-causing event in question. For example, suppose two people survived an earthquake that killed hundreds in their community. One holds a Ph.D. in seismology; the other has never even heard of scientific concepts like plate tectonics. Was the earthquake caused by the activity of "evil" supernatural forces? Which person would be *less* likely to dismiss this possibility outright? The idea here is that people may default to attributing *intentionality* to an unseen agent if they do not see other explanations as plausible. This idea was formally captured in Gray et al.'s (2012 [USA]) concept of "dyadic completion," wherein "otherwise inexplicable suffering should prompt perceptions of moral agency" (p. 111).

Third, as is the case with human perpetrators, an unseen agent is most likely labeled "evil" when the harm to victims attributed to the agent's actions is seen as undeserved or *unjustifiable*. Consider a story from II Samuel 6 in the Hebrew Bible: While pulling the cart on which the Ark of the Covenant (a designated dwelling place of the Israelites' God) was being transported, the oxen stumbled. A man named Uzzah reached out and took hold of the Ark, presumably to prevent it from falling off the cart. According to the storyteller, Uzzah's act violated divine protocol. Thus, even if well-intentioned, the act angered God, and so God killed Uzzah on the spot. In the eyes of the storyteller, God is *not* evil. Rather, God is righteous—or, at most, moody—because Uzzah's slaying was *deserved.*

The Uzzah story is apparently not an isolated example: Even in the face of perceived behaviors suggestive of narcissistic or antisocial personality disorder if a human did them (Varona, 2010 [USA]) or a seeming failure to protect the innocent (Burris et al., 1997 [USA]), believers often search for explanations that preserve the goodness of "God" the actor. For some, this takes the form of blaming Satan for negative outcomes (see Beck & Taylor, 2008 [USA]). Although research has shown that even highly religious individuals' explanations of hypothetical events seldom involve Satan and the demonic (e.g., Lupfer et al., 1996 [USA]), such attributions appear much more common in response to real events that have a devastating personal impact (Krumrei et al., 2011 [USA]; see also Ray et al., 2015 [USA]). Thus, consistent with the three-feature model, unseen evildoers are sometimes blamed for having intentionally caused harm that is perceived to be unjustifiable.

Assumptions About "Evildoers": The Myth of Pure Evil

Whether human or non-human and invisible, labeling an agent "evil" is a consequential step beyond simply labeling one or more of the agent's behaviors as "evil." In fact, Baumeister (1997 [USA]—italics below from pp. 72–74; see also Baumeister, 2012 [USA]) suggested that there exists a rather well-articulated stereotype of "evildoers." Dubbed the "myth of pure evil" (MOPE), this stereotype includes at least six core components. Let's consider how each relates to the three-feature model and informs our understanding of the consequences of labeling an agent "evil":

MOPE component #1: *Evil involves the intentional infliction of harm on people.* This should be quite familiar to you now, as harm and intent are two of the three features of "evil" behavior.

MOPE component #2: *Evil represents the antithesis of order, peace, and stability.* This is arguably an extension of the first component, for remember that harm can be psychosocial as well as physical. The "antithesis of order" is chaos, which can create uncertainty and anxiety. In fact, "destruction of order, chaos, and confusion" was the second most common characterization of evil among Alford's (1997, p. 12) American interviewees.

MOPE component #3: *Evil is driven primarily by the wish to inflict harm merely for the pleasure of doing so*. In other words, it is assumed that the harmful actions of the truly evil are often sadistically motivated (see Chapter 6). Alford (1997, p. 15) cited "pleasure in hurting" as the most common characterization of evil among his interviewees. From the perspective of the three-feature model, this should not be surprising: Whether declared or detected, sadistic motivation is unapologetically self-focused. Thus, it is arguably the *least justifiable* basis someone could have for intentionally inflicting harm.

MOPE component #4: *The victim is innocent and good*. In other words, from the perceiver's perspective, the victim does not deserve to be the target of intentional harm. Any harm inflicted on the victim is therefore likely to be seen as *unjustifiable*. Greig (1996 [Australia]) suggested that a narrative wherein an evil offender harms an innocent victim is a common way of framing episodes of violent criminality. She also noted that people struggle to force-fit some incidents into this narrative, however. For example, in cases involving children who have killed children, confusion and debate often center upon whether a child perpetrator could have foreseen the consequences of their behavior and appreciated its wrongfulness—if not, then of course the young killer would not be labeled "evil."

Note that MOPE #1 through #4 are essentially articulations of the three-feature model of "evil" behavior. Now let's consider the remaining two components.

MOPE component #5: *Evil is the other, the enemy, the outsider, the out-group*. Although this may seem obvious and almost tautological at first glance, let's reframe it slightly: Evil is located outside of oneself and one's inner circle. There are two complementary reasons why we would expect this to be so. First, it's arguably an easier mental task to construct justifications for harmful behavior performed by oneself and one's allies. After all, when it comes to what *we* are thinking, feeling, and intending, each of us as individuals has more direct access than does any other person. Moreover, each of us presumably has better communication and more familiarity with our allies than with strangers or enemies. Second, as we will explore in detail in Chapter 3, the psychosocial costs of being labeled "evil" are considerable, and so people have good reason to deflect the label away from themselves whenever possible.

MOPE component #6: *Evil has been that way since time immemorial.* This theme can be broadened, for although "ancient," "born bad," and "past the point of no return" all tap into different timeframes, they share a common understanding that the "truly evil" are *unchangeably* so. Thus, "evildoers" will continue to do evil—inflicting harm and creating chaos—and they will do little else. They will certainly not do good, and they will probably not do much that is mundane, either. That is, as Greig (2006, p. 149) put it, those who label evildoers become "blind to the strains of normality that invariably coexist with evil." For example, people may find it difficult to imagine a serial killer doing laundry unless it's for a sinister purpose like destroying evidence (see Winter, 2006 [UK]).

One of my students (Kular, 2021) tested this "evil through-and-through" hypothesis experimentally by having over 200 Canadian undergraduates read one of a number of brief descriptions of targets who "would [all] describe themselves as 'pretty average' in most ways." The three "evil" targets—who were depicted as having homicidal fantasies or feeling connected to the beliefs of either a terrorist organization or a hate group—were definitely *not* seen as average when it came to estimating how likely it was that they had engaged in a variety of behaviors in the preceding week. Compared to the "just plain average" target, people (especially those who believed in the MOPE) assumed that "evil" targets were more likely to have done bad things such as lying to someone or getting into an argument. "Evil" targets were also assumed to be less likely to have done good things such as picking up litter or donating to charity. Neither of those results should surprise you. Of greater interest, however, people also assumed that the "evil" targets were less likely to have engaged in mundane self-care activities such as going for a walk or (you guessed it) doing laundry. At the same time, "evil" targets were seen as *more* likely to have recently used public transport, visited a playground or crowded market, or built something. This suggests that participants interpreted the latter activities—benign in and of themselves—as being congruent with preparations for violence or other criminal activity. Indeed, follow-up analyses of open-ended responses confirmed this: Participants tended to list "bad" motives when assuming that "evil" targets had engaged in these behaviors recently, whereas there was no such link for the "average" target.

If evildoers are unchangeable, then it also follows that they're *beyond negotiation, rehabilitation, or redemption.* In the face of what is perceived as unrelenting malicious intent, protecting oneself and one's allies is a sensible priority. Consequently, it's not surprising that containing and eliminating "evildoers" are both seen as rational options. Consistent with this, the more "evil" Canadian undergraduates perceived a child sex offender to be, the more willing they were to express extreme hate toward him—for example, that death wasn't enough, because the world would be better off if every reminder of his existence was destroyed as well (Burris & Rempel, 2011). Webster et al. (2021 [USA]) demonstrated that people who believed in "pure evil" were so focused on dehumanizing and prescribing harsh punishment for an alleged mass shooter that they dismissed the possibility that a brain tumor could be seen as a mitigating factor. Staff who invoked "evil" and related language in reference to offenders in a UK forensic psychiatric facility tended to view these offenders' treatment plans as essentially for show but otherwise pointless (Mason et al., 2002). Ruffles (2004 [Australia]) argued that antisocial personality disorder and psychopathy (see Chapter 4)—clinical labels that capture pervasive, long-term patterns of destructive behavior—are essentially diagnostic proxies for "evil."

Clinical labels aside, how many instances of "evil" behavior does it take to make an "evildoer"—that is, to convince a perceiver that he or she is dealing with someone who embodies the MOPE? To the best of my knowledge, there are no data that address this question directly at the moment. Having said that, the three-feature model makes informed speculation possible: A single "evil" act is probably sufficient if both *perpetrator intentionality and victim harm are seen as extending through time.* For example, if a harmful act is believed to have been premeditated, if it took a while to carry out, and if the perpetrator shows no evidence of genuine remorse such as amends—these all suggest that the act occupies a "thicker slice" of the perpetrator's life and therefore speaks to who that person is at his or her core. Likewise, if the harm caused by the act caused long-term/irreversible damage, then the act also occupies a "thicker slice" of the victim's life and is therefore increasingly more difficult to *justify*.

Consistent with this analysis, Ruffles' review (2004, p. 115) led her to note that "[o]nly one Australian case characterised the very essence of the offender as 'evil'; in R v Dawson [2000] NSWCCA 399, which involved the sentencing of a music teacher for child sex offences, the trial judge viewed the offences as a 'demonstration of an underlying personality trait' that was 'so persistent, so repeated, so premeditated . . . that, indeed, I think it is fair to describe him as . . . 'evil.'" Note here that repetition (that is, multiple harmful acts) is another way by which a diagnostically "thicker slice" of time can be perceived.

The Myth Takes Form: Demons, Satanists, and Serial Killers

Having unpacked the MOPE at length and shown how it is shaped by the three-feature model of "evil" behavior, let's consider three extreme examples of how the MOPE manifests and affects people's responses to "evildoers." Specifically, we will focus on demons, Satanists, and serial killers.

Demons

Manifestations of "possession" by unseen entities appear across many cultural contexts (for a brief overview, see During et al., 2011 [international]). For our purposes, it is not necessary to address the question of whether possessing entities are real in a metaphysical sense. It is critical that we unpack assumptions made by those who believe that *demonic* possession is a genuine phenomenon, however, as these assumptions link to the MOPE and have significant consequences for those presumed to be afflicted.

The first, and foundational, assumption is that there really are unseen entities that can occupy a living human body and take over the person's physical and psychological faculties (cf. Bastian et al., 2015 [international]). Second, although not all possessing entities are evil, some are—and they possess a person in order to cause physical, psychosocial, and spiritual suffering. For example, based on their portrayal across a number of canonical and apocryphal Christian texts, Rosenberg (2007 [Canada]) observed that: "demons . . . seem to act on motivations that do not necessarily appear rational to human comprehension. They seem to have goals including the promotion of heresy and idolatry, committing homicide, perpetrating sexual abuse, and the general infliction of illness and suffering on human beings, perhaps on some occasions out of what might be seen as little beyond a sense of sadism" (p. 98). Further, "[d]emons deprive human beings of their lives, their social networks, their minds, and their humanity" (p. 99). Consequently, "[d]emons are terrifying manifestations of the ultimate evil, in the face of which human beings are utterly helpless" (p. 100).

Third, believers assume that demonic possession is discernible based on a menu of behavioral indicators. As was evident in Rosenberg (2007), many of these indicators involve *harm*, whether the possessed individual is victim or perpetrator. Finally, it is assumed that an "evil" possessing entity can be expelled from the human body it occupies via ritual exorcism, which typically employs a combination of words, symbols/objects, and actions (see Goodwin et al., 1990 [USA]). Note here the crucial importance of attribution: Unless an individual is "diagnosed" as possessed by an evil entity, *exorcism will not be attempted.*

Now here's the critical point: Because possessing demons are unambiguous examples of the MOPE, exorcists sometimes take a "no holds barred" approach. That is, in their attempts to free the allegedly possessed individual, exorcists sometimes utilize extreme techniques. Psychological trauma, serious physical injury, and death have resulted (for an extensive listing of cases, see Rosenberg, 2007, pp. 72–73).

For example, Humphrey (2015, p. 1667) summarized a number of UK-based cases compiled by Stobart (2009; see also Briggs & Whittaker, 2018 [UK]): "Essentially, one or more children in the family were blamed for bringing about the family's misfortunes. This assumed two forms—child witches were believed to have invited an evil spirit into themselves to enhance their own powers to wreak havoc on their families, whilst child victims were believed to have been colonised by an evil spirit against their will." Initially ostracized, the child would often be subject to increasingly severe physical methods of deliverance that included "rubbing chili peppers into bodily orifices on the grounds that these are repugnant to evil spirits; beating, burning or cutting the child to drive the evil spirits out of the body; and starving or semi-strangulating the child to deprive the evil spirits of nutrients and oxygen." To be clear, the relevant issue here is not whether evil spirits were indeed possessing the children. Rather, it is what parents were willing to authorize—and what exorcists were willing to inflict—when they framed the situation as a battle against "ultimate evil."

Satanists

A second application of the MOPE with significant real-world consequences centers on allegations of satanic ritual abuse (SRA) that surged into public consciousness in North America in the 1980s and 1990s (see Humphrey, 2015). Detailed stories emerged of bands of Satan devotees performing covert rituals that involved various combinations of animal sacrifice, sexual violation, and cannibalism. Children were often implicated as witnesses or victims. Authorities at all levels were accused of looking the other way because it was believed that they, too, served Satan. Forensic evidence corroborating the many SRA stories was minimal to nonexistent—and, indeed, often pointed to a different (albeit no less unsettling) narrative. For example, Humphrey noted that "many parents and [sexual abuse] perpetrators exploited children's beliefs in the supernatural by dressing up as horned beasts and ghosts during the abuse, which served the dual purpose of intimidating the children into submission and concealing the identities of the perpetrators" (p. 1666). Further, some allegations were proven to be outright fabrications that were subsequently retracted (e.g., CBC News, 2003 [Canada]).

De Young (2008) analyzed a number of American cases involving alleged SRA, children, and daycare providers using a *moral panic* framework comprising seven core elements. First, she argued that the *emergence* of SRA as a moral panic was based on the linking together of three "master symbols" that represented different facets of uncertainty and anxiety experienced during the 1980s. That is, children made vulnerable by shifting family structures, the sinister presence of the devil in the worldview promoted by conservative Christians, and increasing reliance on trauma as an explanation for negative life circumstances were synthesized into a narrative wherein children were being sexually abused by devil worshipers. Second, so-called *folk devils* were subsequently "recruited" to play the role of corrupting antagonists in the SRA narrative. Many were daycare providers, perhaps because they were the surrogates enlisted to fill in the gaps created by shifting family structures.

Third, *media* played a significant role: "Through the unrestrained use of such words as 'monstrous', 'grotesque' and 'wicked', and the untutored use of such diagnostic terms as 'psychopath', 'pathological liar' and 'pedophile', the media fleshed out the stereotype of the folk devil as quintessentially evil, and went on to depict the alleged victims as innocent and thoroughly traumatized, and thus worthy of more than just sympathy and support, but of rescue and protection" (de Young, 2008, p. 1726). Fourth, *moral entrepreneurs and experts*, whose motives "ranged from professional, to theoretical, to ideological, to personal, to material" (p. 1727), collaborated with media to intensify public outcry and calls for action.

Fifth, *coping and resolution* often took the form of legislation and/or prosecution that was more symbolic than evidence-based. This included new laws that specifically criminalized SRA (which implied that the extant laws for prosecuting abuse of children were inadequate). The accused were subject to lengthy, expensive criminal trials. Most were convicted and given massive sentences—and most of those sentences were overturned as, sixth (*fade away*), SRA was gradually recognized as a moral panic.

Seventh and finally is the *legacy* left by SRA. De Young (2008) argued that none of the problems fueling the anxiety and uncertainty of the period was addressed effectively by anti-SRA activists. Instead, "[i]n the quest to prove day care ritual abuse real, and therefore to justify their claims and activities, moral entrepreneurs and experts usurped children's autobiographies with relentlessly leading interviews, stressed families to the breaking point, tore apart communities, depleted coffers, ruined reputations and hardened attitudes" (pp. 1729–1730; see also Humphrey [2015] for a summary of UK cases during the same timeframe, and Tartari [2013] for an Italian case). The SRA trope has been invoked most recently by followers of QAnon, with suspect political figures serving as the latest folk devils to be targeted (see Miller, 2021 [USA]). Once again, as was the case for exorcists, the key point to note is the extremes to which people are willing to go when they believe they are fighting against pure evil.

Serial killers

As a third example of the MOPE, serial killers should also be mentioned briefly, as we'll tackle distinctions between fact and mythology concerning these individuals in more depth in Chapter 7. For now, the basic point is that, when mythologized, the serial killer is transformed into a sort of modern, secular Satan—complete with an array of not-quite-human qualities and powers (cf. Tithecott, 1997 [USA]). Having been a focus of popular imagination since at least the Whitechapel (London) murders in the late 1800s, the serial killer's "primary persona is that of an immortal and continually lethal presence" according to Caputi (1990 [USA], p. 4)—a "preternatural, enigmatic, eternal genius—[who] has become an ever more common figure in film and fiction" (Caputi, 1993 [USA], p. 102).

When portrayed as elusive and driven by unfathomable motives to destroy human life, the parallel between the serial killer and invisible evil entities becomes even more striking. Indeed, just as the serial killer's anonymity is a key element in avoiding capture, learning the name of a possessing demon is seen as a vital step toward a successful exorcism in many traditions (see Goodwin et al., 1990). And finally, just as Satan and his emissaries were often cast as antagonists in the good-versus-evil plots of medieval European morality plays, so too is the mythic serial killer sometimes now "a central figure in a confluence of apocalyptic narratives" (Caputi, 1993, p. 102; see also Knoll, 2008 [USA]). See Chapter 7 for a discussion of some of the potentially harmful consequences associated with mythologizing serial killers.

Branding "Pure Evil": The Evocative Power of Symbols

In Chapter 1, I made the case that judgments of the justifiability of intentionally harmful acts are often driven by gut reactions (cf. Haidt, 2001 [USA]). For example, many of you may have found it impossible to read about possessing demons, overzealous exorcists, child sex abusers, and serial killers without some mix of fear, anger, and disgust. Indeed, without such emotional reactions, it's an open question whether a meaningful concept of evil—and, by extension, the MOPE—would even exist. Alford (1997; 2006 [USA]) likewise emphasized the important role of (negative) emotion in evil's apperception. In particular, he discussed what he labeled "pre-categorical" evil: personalized representations in which a sense of *dread* figures centrally. For example, many of his interviewees told stories about "evil" that involved going down to the basement as children and *feeling that something was lurking* (see also Mason et al., 2002).

Two observations about these curious basement experiences are relevant here. First, the link between such experiences and the three-feature model of "evil" behavior is tenuous at best. In fact, it seems like the only way to make the link is by assuming that *the sense of dread itself* was the harm inflicted, intentionally and without justification, by whatever bogeyman was down there. Second, although interviewees could have offered a broad range of behavioral examples that better fit the three-feature model, they apparently thought that it was the raw, non-rational reaction to the basements of childhood that best captured what it meant to experience "evil" firsthand. By virtue of their ability, as simply "creepy" places, to evoke unease, the basements of childhood had arguably been transformed into *symbols* of evil.

The idea that a place or an object can evoke strong negative reactions based on its association with an "evil" agent was heralded by Nemeroff and Rozin's (1994 [USA]) early work on symbolic contamination. For example, they showed that many people would be reluctant to try on a sweater that had been previously worn by an "evil" person, even if the sweater in question had been laundered thoroughly. Clearly, physical contamination was not the issue. Rather, the contamination was more of a moral or spiritual nature: "Evil" people can infect objects with their essence.

Greig (1996) suggested that symbols and myths are more closely aligned with "fantasy-based" versus "reality-congruent" knowledge. With this as a backdrop, she observed that "[c]riminal events which encourage the use of the word 'evil' are out of the ordinary, seemingly bizarre, and *highly visual* in the sense that people generally try to recreate imaginatively what they believe has occurred, in order to contain both their fears and their perception of the level of threat" (p. 167, emphasis added). Consequently, she speculated that small details, such as idiosyncrasies of a perpetrator's appearance, can become a particular focus of attention when people construct narratives of "evil" behavior. In turn, these small details may be transformed subsequently into symbols of evil.

I've conducted three studies so far that offer direct experimental support for this line of reasoning. In one (Burris & Rempel, 2011, Study 2), nearly 100 Canadian undergraduates read a rather long description of a convicted child sex offender and his crimes. In one condition, the offender was portrayed as simply enjoying reading; in the other, he was described as being "especially fond of occult literature." This little detail made a big difference among those who regarded evil to be especially threatening: The offender who read occult books was judged to be more "evil."

In a follow-up study (Burris & Rempel, 2011, Study 3), over 100 additional student participants read about a group home worker who was portrayed as engaging in questionable (but not clearly inappropriate) behavior with residents. In one condition, his dress and interests were described as youthful but otherwise unremarkable; in the other, his depiction fit the Goth stereotype (e.g., dyed black hair, a skull ring, fond of horror movies). Because this individual had not clearly crossed the line with those entrusted to him, people gave him some benefit of the doubt, in that he was judged as less "evil" overall compared to the convicted offender in the previous study. Nevertheless, the pattern of results was the same: Among those who regarded evil to be especially threatening, the worker was judged to be more "evil" when he was depicted as Goth.

Although both of these studies clearly showed that appearance cues and interests seem to function as symbols of evil, at least among those who are especially sensitized to it, the results of a third (currently unpublished) study are especially noteworthy. In that study, approximately 80 Canadian undergraduates read a story about watching a shirtless man severely vandalizing a car. As in the previous two studies, there were two conditions: The man had a chest tattoo that was shaped either like a swastika or a "+." As you might have guessed by now, the vandal was seen as more "evil" when he had the swastika tattoo.

So what's going on here? In all three studies, the protagonists' association with culturally designated "evil" symbols appeared *voluntary*. Therefore, people may have assumed that such choices—getting a swastika tattoo, for example—tell them something about the kind of person that they are dealing with. Indeed, Burris and Rempel (2011, Study 1) showed that "evil" symbols make the MOPE more cognitively accessible: In a study involving nearly 150 Canadian undergraduates, those exposed to "evil" symbols such as the Sigil of Baphomet (Satanism) and "666" (Anti-Christ) scored higher on a MOPE endorsement scale created for the study compared to those exposed to either traditional religious or neutral symbols (see Webster & Saucier, 2013 [USA], for an alternate approach to measuring "belief in pure evil"). Once the MOPE is mentally online, people may use it to fill in the gaps concerning what a suspected "evildoer" is like—and, importantly, how they should respond to that person.

This helps explain one additional finding from the unpublished study described above: Not only did participants rate the car vandal as more "evil" when he sported the swastika tattoo, they also rated his behavior as more "evil." This is a big deal because *his behavior was absolutely identical in the two versions of the story*. On the surface, of course, this doesn't seem logical, but it makes sense if "evil" symbols activate the MOPE and evoke negative emotions. Under such circumstances, everything the target person says or does may be regarded with greater suspicion and disdain.

It's worth noting that some "evil" symbols are shared, often based on socialization from a very young age (see content analysis of feature-length Disney films by Fouts et al., 2006 [Canada]; see also Obiols-Suari & Marco-Pallarés, 2021 [Spain]). Marion et al. (2018 [USA]) demonstrated that film depictions of transformation from good to evil are often signified by the onset of a variety of dermatological conditions—in other words, bad character yields bad (evil?!) skin. On the other hand, some "evil" symbols—like a childhood basement—are undoubtedly idiosyncratic, possibly stamped in by one or more specific traumatic experiences. Once in place, however, symbols can function as powerful emotional shorthand. That is, their mere presence may evoke a gut reaction that can render three-feature assessments of a target's behavior irrelevant: "That person's evil . . . just look at 'em."

Bringing It Back (Too Close to) Home

We've spent a fair bit of time on "evildoers" and the symbols associated with them in this chapter. As a reader, perhaps you think that this has been an interesting intellectual exercise or, at most, that you have learned a bit more about when and why you might be especially likely to label *someone else* as "evil." After all, as Baumeister (1997) noted, people rarely see *themselves* as "evil."

Remember, however, that *any* behavior can be labeled "evil" if it is judged by a perceiver to match the three-feature prototype of intentional, unjustifiable harm. Recall also my argument that it's often a small jump from "evil" behavior to "evildoer"—and that the consequences of this label are often severe for the target.

This sets up a profound dilemma: All of us, at one time or another, will engage in behavior that promotes our own self-interest at the expense of others' well-being. It is quite reasonable to expect that someone, somewhere will perceive that behavior to be unjustifiable. Thus, *anyone's behavior can be labeled "evil."* Consequently, any perceived "evildoer" is potentially subject to unbridled punishment. The motive to sidestep the "evil" label is therefore most likely a powerful one. We'll examine this motive in detail in the next chapter.

References

Alford, C. F. (1997). The political psychology of evil. *Political Psychology, 18*(1), 1–17. doi:10.1111/0162-895X.00042

Alford, C. F. (2006). Talking about evil, even when it is not supposed to exist. In T. Mason (Ed.), *Forensic psychiatry: Influences of evil* (pp. 313–326). Humana Press.

Bastian, B., Bain, P., Buhrmester, M. D., Gómez, Á., Vásquez, A., Knight, C. G., & Swann, W. B., Jr. (2015). Moral vitalism: Seeing good and evil as real, agentic forces. *Personality and Social Psychology Bulletin, 41*(8), 1069–1081. doi:10.1177/0146167215589819

Baumeister, R. F. (1997). *Evil: Inside human cruelty and violence*. W. H. Freeman.

Baumeister, R. F. (2012). Human evil: The myth of pure evil and the true causes of violence. In M. Mikulincer & P. R. Shaver (Eds.), *The social psychology of morality: Exploring the causes of good and evil* (pp. 367–380). American Psychological Association.

Baumeister, R. F., Bratslavsky, E., Finkenauer, C., & Vohs, K. D. (2001). Bad is stronger than good. *Review of General Psychology, 5*(4), 323–370. doi:10.1037/1089-2680.5.4.323

Beck, R., & Taylor, S. (2008). The emotional burden of monotheism: Satan, theodicy, and relationship with God. *Journal of Psychology and Theology, 36*(3), 151–160. doi:10.1177/009164710803600301

Briggs, S., & Whittaker, A. (2018). Protecting children from faith-based abuse through accusations of witchcraft and spirit possession. *British Journal of Social Work, 48*, 2157–2175. doi:10.1093/bjsw/bcx155

Burris, C. T., Harmon-Jones, E., & Tarpley, W. R. (1997). "By faith alone": Religious agitation and cognitive dissonance. *Basic and Applied Social Psychology, 19*(1), 17–31. doi:10.1207/s15324834basp1901_2

Burris, C. T., & Rempel, J. K. (2011). "Just look at him": Punitive responses cued by "evil" symbols. *Basic and Applied Social Psychology, 33*(1), 69–80. doi:10.1080/01973533.2010.539961

Caputi, J. (1990). The new Founding Fathers: The lore and lure of the serial killer. *Journal of American Culture, 13*(3), 1–12. doi:10.1111/j.1542-734X.1990.1303_1.x

Caputi, J. (1993). American psychos: The serial killer in contemporary fiction. *Journal of American Culture, 16*(4), 101–112. doi:10.1111/j.1542-734X.1993.t01-1-00101.x

CBC News (2003, December 31). Judge rules child sex prosecution was malicious. http://www.cbc.ca/news/canada/judge-rules-child-sex-prosecution-was-malicious-1.365154

de Young, M. (2008). The day care ritual abuse moral panic: A sociological analysis. *Sociology Compass, 2*(6), 1719–1733. doi:10.1111/j.1751–9020.2008.00169.x

During, E. H., Elahi, F. M., Taieb, O., Moro, M.-R., & Baubet, T. (2011). A critical review of dissociative trance and possession disorders: Etiological, diagnostic, therapeutic, and nosological issues. *Canadian Journal of Psychiatry, 56*(4), 235–242. doi:10.1177/070674371105600407

Ellard, J. H., Miller, C. D., Baumle, T.-L., & Olson, J. M. (2002). Just world processes in demonizing. In M. Ross & D. T. Miller (Eds.), *The justice motive in everyday life* (pp. 350–364). Cambridge University Press. doi:10.1017/CBO9780511499975

Fouts, G., Callan, M., Piasentin, K., & Lawson, A. (2006). Demonizing in children's television cartoons and Disney animated films. *Child Psychiatry and Human Development, 37*, 15–23. doi:10.1007/s10578-006-0016-7

Goodwin, J., Hill, S., & Attias, R. (1990). Historical and folk techniques of exorcism: Applications to the treatment of dissociative disorders. *Dissociation, 3*(2), 94–101.

Gray, K., Young, L., & Waytz, A. (2012). Mind perception is the essence of morality. *Psychological Inquiry, 23*(2), 101–124. doi:10.1080/1047840X.2012.651387

Greig, D. (1996). Criminal responsibility and the concept of evil. *Psychiatry, Psychology and Law, 3*(2), 163–178. doi:10.1080/13218719609524886

Greig, D. N. (2006). Madness, badness, and evil. In T. Mason (Ed.), *Forensic psychiatry: Influences of evil* (pp. 135–152). Humana Press.

Haidt, J. (2001). The emotional dog and its rational tail: A social intuitionist approach to moral judgment. *Psychological Review, 108*(4), 814–834. doi:10.1037/0033-295X.108.4.814

Humphrey, C. (2015). Evil, child abuse and the caring professions. *Journal of Religion and Health, 54*, 1660–1671. doi:10.1007/s10943-014-9898-z

Knoll, J. L. (2008). The recurrence of an illusion: The concept of "evil" in forensic psychiatry. *Journal of the American Academy of Psychiatry and Law, 36*(1), 105–116.

Krumrei, E. J., Mahoney, A., & Pargament, K. I. (2011). Demonization of divorce: Prevalence rates and links to post-divorce adjustment. *Family Relations, 60*(1), 90–103. doi:10.1111/j.1741–3729.2010.00635.x

Kular, S. (2021). *Evil through and through: Lay prediction of "evil" individuals' everyday behaviours* [Unpublished honors thesis]. University of Waterloo.

Lupfer, M. B., Tolliver, D., & Jackson, M. (1996). Explaining life-altering occurrences: A test of the "God of the Gaps" hypothesis. *Journal for the Scientific Study of Religion, 35*(4), 379–391. doi:10.2307/1386413

Marion, T., Reese, V., & Wagner, R. F. (2018). Dermatologic features in good film characters who turn evil: The transformation. *Dermatology Online Journal, 24*(9), 1–8. doi:10.5070/D3249041411

Mason, T., Richman, J., & Mercer, D. (2002). The influence of evil on forensic clinical practice. *International Journal of Mental Health Nursing, 11*, 80–93. doi:10.1046/j.1440-0979.2002.00231.x

Miller, D. T. (2021). Characterizing QAnon: Analysis of YouTube comments presents new conclusions about a popular conservative conspiracy. *First Monday, 26*(2). doi: 10.5210/fm.v26i2.10168

Nemeroff, C., & Rozin, P. (1994). The contagion concept in adult thinking in the United States: Transmission of germs and of interpersonal influence. *Ethos, 22*(2), 158–186. doi:10.1525/eth.1994.22.2.02a00020

Obiols-Suari, N., & Marco-Pallarés, J. (2021). Does it look good or evil? Children's recognition of moral identities in illustrations of characters in stories. *Frontiers in Psychology, 12*, 1358. doi:10.3389/fpsyg.2021.552387

Ray, S. D., Lockman, J. D., Jones, E. J., & Kelly, M. H. (2015). Attributions to God and Satan about life-altering events. *Psychology of Religion and Spirituality, 7*(1), 60–69. doi:10.1037/a0037884

Rosenberg, E. (2007). *The representation and role of demon possession in Mark* [Unpublished master's thesis]. McGill University.

Ruffles, J. (2004). Diagnosing evil in Australian courts. *Psychiatry, Psychology and Law, 11*(1), 113–121. doi:10.1375/pplt.2004.11.1.113

Stobart, E. (2009). Child abuse linked to accusations of "possession" and "witchcraft." In J. La Fontaine (Ed.), *The devil's children* (pp. 151–172). Routledge.

Tartari, M. (2013). Moral panic and ritual abuse: Where's the risk? Findings of an ethnographic research study. In C. Critcher, J. Hughes, J. Petley, & A. Rohloff (Eds.), *Moral panics in the contemporary world* (pp. 193–213). Bloomsbury Collections. doi:10.5040/9781628928204.ch-009

Tithecott, R. (1997). *Of men and monsters: Jeffrey Dahmer and the construction of the serial killer*. University of Wisconsin Press.

van Prooijen, J.-W., & van de Veer, E. (2010). Perceiving pure evil: The influence of cognitive load and prototypical evilness on demonizing. *Social Justice Research, 23*(4), 359–271. doi:10.1007/s11211-010-0119-y

Varona, A. (2010, August). *YHWH: A structured personality assessment of the God depicted in the Bible*. Paper presented at the International Association for the History of Religion Conference, Toronto, Canada.

Webster, R. J., & Saucier, D. A. (2013). Angels and demons are among us: Assessing individual differences in belief in pure evil and belief in pure good. *Personality and Social Psychology Bulletin, 39*(1), 1455–1470. doi:10.1177/0146167213496282

Webster, R. J., Vasturia, D., & Saucier, D. A. (2021). Demons with guns: How belief in pure evil relates to attributional judgments for gun violence perpetrators. *Applied Cognitive Psychology, 35*(3), 809–818. doi:10.1002/acp.3795

Winter, D. A. (2006). Destruction as a constructive choice. In T. Mason (Ed.), *Forensic psychiatry: Influences of evil* (pp. 153–178). Humana Press.

3
The "Mark of Cain"

Why do people often seem agitated when called out for behaving badly? How do *you* feel when you're the one being called out? How do you deal with such situations?

The "First" True Crime Story

Cain and Abel. If you come from a faith, a family, or even just a culture that puts stock in the Hebrew Bible, you are probably familiar with the basics of the storyline in the Book of Genesis that centers on these two characters: Possibly motivated by jealousy, Cain killed his brother Abel. When confronted by God, Cain lied by professing no knowledge of his brother's whereabouts. God exposed the lie and announced the punishment to be bestowed: Cain would be stripped of his agricultural vocation and made a "restless wanderer"—essentially, rendered homeless. Cain lamented that the punishment was more than he could bear, and further voiced fears that he himself would be killed. In response, God marked Cain so that he would not be killed.

Multiple elements of this story point to principles that have broad implications for a psychological understanding of evil. This was the first recorded act of intentional interpersonal harm within the sacred text, and God's dialogue with Cain clearly suggests that God perceived the act as unjustified. Thus, for God, Abel's murder fit the three-feature model of "evil" behavior. God responded with total castigation, so that Cain was forced to give up his livelihood, his rootedness, and his access to God. Cain experienced the prospect of all of this as *unbearable*, and his expressions of concern about being killed clearly suggested that he also felt unsafe, perhaps verging on paranoia. That God subsequently marked Cain was not necessarily merciful, however, for although doing so may have kept Cain alive, it also reinforced his stigma.

Evil in Mind. Christopher T. Burris, Oxford University Press. © Oxford University Press 2022.
DOI: 10.1093/oso/9780197637180.003.0003

Elaborations on Cain's fate in apocryphal sources from the Latter-Day Saints tradition (Bowman, 2007 [USA]) bring in elements of the "myth of pure evil" (MOPE). That is, he is portrayed as "occasionally pitiable . . ., but almost always he is presented as more demon than man, twisted by evil, unredeemably subhuman" (p. 73). Moreover, according to Bowman, claims persisted into the 1990s that "big and hairy" Cain never died. Rather, he appeared in western North America as Bigfoot/Sasquatch—less demonic but more bestial, and still beyond the human fringe.

"Evil" as the "Mark of Cain"

In Chapter 2, I argued that it is often only a small jump from "evil" behavior to "evildoer," and that evildoers—incarnations of the MOPE—are judged without mercy. Add to this the fact that humans have a hard-wired need to belong (Baumeister & Leary, 1995 [USA]), so much so that rejection/exclusion is physically as well as emotionally painful (MacDonald & Leary, 2005 [Australia/USA]). With these things in mind, Cain's experience of his banishment and stigma as unbearable makes perfect sense: *Being labeled "evil" is the ultimate signifier of social rejection, equivalent to being branded with the "Mark of Cain"* (cf. Barry, 2013 [USA]). Thus, we humans have a legitimate, deep-seated reason to avoid being seen as "evil" when possible.

Although people are sensitized to the impact that others' judgment might have on them, they also carry internal audiences inside the head (e.g., Mitchell, 1994 [USA]). These internal audiences may function as a first line of defense against engaging in behavior that could result in being branded with the Mark of Cain. For example, Mazar et al. (2008 [Canada/USA]) showed that although many of their student participants were willing to cheat *a little bit* for monetary gains when the opportunity presented itself, doing more than this would contradict their own image of themselves as "honest." Mazar et al. also showed that reminders of moral standards—drawing their student participants' attention to an (actually nonexistent) honor code beforehand, for example—tended to eliminate cheating even when there were no explicitly objective consequences for violating such standards. Because there is at least a rough correspondence between self-appraisals by internal audiences and appraisals by external others (e.g., Leary et al., 1995 [USA]), it follows that *people usually don't want to see themselves as "evil," either.*

Deflecting the Mark of Cain

If people generally do not wish to see themselves—or be seen by others—as "evil," then we should expect them to try to deflect the label away from themselves most of the time. How do they do this? Let's look at the menu of strategies.

Moral licensing

One approach is to engage in questionable behavior only after having established one's credentials as a moral person—an effect that Merritt et al. (2010 [USA]) referred to as *moral licensing*. The idea here is that if one is "basically a good person," then one should be granted some leeway or benefit of the doubt when engaging in problematic behavior. Although research has demonstrated moral licensing effects with reasonable consistency (see Mullen & Monin, 2016 [USA]), it seems easy to imagine how this technique could backfire, especially when external audiences are involved. After all, how can one be *certain* that his or her moral reputation is solid enough in others' eyes to withstand the hit from engaging in behavior that others could perceive as "evil"?

Denying one's role

There are other options. For example, when external audiences are involved, the most obvious, least sophisticated technique to deflect the "evil" label is to *deny any role in a negative outcome*, epitomized by the child's exclamation of "I didn't do it!" If internal audiences are the focus, however, this technique requires greater sophistication, with a focus on recall. That is, in the aftermath of engaging in questionable behavior, a person's memory of the event needs to be either *absent* ("that didn't happen") or *distorted* ("that didn't happen the way you say it did").

For example, some television talk shows have routinely featured families in crisis. Not uncommonly, parents accused of severe abuse and neglect in years past by their now-adult children insist that such events never happened. The possible explanations for such discrepancies are few. The simplest, of course, is that the adult children's accusations are essentially accurate and the parents are blatantly lying. After all, from a Mark of Cain standpoint, admitting before millions of viewers that one has been an abusive parent could feel unbelievably risky. In other instances, however, adult children retract their accusations, sometimes based on their own emerging sense that their accusations are substantively false (see Ost, 2017 [UK]). But there is also a third possibility, a sort of in-between whereby a parent can state, truthfully and with conviction, that they have no recall of incidents of abuse that actually happened.

Lapses in recall apparently occur among victims as well as perpetrators. For example, Anderson and Huddleston (2012 [UK]) pointed to research suggesting a "higher incidence of self-reported forgetting for people abused by a parent than by a stranger" (p. 108). Inspired by this finding, these authors made a simple but compelling argument: People generally want to avoid negative experiences, and because many such experiences are rooted in memories of past negative events, people are often motivated to forget those memories. Because abuse by parents is, among other things, a bigger betrayal of trust than abuse by strangers, people may be more motivated to forget it.

So how does "motivated forgetting" work? Pointing to the robust experimental literature showing that people make use of inhibition mechanisms to override well-learned or reflexive behaviors, Anderson and Huddleston (2012) argued that (at least some) people make use of a similar toolset to deal with the prospect of unpleasant memories. Thus, people can *willfully interfere with the encoding process* in an effort to prevent memory formation. Failing that, they can *willfully suppress its retrieval*. Failing that, they can create a mental diversion by *substituting neutral thoughts* for the memories tagged as needing to be forgotten.

Although Anderson and Huddleston (2012) reviewed a number of lab studies (including some involving neuroimaging) that offered evidence of motivated forgetting, most focused on the forgetting of simple, innocuous stimuli such as lists of words. Nevertheless, Anderson and Hanslmayr (2014 [Germany/UK]) pointed to a small but growing body of research suggesting that motivated forgetting can affect (at minimum, distort) autobiographical memories as well. They further suggested that lab studies probably underestimate real-world forgetting effects when greater spans of time pass and self-focused motives are engaged. They specifically mentioned motives such as "regulating negative affect," "justifying inappropriate behavior," "deceiving others and oneself," and "preserving self-image" (p. 289, Box 4; see also "failure of integration" as discussed by Wainryb, 2000 [USA]). Note how the latter three motives in particular are consistent with a desire to avoid the Mark of Cain.

Anderson and Huddleston (2012) cautioned that, at least based on lab studies, the ability to engage in motivated forgetting varies across individuals: Some people are quite good at employing the techniques identified above, and some aren't. There are other techniques that can kill the past, however. For example, substance use may help make memories of an event's occurrence, or one's involvement in it, inaccessible (e.g., D'Argembeau et al., 2006 [Belgium/Switzerland]; Nandrino et al., 2016 [France]). Dissociation (i.e., directing one's attention away from one's usual experience of self or surroundings) may serve a similar function, although the results of relevant studies appear mixed (see Giesbrecht et al., 2008 [Netherlands/USA]). Nevertheless, the bulk of the research reviewed suggests that denials of wrongdoing can be *psychologically* veridical (cf. Stillwell & Baumeister, 1997 [USA]). That is, given sufficient motivation, ability, and time, some perpetrators may indeed be capable of stating—truthfully—that they *don't remember* doing whatever they stand accused of, even if such accusations can be substantiated.

More speculatively, there may be a third strategy for denying one's role in a negative outcome that is distinct from both the *absent* ("that didn't happen") and the *distorted* ("that didn't happen the way you say it did") strategies described above: Replace the actual event narrative with a completely different, benign one. Let's call this the *swapped* strategy ("*that* didn't happen—*this* happened"). To illustrate, some years ago on a television talk show featuring allegedly out-of-control children, hidden cameras showed a young adolescent girl stealing a planted necklace from a drawer inside a studio lounge room. Necklace in hand, the girl sat down and calmly said aloud to herself: "My grandma gave me this."

There was nothing in the admittedly limited footage to suggest that the girl was delusional due to mental illness. Perhaps she was simply rehearsing a lie to be told, as needed, to any would-be inquirers. Nevertheless, there is once again an interesting in-between possibility: It has been well established that at least some people can be induced by others to adopt false memories (see Belli, 2012 [USA]). By extension, perhaps it is also possible for such memories to be *self-induced*—a (false) story told to oneself. In the absence of attention drawn to contradictory (objective) evidence, such storytelling could appease both internal and external audiences. Indeed, von Hippel and Trivers (2011 [Australia/USA]) have argued that humans acquired the ability to deceive themselves because that makes it easier to deceive others. That is, whereas unmasked lies intended to conceal selfish behavior magnify the risk of condemnation by others, self-deception allows for advancement of an individual's self-interest *and* decreases the likelihood that the deception itself will be detected. Remember the saying: "It's not a lie if you believe it."

Of course, both obliterating memory of a harm-producing event and swapping it for a different, benign event are decidedly extreme strategies for avoiding the Mark of Cain. A more moderate—and probably more frequent—approach is to *dismantle the three features of "evil" behavior* (i.e., harmful, intentional, unjustifiable) when giving an account of one's involvement in a harm-producing event to internal or external audiences. Let's look at these three strategies, one at a time (for a different, yet overlapping, parsing of strategies of "moral disengagement," see Bandura et al., 1996 [Italy/USA]).

Minimizing perceived harm

As is so often the case in this book, "perceived" is a key qualifier. Sometimes structural factors and built-in limitations of human information processing obscure the potentially harmful consequences of our behavior, and so there's no push to minimize them. As an example of structural factors, consider humans' use of animals for food. The average urban dweller is far removed from the various steps involved in meat production, particularly the necessary act of killing an animal, so "chicken comes from the grocery store." Once children "connect the dots" concerning meat production, however, some choose to become vegetarian (see Bray et al., 2016 [Australia]). As another example of structural factors, Mazar et al. (2008) showed that people were more willing to cheat *to obtain tokens to be exchanged for cash* versus to obtain an identical amount of cash directly. Adding one extra step was apparently sufficient to nudge their participants in the direction of greater dishonesty.

Concerning the limitations of human information processing, people are generally bad at tracking gradual changes over time (cf. the "just noticeable difference": see Stern & Johnson, 2010 [USA]). Likewise, people are also bad at mentally modeling the cumulative effect of a large number of individuals' behaviors. Both phenomena can feed into good-faith underestimation of the negative environmental impact of one's choices, for example (see Goleman, 2010 [USA]).

Cynical overseers sometimes leverage structural factors and perceptual constraints to foster participation in, or quell objections to, large-scale acts of harm *by making the harm less discoverable* (see Chapter 8). But let's bring it back around to people for whom harm has not been obscured by factors or forces beyond their control. What might *they* do?

One way to reduce a blatant sense of the harmfulness of one's deeds is to *choose to engage in unethical behaviors that can be framed, at least superficially, as victimless.* Indeed, Ruedy et al. (2013 [UK/USA], p. 532) observed that "voluntary unethical acts without salient victims and obvious harm not only fail to elicit negative affect but may actually evoke positive affect"—an effect that they dubbed the "cheater's high." Of course, the effectiveness of this technique depends upon people's ability to convince themselves and others that their behaviors are indeed comparatively harmless. For example, fraudulently withholding owed taxes may not seem like a big deal, especially given people's previously noted tendency to underestimate the collective impact of many individuals' choices, *unless* one explicitly acknowledges that tax cheating means less available funding for advancing the common good, including society's most vulnerable.

Another technique for reducing the salience of potentially harmful consequences of one's behavior is *preemptively redirecting one's attention.* Typically, takes the form of a *concrete, short-term* focus. Unlike a more long-term, abstract focus, a here-and-now focus psychologically unhooks a specific act from the causal chains that imply that one's act could have negative, and potentially long-lasting, consequences for others (cf. Baumeister's, 1997 [USA], concepts of "low-level thinking" and "elastic timeframe"). Telling thoughts include: "I may never get another chance like this" and "Nobody will ever find out."

Two other harm-related options are victim-focused. First, the target of harm can be depicted (within one's own mind and/or to others) as being relatively *incapable of experiencing pain* (e.g., Gray & Wegner, 2009 [USA])—the idea being that *harm without suffering* is less problematic. For example, the inferred incapacity to feel pain among non-human species such as fish is a central factor in defining their ethical treatment (Key, 2016 [Australia]; see also Xu et al., 2009 [China], who found neural evidence that both Chinese and Caucasian individuals experience less empathic pain in response to pain experienced by outgroup versus ingroup members).

Second, a perpetrator can go a step further in his or her attempt to minimize perceived harm. Specifically, *active reversal* is a framing strategy wherein the supposed "victims" are not, in fact, victims. That is, they did not suffer or experience other negative consequences, but instead may have experienced pleasure and other positive consequences. Active reversal is often evident among individuals who commit sex offenses against children. Indeed, in their influential theoretical work, Ward and Keenan (1999 [Australia/New Zealand]) identified minimization of harm to (child) victims as one of the orienting assumptions that help initiate and sustain offenders' behavior (see also Gannon et al., 2007 [New Zealand/UK]). For example, one of Sullivan and Sheehan's (2016 [UK/USA]) interviewees who molested his infant son and posted images of the abuse online stated: "I didn't want to, as I saw it, hurt or harm anybody and he was young enough that I figured he would have no memory of it, therefore there would be no harm in it" (p. 83). Another interviewee who had paid pimps for access to children declared: "I'm not hurting anybody. I never penetrated a child. I never broke a hymen. I never did things that would cause pain. So I said I'm justified I'm not causing them pain. They are enjoying what they are doing and so there is nothing wrong with this" (p. 82). Harm minimization has also been observed in other male offender samples from the UK (Kettleborough & Merdian, 2017), as well as from Canada (Nunes & Jung, 2012), Japan (Katsuta & Hazama, 2016), and the Netherlands (Hempel et al., 2015). It has also been noted among females who have offended against children (Gannon & Alleyne, 2013 [UK]) and males who have offended against adults (Scully & Marolla, 1984 [USA]).

So we see that the possible contributors to reduced harm salience span a rather wide continuum—from structural and perceptual factors beyond an individual's control to preemptive choices and real-time framing techniques that an individual marshals during and after engaging in a harmful act. Reduced harm salience is arguably a notable contributor to the "magnitude gap" previously described by Baumeister (1997), wherein the import of a harm-causing incident is typically experienced as much greater by victims versus perpetrators. (For a comparison of victim and perpetrator accounts offered by children in conflict situations, see Wainryb et al., 2005 [Canada/USA].)

Decreasing perceived intent

Sometimes the magnitude of victim harm (whether forecast or post hoc) cannot be minimized sufficiently to deflect the Mark of Cain by the means described in the previous section. In such cases, it may be possible for individuals to *decrease their sense of agency* (e.g., Morsella et al., 2011 [USA])—that is, the sense that "I am in control of my behavior"—in the midst of an event that has harmful outcomes.

For example, Chapman and Maclean (2015) reviewed a number of Canadian criminal cases involving defense claims that serious offenses, including sexual assault and murder, occurred when the accused was in a state of *automatism*, or "involuntary conduct resulting from some form of impaired consciousness" (McSherry, 2003 [Australia], p. 587). Such impairment appears to be linked often to parasomnias—atypical sleep states wherein individuals are capable of performing relatively complex behavioral sequences such as walking, eating, driving, and even sexual activity (e.g., Andersen et al., 2007 [Brazil/Canada]; Cicolin et al., 2011 [Italy]; Shapiro et al., 2003 [Canada])—while in a state that has been described as "not quite wakefulness and not quite sleep" (Pressman et al., 2007 [USA], p. 199).

Typically, defendants whose offenses are deduced to have occurred in a state of automatism are found to be not criminally responsible, and therefore not subject to punishment. This makes sense from a prototype perspective, in that the intentionality feature of behavior judged to be "evil" is absent. Pressman et al. (2007) argued that bona fide cases of automatism-induced criminal behavior are quite rare, however, and based on their review of the relevant medical literature, they were particularly skeptical of legal defenses claiming automatisms triggered by excessive alcohol use. Indeed, they noted that a "conservative estimate would be that alcohol alone is five million times more likely than sleepwalking or confusional arousals to be the cause of violent behavior" (p. 210). They further argued that if an individual believes that substance use has triggered past parasomnic episodes, that person should be considered reckless or negligent if an offense episode in question was preceded by substance use.

This legal argument points to a key issue here—that is, the extent to which individuals can *self-induce* states of automatism through chemical or other means. A suggestive, albeit indirect, case can be made for chemical means. Specifically, Droutman et al. (2015 [USA]) reviewed neuroimaging studies showing evidence of structural damage to the insula, as well as decreased insular function during decision-making tasks, among substance abusers. In turn, the insula has been linked to a sense of agency (Sperduti et al., 2011

[France]). Thus, it seems plausible that substance use, via its impact on the insula, could lead to a decreased sense of agency during the commission of a harmful act.

In addition, although the mechanisms responsible deserve much additional research, neuroimaging studies have gone a long way toward establishing that the effects of hypnosis—for at least some individuals, some of the time—are real (see Oakley & Halligan, 2013 [UK]). This is important here for two reasons. First, a central feature of what are regarded as the "classical suggestion effects" of hypnosis—including alterations in beliefs, perceptions, and (importantly) behavior—is that they are experienced as *involuntary*. Second, autohypnosis or self-hypnosis is not merely possible, but arguably foundational to hypnotic effects even when an external agent is the designated hypnotist (see Oakley, 1999 [UK]). Thus, it seems plausible that individuals with the capacity for self-hypnosis could preemptively will themselves toward experiencing their own harmful behavior as automatic or perhaps even controlled by an external force (such as a demon, for example). The experience of automaticity may be especially strong when highly hypnotizable individuals also have dissociative tendencies (see Terhune et al., 2016 [international]). Given that the latter have been linked to a propensity for violence across a wide variety of populations (Moskowitz, 2004 [New Zealand]), the role of dissociation as a potentiator of self-induced states of automaticity seems especially noteworthy.

Although phenomena such as automatism and self-hypnosis may seem exotic and fascinating, the human tendency to distance oneself from negative outcomes typically manifests in much more mundane ways. Some such manifestations are rooted in the "temporal binding" effect. This small perceived gap in time between an intended behavior and a real-world outcome has been convincingly linked to humans' sense of agency (see Moore & Obhi, 2012 [Canada/UK], for a review). With this in mind, consider results from a pair of remarkable studies by Yoshie and Haggard (2013 [Japan/UK]): Over a number of trials while watching an onscreen timer, people heard either negative (angry or disgusted voices), positive (approving or amused voices), or neutral sounds (simple tones) after pressing a computer key. People tended to perceive a greater time gap between their key presses and negative sounds (that is, they showed less temporal binding) compared to when positive or neutral sounds followed their key presses.

These results speak directly to the Mark of Cain phenomenon as described: The tendency to downplay one's own sense of intentionality in response to others' negative reactions (like the angry or disgusted voices used in these studies) may be the default. Moreover, given the tiny spans of time involved the observed effect (a few milliseconds more, on average), this tendency is quite possibly reflexive. To be sure, parasomnias, chemicals, and willful dissociation may produce more dramatic effects, but they may not differ in kind all that much.

Invoking justifications

Minimizing perceived harm and decreasing perceived intent may work for *internal* audiences at least some of the time, but both are hard sells for *external* audiences. For victims especially, the magnitude and persistence of harm may be impossible to ignore. Likewise, perpetrators' claims of a nonexistent sense of agency during the commission of a harmful act may fail to impress listeners. Indeed, the [agency → behavior → outcome] sequence seems intuitive for most people, especially when outcomes are judged to be negative (Gray et al., 2012 [USA]). American television personality Judge Judy summed this up nicely in her catchphrase "don't pee on my leg and tell me it's raining" (Sheindlin, 1996).

Remember that intentional harm minus adequate justification perfectly matches the prototypic features of "evil" behavior. Indeed, at the extreme, such behavior is likely to be perceived as consistent with the MOPE: It is done "for shits and giggles." That is, it is gratuitous and sadistic (see Chapter 6). If people don't want to be seen—or see themselves—as "evil," then they should be motivated to justify their behavior when perceptions of harm and intent are not open to negotiation. *Invoking justifications* is thus the fail-safe for deflecting the Mark of Cain.

In fact, Henriques (2003 [USA]) made the bold claim that humans are justifying organisms—that is, that our self-awareness arose in response to the demand to justify our behavior to each other. According to this perspective, a justification is not a dispassionate explanation to a dispassionate audience. Different explanations have different social consequences, and so humans are more like defense attorneys than court reporters. That is, their goal is to generate explanations for defendants' (that is, their own) behavior that are simultaneously plausible *and* benign, at least ideally. Of course, a plausible explanation is not necessarily a truthful one. For example, people may be consciously aware that they harbor selfish or malevolent motives but disavow them, or they may not be able to pinpoint with confidence their actual motives. At the same time, dishonesty in and of itself does not invariably result in censure: Lying is sometimes seen as more moral than telling the truth, at least when it is perceived as emerging from benevolent rather than selfish intentions (Levine & Schweitzer, 2014 [USA]).

Remember my suggestion that people's actions are subject to evaluation by internal as well as external audiences? If this is true, then justifications for behaviors perceived as intentional and harmful must be directed to one or both. Depending on the audience and on the specific circumstances, justifications may range from *good reasons* to *good enough reasons* (cf. Malle et al.'s, 2014 [USA], model of blame). Let's look at these.

"I am good"

Employing *good reasons* is intended to create maximum distance between oneself and the Mark of Cain. The basic principle is to frame the harmful act as being *in the service of a greater good that transcends both the actor and the target.*

Consider the case of an American woman who attempted online solicitation of a hitman to kill a random person wearing fur in order to make a statement concerning animal rights (Lewin, 2012). Clearly, she perceived protecting animals as the *right* thing to do. Her *moral conviction* fueled the perceived import and urgency to further her cause. Moreover—and of greatest importance for our purposes here—"strong moral convictions are associated with accepting any means to achieve preferred ends" (Skitka, 2010 [USA], p. 278). Thus, setting aside the multiple indicators of disorganized thinking apparent in her plans as she articulated them (e.g., requesting that the killing take place in a local library while she was present so that she could pass out animal cruelty pamphlets afterwards), the would-be perpetrator seemed to have convinced herself that promoting the cause of animal rights completely justified the murder of a stranger.

Importantly, not all ends can justify harm-producing means while allowing actors to promote their own goodness. Heroes don't act in self-defense. Rather, they defend the innocent and defenseless. The key is to frame one's motivation as *beyond (the individual) self.* As *good reasons* for harmful behavior, abstract entities or principles (e.g., God, justice, honor) and collectives (e.g., country, family, the unborn) are especially effective, for two reasons. First, the larger they are, the more likely it is that audiences can relate and therefore accept the justification. Second, positioning oneself as acting on behalf of an ultimate good sets up an implied binary. That is, those who stand in the way of ultimate good are very likely evil and thus deserving of harm. Thus, acting with a *good reason* allows the perpetrator to embrace *intentionality* heartily and simply contextualize *harm* inflicted on others without diminishing it.

"I am not bad"

Employing *good enough* reasons for harmful behavior can also deflect the Mark of Cain—not by reinforcing the perception that "I am good," but rather the perception that "I am not bad." Self-focused goals assume greater centrality in *good enough* reasons. Thus, although killing in self-defense may not be seen as virtuous or heroic, it is understandable and certainly not *evil* (see Quiles et al., 2010 [Belgium/Spain]).

A theme common to many *good enough* reasons, such as acting in self-defense, is that the *self is under duress or otherwise disadvantaged*. This is a "victim" narrative in the broadest possible sense. Versions of this include the following.

"The target has victimized me"

That is, "the target hurt me (directly or indirectly), so I will hurt the target." The goal here isn't particularly noble: It's not about justice for someone else. Rather, it's about *revenge*. Combined with the magnitude gap (Baumeister, 1997) and a sense of identity of oneself or one's group as a victim, revenge can perpetuate a conflict as well as escalate its severity.

"The world (including the target) could victimize me"

Here the focus is *protection*: "Bad things could happen to me or those close to me unless I prevent them by hurting the target." Thus, one's behavior is claimed as a near-necessity given the circumstances. Do not confuse this with a decreased sense of agency described earlier. When used here, the assertion that "I had no choice" means that the individual did not want to deal with the anticipated negative consequences of making a different choice, not that they experienced an inability to control their own behavior (as in automatism).

Sometimes the target of harm and the source of threat are different. In such instances, the victim narrative takes this form: "If I didn't hurt the target, then the (power-wielding individuals/groups in my) world would have hurt me." This is the exact formula by which some of Alford's (1997 [USA]) interviewees justified Adolf Eichmann's behavior in Chapter 1.

"The world (not necessarily the target) has victimized me"

The focus here is *compensation*: "I've been hard done by, and *somebody* needs to pay for that." That is, individuals perceive themselves (and/or wish to be perceived by others) as wounded or disadvantaged, and this entitles them to increased benefits and/or decreased accountability in other contexts.

A number of research examples illustrate the compensation narrative in action. For example, Zitek et al. (2010 [USA]) showed that a salient sense of unfairness (even when caused by a computer glitch rather than a person) increased selfish behavior via an increased sense of entitlement. Similarly, an intimate partner's failure to meet emotional or sexual needs is an oft-cited justification for seeking extra-relational affairs; tit-for-tat revenge is mentioned much less frequently (see Omarzu et al., 2012 [USA]).

In one American study reported by Mullen and Nadler (2008), participants with a strong pro-choice moral mandate read about a doctor who was facing trial for administering a late-term abortion, and who was either convicted or acquitted. One in four conviction condition participants (25%) subsequently failed to return a pen borrowed from the experimenter, whereas none (0%) of the acquittal participants failed to do so; participants lacking a pro-choice moral mandate did not show this pattern. In a second study, 76% of participants who recalled and wrote about someone who had angered them by acting immorally reported a "tails" result of a coin toss, which they believed would qualify them for a cash-earning trivia game. This was statistically higher than the expected 50%, suggesting that participants cheated. In contrast, participants who wrote about being angered by encountering task obstacles, as well as participants who wrote about a neutral topic, did not differ statistically from the expected 50%. Thus, people appeared more likely to engage in questionable behavior after learning that morals that they champion had been violated.

According to Hendin and Cheek (1997 [USA]), "I don't worry about other people's problems—I've got enough of my own" is a mantra of *covert narcissists*. Thus, the sense of being hard-done-by is sometimes used as a justification for inaction (that is, negligence) as well as action that causes harm.

The compensation narrative is also observable in intergroup contexts. In particular, Noor et al. (2012 [Israel/UK]) suggested that groups that perceive themselves to have been mistreated can subsequently embrace an "ideology of entitlement" fueled by a sense of collective victimhood.

Even arguably minor episodes of physical discomfort may be enough to mobilize the compensation narrative. For example, in a study by Ong et al. (2017), Dutch participants were randomly assigned to stick their hand in either warm or painfully cold water, then roll a die three times and report the outcome of the first roll. They were told that they would be paid one euro per die pip. Average reports in the cold condition (4.34) exceeded expected results based on chance (3.50), whereas average reports in the warm condition did not (3.68). Those who experienced pain therefore appeared more likely to cheat, plausibly because they felt like they "earned" higher payment by suffering.

Like pain, fatigue may serve as grounds for seeking illicit compensation. For example, in the two American studies reported by Mead et al. (2009), participants were first asked to write a short essay with either challenging (don't use the letters A or N) or easy (don't use the letters X or Z) instructions. They subsequently completed a set of computational tasks. Some participants were scored and paid by the researcher for the number of correct solutions; others were allowed to self-score and pay themselves. In other words, they were given the opportunity to cheat. Those who had completed the challenging essay—and, thus, who were presumably more fatigued—were more likely to cheat. They were also more likely to seek out a cheating opportunity when possible.

What's left?

So far in this chapter we've looked at the Mark of Cain and sampled some deflection strategies—in particular, those based on dismantling the three prototypic features of "evil" behavior (that is, minimizing perceived harm, decreasing attributions of intent, and framing one's actions as justifiable). To be sure, not all strategies are equally effective when dealing with internal and external audiences. For example, as I noted earlier, diminishing the sense of agency is likely an easier sell when the audience is internal. Even in cases wherein deflection techniques prove ineffective, however, the fact that a harm-doer uses them suggests that they have accepted the legitimacy of the audience and its capacity to pass judgment. To complete the picture, let's look at two alternative strategies for neutralizing the Mark of Cain that are designed to undermine this legitimacy.

"I am Cain (and So Are You)"

> I am only what you made me. I am only a reflection of you.
>
> Testimony of Charles Manson in the Tate-LaBianca Murder Trial, n.d.

People are especially likely to apply the "evil" label to behavior that they regard as morally inexplicable (see Chapter 2). Labeling someone "evil" is the functional equivalent of branding with the Mark of Cain, transforming that person into a moral outcast. With this as a backdrop, the first alternative strategy delegitimizes the Mark of Cain *by turning the judgment back onto the audience* (cf. "condemning the condemners" in Sykes & Matza, 1957 [USA]). Thus, unlike the previous strategies, the actor acknowledges wrongdoing in its totality and makes no attempt to justify it, but redirects attention toward others' wrongdoing, which is depicted as comparable or greater in magnitude. In simple terms, one concedes that one's behavior is bad but not exceptional, and so one doesn't deserve to be stigmatized and outcast for it. This technique is probably most effective when the comparison is *in kind* (that is, petty theft versus petty theft rather than petty theft versus relational indiscretion).

At its core, the Mark of Cain is an interpersonal phenomenon, and so external audiences are the ultimate focus of deflection or neutralization attempts. Nevertheless, an important first step may be to appease one's internal audience by normalizing the behavior in question—that is, that "everybody (or, at least, my ingroup) does it" (see Gino et al., 2009 [USA]; Moore & Gino, 2013 [UK/USA]). Having soothed themselves, an actor can then employ what might be referred to as "meta-moral hypocrisy" by accusing the external audience of applying a double standard—that is, judging the actor for the same behavior that they would tolerate among themselves (for a consideration of moral hypocrisy proper, see Valdesolo & Desteno, 2007, 2008 [USA]; see also Barkan et al., 2012 [Israel/USA], for evidence of the "pot calling the kettle black" phenomenon, wherein one judges others more harshly for engaging in the same questionable behavior of which one is guilty). In effect, the Mark of Cain is rendered meaningless.

"I am Cain (and I Could Kill You, Too)"

> Only God can judge me now. Nobody else, nobody else. All you other motherfuckers get out of my business.
>
> Shakur, 1999 (USA)

The Mark of Cain works as a tool for censure only if the target's well-being can be substantively affected by the judging audience. Thus, the second alternative strategy is to *dismiss the consequentiality of the audience's judgment*. Once again, behavior that causes harm is owned. No attempt is made to justify it. There is no need to justify it, for the actor asserts their invulnerability to social evaluation, often accompanied by displays of power (cf. Baumeister's, 1997, discussion of the badass). Indeed, perception of oneself as powerful has been shown to fuel moral hypocrisy (i.e., a more lenient standard for one's own, versus others', behavior: Lammers et al., 2010 [Netherlands/USA]), to increase social distance (Lammers et al., 2012 [Netherlands/USA]), to lessen emotional responsiveness to others perceived as less powerful (van Kleef et al., 2008 [Netherlands/USA]), and to lead to discounting the value of expert advice (Tost et al., 2012 [USA]).

At first glance, employing this strategy seems to create a perceived disconnect between the Mark of Cain and the "evil" label because the individual embraces elements of the MOPE rather than casting them off. Beneath the surface, however, the strategy often appears to have a reactive, defensive quality: If one is *truly* unaffected by others' judgment, why must one assert that this is so with such vigor?

For example, some artists identified with the black metal musical genre have been linked to church burnings, torture, and murder interwoven with religious (particularly anti-Christian) blasphemy (see Hartmann, 2011 [international]). Thus, for some, black metal is not simply a musical style but a lifestyle characterized by defiance of law and the sacred. It has been characterized by Venkatesh et al. (2014 [Canada/USA], p. 77) as an outlet for "feral individualism" and "a vehicle for . . . non-belonging and constant revolt against dominant social sign systems." The willful embrace of the trappings of evil by some black metal adherents therefore appears to be a reactive undertaking, one that is intended to boost a sense of personal power (cf. Burris & Rempel, 2012 [Canada]).

Consider also a violent Australian offender described by Greig (2006, p. 146): "[H]e used every opportunity to highlight the potential danger he appeared to represent, reinforcing this view with grandiose and wide-ranging threats against the community and public figures, and implying that he possessed both the capacity and desire to inflict boundless violence." The offender clearly appeared to embrace elements of the MOPE. He took things a step further, however, by inflicting violence on himself, mutilating his ears, nipple, and genitals. Although self-harm does not map clearly onto the MOPE, it could be construed as the ultimate assertion of the inconsequentiality of the audience's judgment: "*You can't hurt me (any more than I can hurt myself).*" Indeed, Greig argued that the offender's self-mutilation accorded him a kind of status within the prison system, and she suggested that although he "vehemently argued that an oppressive state power was denying him his freedom, he was equally afraid of confronting the world outside and used strategies to ensure that his incarceration continued" (p. 143). In this regard, he sounds a lot like Cain himself, focused on self-protection.

Summing Up: Bearing Cain's Pain

The desire to avoid the Mark of Cain—being labeled "evil"—is a powerful motive because it is linked to the pain of social rejection. It moves us to want to "'morally satisfice,' to achieve a socially acceptable minimum amount of moral acceptance from others" (Hitlin, 2008 [USA], p. 39). We seem fully prepared to use what Hitlin (see also Mercier & Sperber, 2011 [USA/France]) referred to as "lawyer logic" to accomplish this. That is, we may employ any combination of tactics outlined in this chapter to convince an audience (or ourselves) that we are okay—even if what we do ensures that others are not. We will even sometimes extend ourselves in this way on behalf of ingroup members. For example, Coman et al. (2014) found that Americans tended to forget justifications for atrocities offered by a presumed outgroup member (an Afghan soldier), but remembered those same justifications when offered by a U.S. soldier.

It's worth emphasizing that just because people are often motivated to sidestep judgment when accounting for their own harm-producing behavior, this doesn't necessarily mean that the details of such accounts are disingenuous or demonstrably wrong. Indeed, *sometimes perpetrators say that they're victims because they've been victimized.* It's an open question whether the narrative(s) constructed will be deemed sufficient by others to spare "victimized perpetrators" judgment for the harm that the perpetrators themselves have caused, however.

Given the noxious power of the Mark of Cain and the consequent push to go to occasionally great lengths to avoid it, why would someone decide to put themselves in this position in the first place? That is, what moves an individual to choose behavior that harms others? The answers are less mysterious than you might wish them to be. We'll explore them in the next chapter.

References

Alford, C. F. (1997). The political psychology of evil. *Political Psychology, 18*(1), 1–17. doi:10.1111/0162-895X.00042

Anderson, M. C., & Hanslmayr, S. (2014). Neural mechanisms of motivated forgetting. *Trends in Cognitive Sciences, 18*(6), 279–292. doi:10.1016/j.tics.2014.03.002

Anderson, M. C., & Huddleston, E. (2012). Towards a cognitive and neurobiological model of motivated forgetting. In R. F. Belli (Ed.), *True and false recovered memories: Toward a reconciliation of the debate, Nebraska Symposium on Motivation* (pp. 53–120). Springer Science + Business Media. doi:10.1007/978-1-4614-1195-6_3

Andersen, M. L., Poyares, D., Alves, R. S. C., Skomro, R., & Tufik, S. (2007). Sexsomnia: Abnormal sexual behavior during sleep. *Brain Research Reviews, 56*(2), 271–282. doi:10.1016/j.brainresrev.2007.06.005

Bandura, A., Barbaranelli, C., Caprara, G. V., & Pastorelli, C. (1996). Mechanisms of moral disengagement in the exercise of moral agency. *Journal of Personality and Social Psychology, 71*(2), 364–374. doi:10.1037/0022-3514.71.2.364

Barkan, R., Ayal, S., Gino, F., & Ariely, D. (2012). The pot calling the kettle black: Distancing response to ethical dissonance. *Journal of Experimental Psychology: General, 141*(4), 757–773. doi:10.1037/a0027588

Barry, P. B. (2013). *Evil and moral psychology*. Routledge.

Baumeister, R. F. (1997). *Evil: Inside human cruelty and violence*. W. H. Freeman.

Baumeister, R. F., & Leary, M. R. (1995). The need to belong: Desire for interpersonal attachments as a fundamental human motivation. *Psychological Bulletin, 117*(3), 497–529. doi:10.1037/0033-2909.117.3.497

Belli, R. F. (2012). *Nebraska Symposium on Motivation: Vol. 58. True and false recovered memories: Toward a reconciliation of the debate*. Springer Science + Business Media. doi:10.1007/978-1-4614-1195-6

Bowman, M. (2007). A Mormon Bigfoot: David Patten's Cain and the conception of evil in LDS folklore. *Journal of Mormon History, 33*(3), 62–82.

Bray, H. J., Zambrano, S. C., Chur-Hansen, A., & Ankeny, R. A. (2016). Not appropriate dinner table conversation? Talking to children about meat production. *Appetite, 100*, 1–9. doi:10.1016/j.appet.2016.01.029

Burris, C. T., & Rempel, J. K. (2012). Good and evil in religion: The interpersonal context. In L. Miller (Ed.), *The Oxford handbook of the psychology of religion and spirituality* (pp. 123–137). Oxford University Press. doi:10.1093/oxfordhb/9780199729920.013.0008

Chapman, F. E., & MacLean, J. (2015). Parasomnia, sexsomnia, and automatism in *R. v. Hartman*. *Criminal Reports, 21*, 299–315.

Cicolin, A., Tribolo, A., Giordano, A., Chiarot, E., Peila, E., Terreni, A., Bucca, C., & Mutani, R. (2011). Sexual behaviors during sleep associated with polysomnographically confirmed parasomnia overlap disorder. *Sleep Medicine, 12*(5), 523–528. doi:10.1016/j.sleep.2011.02.002

Coman, A., Stone, C. B., Castano, E., & Hirst, W. (2014). Justifying atrocities: The effect of moral-disengagement strategies on socially shared retrieval-induced forgetting. *Psychological Science, 25*(6), 1281–1285. doi:10.1177/0956797614531024

D'Argembeau, A., Van der Linden, M., Verbanck, P., & Noël, X. (2006). Autobiographical memory in non-amnesic alcohol-dependent patients. *Psychological Medicine, 36*(12), 1707–1715. doi:10.1017/S0033291706008798

Droutman, V., Read, S. J., & Bechara, A. (2015). Revisiting the role of the insula in addiction. *Trends in Cognitive Science, 19*(7), 414–420. doi:10.1016/j.tics.2015.05.005

Gannon, T. A., & Alleyne, E. K. A. (2013). Female sexual abusers' cognition: A systematic review. *Trauma, Violence, and Abuse, 14*(1), 67–79. doi:10.1177/1524838012462245

Gannon, T. A., Ward, T., & Collie, R. (2007). Cognitive distortions in child molesters: Theoretical and research developments over the past two decades. *Aggression and Violent Behavior, 12*(4), 402–416. doi:10.1016/j.avb.2006.09.005

Giesbrecht, T., Lynn, S. J., Lilienfield, S. O., & Merckelbach, H. (2008). Cognitive processes in dissociation: An analysis of core theoretical assumptions. *Psychological Bulletin, 134*(5), 617–647. doi:10.1037/0033-2909.134.5.617

Gino, F., Ayal, S., & Ariely, D. (2009). Contagion and differentiation in unethical behavior: The effect of one bad apple on the barrel. *Psychological Science, 20*(3), 393–398. doi:10.1111/j.1467-9280.2009.02306.x

Goleman, D. (2010). *Ecological intelligence: The hidden impacts of what we buy*. Crown Business Publishing.

Gray, K., Waytz, A., & Young, L. (2012). The moral dyad: A fundamental template unifying moral judgment. *Psychological Inquiry, 23*(2), 206–215. doi:10.1080/1047840X.2012.686247

Gray, K., & Wegner, D. (2009). Moral typecasting: Divergent perceptions of moral agents and moral patients. *Journal of Personality and Social Psychology, 96*(3), 505–520. doi:10.1037/a0013748

Greig, D. N. (2006). Madness, badness, and evil. In T. Mason (Ed.), *Forensic psychiatry: Influences of evil* (pp. 135–152). Humana Press.

Hartmann, G. (2011, February 17). Top 10 worst crimes committed by Black Metal musicians. https://metalinjection.net/lists/top-10-crimes-committed-black-metal-musicians

Hempel, I. S., Buck, N. M. L., van Vugt, E. S., & van Marle, H. J. C. (2015). Interpreting child sexual abuse: Empathy and offense-supportive cognitions among child sex offenders. *Journal of Child Sexual Abuse, 24*(4), 354–368. doi:10.1080/10538712.2015.1014614

Hendin, H. M., & Cheek, J. M. (1997). Assessing hypersensitive narcissism: A reexamination of Murray's Narcissism Scale. *Journal of Research in Personality, 31*(4), 588–599. doi:10.1006/jrpe.1997.2204

Henriques, G. (2003). The tree of knowledge system and the theoretical unification of psychology. *Review of General Psychology, 7*(2), 150–182. doi:10.1037/1089-2680.7.2.150

Hitlin, S. (2008). *Moral selves, evil selves: The social psychology of conscience*. Palgrave MacMillan.

Katsuta, S., & Hazama, K. (2016). Cognitive distortions of child molesters on probation or parole in Japan. *Japanese Psychological Research, 58*(2), 163–174. doi:10.1111/jpr.12107

Kettleborough, D. G., & Merdian, H. L. (2017). Gateway to offending behaviour: Permission-giving thoughts of online users of child sexual exploitation material. *Journal of Sexual Aggression, 23*(1), 19–32. doi:10.1080/13552600.2016.1231852

Key, B. (2016). Why fish do not feel pain. *Animal Sentience, 3*, 1–33.

Lammers, J., Galinsky, A. D., Gordijn, E. H., & Otten, S. (2012). Power increases social distance. *Social Psychological and Personality Science*, *3*(3), 282–290. doi:10.1177/1948550611418679

Lammers, J., Stapel, D. A., & Galinsky, A. D. (2010). Power increases hypocrisy: Moralizing in reasoning, immorality in behavior. *Psychological Science*, *21*(5), 737–744. doi:10.1177/0956797610368810

Leary, M. R., Tambor, E. S., Terdal, S. K., & Downs, D. L. (1995). Self-esteem as an interpersonal monitor: The sociometer hypothesis. *Journal of Personality and Social Psychology*, *68*(3), 518–530. doi:10.1037/0022-3514.68.3.518

Levine, E. E., & Schweitzer, M. E. (2014). Are liars ethical? On the tension between benevolence and honesty. *Journal of Experimental Social Psychology*, *53*, 107–117. doi:10.1016/j.jesp.2014.03.005

Lewin, K. (2012, February 22). Woman accused of hiring hit man to kill random fur-wearer. http://www.cnn.com/2012/02/22/justice/ohio-anti-fur-plot-arrest/index.html

MacDonald, G., & Leary, M. R. (2005). Why does social exclusion hurt? The relationship between social and physical pain. *Psychological Bulletin*, *131*(2), 202–223. doi:10.1037/0033-2909.131.2.202

Malle, B. F., Guglielmo, S., & Monroe, A. E. (2014). A theory of blame. *Psychological Inquiry*, *25*(2), 147–186. doi:10.1080/1047840X.2014.877340

Mazar, N., Amir, O., & Ariely, D. (2008). The dishonesty of honest people: A theory of self-concept maintenance. *Journal of Marketing Research*, *45*(6), 633–644. doi:10.1509/jmkr.45.6.633

McSherry, B. (2003). Voluntariness, intention, and the defence of mental disorder: Toward a rational approach. *Behavioral Sciences and the Law*, *21*(5), 581–599. doi:10.1002/bsl.552

Mead, N. L., Baumeister, R. F., Gino, F., Schweitzer, M. E., & Ariely, D. (2009). Too tired to tell the truth: Self-control resource depletion and dishonesty. *Journal of Experimental Social Psychology*, *45*(3), 594–597. doi:10.1016/j.jesp.2009.02.004

Mercier, H., & Sperber, D. (2011). Why do humans reason? Arguments for an argumentative theory. *Behavioral and Brain Sciences*, *34*(2), 57–111. doi:10.1017/S0140525X10000968

Merritt, A. C., Effron, D. A., & Monin, B. (2010). Moral self-licensing: When being good frees us to be bad. *Social and Personality Psychology Compass*, *4*(5), 344–357. doi:10.1111/ j.1751-9004.2010.00263.x

Mitchell, R. W. (1994). Multiplicities of self. In S. T. Parker, R. W. Mitchell, & M. L. Boccia (Eds.), *Self-awareness in animals and humans: Developmental perspectives* (pp. 81–107). Cambridge University Press.

Moore, C., & Gino, F. (2013). Ethically adrift: How others pull our moral compass from true North, and how we can fix it. *Research in Organizational Behavior*, *33*, 53–77. doi:10.1016/j.riob.2013.08.001

Moore, J. W., & Obhi, S. S. (2012). Intentional binding and the sense of agency: A review. *Consciousness and Cognition*, *21*(1), 546–561. doi:10.1016/j.concog.2011.12.002

Morsella, E., Berger, C. C., & Krieger, S. C. (2011). Cognitive and neural components of the phenomenology of agency. *Neurocase*, *17*(3), 209–230. doi:10.1080/13554794.2010.504727

Moskowitz, A. (2004). Dissociation and violence: A review of the literature. *Trauma, Violence, and Abuse*, *5*(1), 21–46. doi:10.1177/1524838003259321

Mullen, E., & Monin, B. (2016). Consistency versus licensing effects of past moral behavior. *Annual Review of Psychology*, *67*, 363–385. doi:10.1146/annurev-psych-010213-115120

Mullen, E., & Nadler, J. (2008). Moral spillovers: The effect of moral violations on deviant behavior. *Journal of Experimental Social Psychology*, *44*(5), 1239–1245. doi:10.1016/j.jesp.2008.04.001

Nandrino, J.-L., El Haj, M., Torre, J., Naye, D., Douchet, H., Danel, T., & Cottonçin, O. (2016). Autobiographical memory deficits in alcohol-dependent patients with short- and long-term abstinence. *Alcoholism: Clinical and Experimental Research*, *40*(4), 856–873. doi:10.1111/acer.13001

Noor, M., Shnabel, N., Halabi, S., & Nadler, A. (2012). When suffering begets suffering: The psychology of competitive victimhood between adversarial groups in violent conflicts. *Personality and Social Psychology Review*, *16*(4), 351–374. doi:10.1177/1088868312440048

Nunes, K. L., & Jung, S. (2012). Are cognitive distortions associated with denial and minimization among sex offenders? *Sexual Abuse: A Journal of Research and Treatment*, *25*(2), 166–188. doi:10.1177/1079063212453941

Oakley, D. A. (1999). Hypnosis and conversion hysteria: a unifying model. *Cognitive Neuropsychiatry*, *4*(3), 243–265. doi:10.1080/135468099395954

Oakley, D. A., & Halligan, P. W. (2013). Hypnotic suggestion: Opportunities for cognitive neuroscience. *Nature Reviews: Neuroscience*, *14*, 565–576. doi:10.1038/nrn3538

Omarzu, J., Miller, A. N., Schultz, C., & Timmerman, A. (2012). Motivations and emotional consequences related to engaging in extramarital relationships. *International Journal of Sexual Health*, *24*(2), 154–162. doi:10.1080/19317611.2012.662207

Ong, H. H., Nelisson, R. M. A., & van Beest, I. (2017, January). *Physical pain increases dishonest behavior*. Poster presented at the Annual Meeting of the Society for Personality and Social Psychology, San Antonio, Texas.

Ost, J. (2017). Adults' retractions of childhood sexual abuse allegations: High-stakes and the (in)validation of recollection. *Memory*, *25*(7), 900–909. doi:10.1080/09658211.2016.1187757

Pressman, M. R., Mahowald, M. W., Schenck, C. H., & Bornemann, M. C. (2007). Alcohol-induced sleepwalking or confusional arousal as a defense to criminal behavior: A review of scientific evidence, methods and forensic considerations. *Journal of Sleep Research*, *16*(2), 198–212. doi:10.1111/j.1365-2869.2007.00586.x

Quiles, M. N., Morera, M. D., Correa, A. D., & Leyens, J. P. (2010). What do people mean when speaking of evilness? *Spanish Journal of Psychology*, *13*(2), 788–797. doi:10.1017/S1138741600002444

Ruedy, N. E., Moore, C., Gino, F., & Schweitzer, M. E. (2013). The cheater's high: The unexpected affective benefits of unethical behavior. *Journal of Personality and Social Psychology*, *105*(4), 531–548. doi:10.1037/a0034231

Scully, D., & Marolla, J. (1984). Convicted rapists' vocabulary of motive: Excuses and justifications. *Social Problems*, *31*(5), 530–544. doi:10.1525/sp.1984.31.5.03a00050

Shakur, T. (1999). Only God can judge me [Song]. On *Only God can judge me* [Album]. No Limit/Priority/EMI Records.

Shapiro, C. M., Trajanovic, N. N., & Federoff, J. P. (2003). Sexsomnia—a new parasomnia? *Canadian Journal of Psychiatry*, *48*(5), 311–317. doi:10.1177/070674370304800506

Sheindlin, J. (1996). *Don't pee on my leg and tell me it's raining: America's toughest family court judge speaks out*. HarperCollins Publishers.

Skitka, L. J. (2010). The psychology of moral conviction. *Social and Personality Psychology Compass*, *4*(4), 267–281. doi:10.1111/j.1751-9004.2010.00254.x

Sperduti, M., Delaveau, P., Fossati, P., & Nadel, J. (2011). Different brain structures related to self- and external-agency attribution: A brief review and meta-analysis. *Brain Structure and Function*, *216*(2), 151–157. doi:10.1007/s00429-010-0298-1

Stern, M. K., & Johnson, J. H. (2010). Just noticeable difference. In I. B. Weiner & W. E. Craighead (Eds.), *The Corsini encyclopedia of psychology* (pp. 886–887). John Wiley & Sons.

Stillwell, A. M., & Baumeister, R. F. (1997). The construction of victim and perpetrator memories: Accuracy and distortion in role-based accounts. *Personality and Social Psychology Bulletin*, *23*(11), 1157–1172. doi:10.1177/01461672972311004

Sullivan, J., & Sheehan, V. (2016). What motivates sexual abusers of children? A qualitative examination of the spiral of sexual abuse. *Aggression and Violent Behavior*, *30*, 76–87. doi:10.1016/j.avb.2016.06.015

Sykes, G. M., & Matza, D. (1957). Techniques of neutralization: A theory of delinquency. *American Sociological Review*, *22*, 664–670. doi:10.2307/2089195

Terhune, D. B., Polito, V., Barnier, A. J., & Woody, E. Z. (2016). Variations in the sense of agency during hypnotic responding: Insights from latent profile analysis. *Psychology of Consciousness: Theory, Research, and Practice*, *3*(4), 293–302. doi:10.1037/cns0000107

Testimony of Charles Manson in the Tate-LaBianca Murder Trial (n.d.). Famous Trials by Professor Douglas O. Linder. https://www.famous-trials.com/manson/258-mansontestimony

Tost, L. P., Gino, F., & Larrick, R. (2012). Power, competitiveness, and advice taking: Why the powerful don't listen. *Organizational Behavior and Human Decision Processes*, *117*(1), 53–65. doi:10.1016/j.obhdp.2011.10.001

Valdesolo, P., & Desteno, D. (2007). Moral hypocrisy: Social groups and the flexibility of virtue. *Psychological Science*, *18*(8), 689–690. doi:10.1111/j.1467-9280.2007.01961.x

Valdesolo, P., & Desteno, D. (2008). The duality of virtue: Deconstructing the moral hypocrite. *Journal of Experimental Social Psychology*, *44*(5), 1334–1338. doi:10.1016/j.jesp.2008.03.010

van Kleef, G.A., Oveis, C., van der Löwe, I., LuoKogan, A., Goetz, J., & Keltner, D. (2008). Power, distress, and compassion: Turning a blind eye to the suffering of others. *Psychological Science*, *19*(12), 1315–1322. doi:10.1111/j.1467-9280.2008.02241.x

Venkatesh, V., Podoshen, J. S., Urbaniak, K., & Wallin, J. J. (2014). Eschewing community: Black Metal. *Journal of Community and Applied Social Psychology*, *25*(1), 66–81. doi:10.1002/casp.2197

von Hippel, W., & Trivers, R. (2011). The evolution and psychology of self-deception. *Behavioral and Brain Sciences*, *34*(1), 1–56. doi:10.1017/S0140525X10001354

Wainryb, C. (2000). Values and truths: The making and judging of moral decisions. In M. Laupa (Ed.), *New directions for child and adolescent development*, vol. 89 (pp. 33–46). Jossey-Bass.

Wainryb, C., Brehl, B. A., & Matwin, S. (2005). Being hurt and hurting others: Children's narrative accounts and moral judgments of their own interpersonal conflicts. *Monographs of the Society for Research in Child Development*, *70*, 1–114. doi:10.1111/j.1540-5834.2005.00350.x

Ward, T., & Keenan, T. (1999). Child molesters' implicit theories. *Journal of Interpersonal Violence*, *14*(8), 821–838. doi:10.1177/088626099014008003

Xu, X., Zuo, X., Wang, X., & Han, S. (2009). Do you feel my pain? Racial group membership modulates empathic neural responses. *Journal of Neuroscience, 29*(26), 8525–8529. doi:10.1523/jneurosci.2418-09.2009

Yoshie, M., & Haggard, P. (2013). Negative emotional outcomes attenuate sense of agency over voluntary actions. *Current Biology, 23*(20), 2028–2032. doi:10.1016/j.cub.2013.08.034

Zitek, E. M., Jordan, A. H., Monin, B., & Leach, F. R. (2010). Victim entitlement to behave selfishly. *Journal of Personality and Social Psychology, 98*(2), 245–255. doi:10.1037/a0017168

4
Becoming Evil

Are you evil?

I suspect that the overwhelming majority of you answered "no." Some of you probably answered "hell, no!" and want to toss this book in the trash right now because you feel insulted that I would even ask such a thing. Given the stigmatizing power of the Mark of Cain that I described in Chapter 3, neither of us should be surprised if the question makes you uncomfortable.

But if you're still reading, let's dig a little deeper. Remember from Chapter 1 that the label "evil" is most likely applied when behavior meets certain criteria. So let me ask you a slightly different question: Has your choice to act (or not to act) ever had consequences that were perceived by at least one other person as *harmful* and *inadequately justified*—perhaps even *completely unjustifiable*? That is, do you think that anyone has ever judged your behavior to be "evil"?

"Yes, but . . ." Dread of the Mark of Cain may be spiking in you right now, and so you may be making full use of the deflection tools I described in Chapter 3. You're still basically a good person. It really wasn't a big deal. You weren't in your right mind. You had a good (enough) reason for doing what you did. It was no worse than what other people do. It doesn't matter what other people think of you.

But take a breath and consider, for just a moment, whether the person judging you had a point: Were you in the *best* position to gauge the full impact of your behavior on other people? Were you *really* out of your mind then? Although it may have "seemed like a good idea at the time," can you *truly* stand by that assessment of your actions now? Even supposing that other people have done the same (or worse) things, does that make the negative impact of your actions any *less*? Why might it feel important for you to insist those who judge you *can't* actually hurt you?

The point here is that, despite the risk of being branded with the Mark of Cain, most—probably all—people have done something that someone else would label "evil" at one time or another. Were this not so, we could congratulate ourselves on being *good* people and lament and puzzle over *bad* people,

Evil in Mind. Christopher T. Burris, Oxford University Press. © Oxford University Press 2022.
DOI: 10.1093/oso/9780197637180.003.0004

and this book would tell a very different story. The question, then, is: What moves people to engage in behaviors that others might label "evil"?

The "Mind over Matter" Principle

One of my grade-school teachers answered this question years ago, although neither he nor I realized it at the time. When a classmate asked why they were being denied permission to visit the drinking fountain off-schedule, my teacher replied: "It's mind over matter—*I don't mind and you don't matter*." Translated into more formal terms that apply here, that sarcastic declaration looks like this: A person is especially likely to engage in evil behavior when the *expected* net benefits to self (or ingroup) outweigh the *expected* costs to the victim(s). However simple (or even simplistic) this "Mind over Matter" (MioMa) principle may sound, it has profound implications, so let me unpack it a bit.

"You don't matter *enough*"

Situations that spawn evil behavior are often not as stark as implied by the MioMa principle in its most compact form. That is, in many situations, it's not that the persons suffering harm do not matter *at all* to an actor—rather, it's that they don't matter *enough*. So let's say you value someone else at a level of "9" on a 10 scale. For you to act against that person's best interest, you don't necessarily have to drop them down to a "1," or even an "8." You simply have to rate something else a "10," even if only for a brief span of time.

This can create a kind of magnitude gap that differs from the harm-focused one that I described in Chapter 3: Although a victim may feel permanently and totally devalued (like a "1"), a perpetrator *at most* may be aware only of a temporary shift in priorities. It seems easy to imagine the disputes that can result from this. For example, suppose an unfaithful partner claims to have "never stopped loving" the betrayed partner. Given the act of betrayal, it's clear that the unfaithful partner did not love the betrayed partner *enough* to make different choices. Nevertheless, an assertion of love without interruption could feel completely true to the unfaithful partner but sound completely false to the betrayed partner.

"Not mattering" can foster negligence and inaction as well as action

Sometimes would-be victims are deliberately devalued and targeted for harm by perpetrators. In other instances, "not mattering" means that victims are given very little thought. Thus, harm can result or worsen as a result of someone acting negligently or *doing nothing*. Two cases illustrate this point. First, a 2-year-old Canadian girl died from heatstroke after 7 hours inside a locked vehicle midsummer, having been "forgotten" by her daycare provider (who subsequently lied about the death discovery circumstances: Canadian Press, 2017). Second, approximately 40 individuals watched a live-streamed broadcast of a 15-year-old American girl being sexually assaulted and did not contact authorities (Associated Press, 2017).

Because both cases center on *inaction*, establishing intentionality is difficult. Thus, people's judgments concerning evilness may be more variable compared to when harm is the result of direct action. Nevertheless, I suspect that judgments of evil are more likely to the extent that one concludes that the daycare provider *should have* been more attentive and the assault viewers *should have* contacted authorities: Failing to act in a way to show that the victim mattered (enough) is likely seen as *unjustifiable* in such instances. And then, for those who feel sympathy for the victims, it's just a short jump to the question of "what kind of person would let that happen?" (see Chapter 2).

"Expected" is not the same as "actual"

Although this is perhaps obvious, the implications are worth spelling out. First, consider expected costs to the victim: The less the would-be victims are a focus of attention, the easier it is *not* to expect that one's own actions will cause them harm. In contrast, the more that would-be victims are a focus of attention, anticipated harm must be either minimized or justified (see Chapter 3).

Second, consider expected costs to the perpetrator. Two key issues here are the would-be perpetrator's *awareness of possible costs to self* and their *estimates concerning the likelihood of actually experiencing those costs*. It's certainly the case that concerns about getting caught are at least somewhat of a deterrent for people considering criminal activity (e.g., Horney & Marshall, 1992

[USA]; Svensson, 2015 [Sweden]; Wikström et al., 2011 [Greece/UK]). The relationship is far from perfect, however. The *Dumbest Criminals* television franchise attempted to capitalize on this, as the title implies, by suggesting that the show's presenters and viewers have something in common: They're smarter than the bungling offenders.

This isn't really a fair comparison, however: An after-the-fact perspective of an informed, disinterested third party can differ quite dramatically from that of a perpetrator in the middle of a situation. Consequently, people tend to be rather bad at what has been labeled *moral forecasting*—that is, predictions concerning how ethically they would behave in a given situation. Typically, people forecast based on what they think that they *should* do, whereas what they *want* to do is often the bigger influence once they are in the actual situation (see Sezer et al., 2015 [USA]).

An unsettling example of how the specifics of a situation can shift ethical decision-making comes from a study by Ariely and Loewenstein (2006), who asked undergraduate heterosexual American men to answer sex-related questions once while not in a sexually aroused state, and at a different time while they (the *same* men) had masturbated nearly to orgasm. Suggestive of a heightened urgency for sexual release, the men reported a wider range of sexual targets and activities to be arousing when answering questions while masturbating. They reported less positive attitudes toward condom use as well. More disturbingly, they also reported a greater willingness to use manipulative and coercive means to obtain sexual gratification. For example, when in an aroused (versus non-aroused) state, five times as many (of the *same*) men admitted that they would be willing to drug a date to increase their chances of having sex with her.

Thus, sexual arousal appeared to create a kind of "tunnel-vision where goals other than sexual fulfilment [such as ethical treatment of a potential partner] become eclipsed by the motivation to have sex" (Ariely & Loewenstein, 2006, p. 95, brackets inserted). That is, when the men were aroused, it was more likely that they *didn't mind* and women *didn't matter*. This arousal-driven tunnel vision also appears to decrease expectancy of costs to the self, such as the estimated likelihood of contracting a sexually transmitted infection (Blanton & Gerrard, 1997 [USA]). Indeed, Skakoon-Sparling et al. (2016 [Canada]) showed that sexual arousal seems to increase both sexual and non-sexual risk-taking (but not necessarily overtly unethical behavior) among women as well as men. It is unlikely that this tunnel-vision phenomenon is exclusive to sexual arousal—rather, any high-intensity motivational state (to avoid the aversive effects of substance withdrawal, for example) might be expected to radically reshuffle a person's priorities.

Complementarily, would-be perpetrators may seek to *manage potential costs*. In what is perhaps its most problematic form, this involves setting up circumstances so that the brunt of negative consequences of one's behavior falls onto others rather than the perpetrator. At the interpersonal level, Peck (1983 [USA], p. 129) identified "consistent destructive, scapegoating behavior, which may often be quite subtle" as one of the diagnostic criteria for his proposed "evil personality disorder." Beyond the interpersonal level, the practice is so common in business contexts (for example, production practices that have an adverse impact on the surrounding environment) that the term *negative externality* has been coined to refer to it (e.g., Biglan, 2011 [USA]). Given this, it should not be surprising that (especially large) organizational entities are often labeled "evil" (e.g., Hamilton & Sanders, 1999 [USA]; Litowitz, 2003–2004 [USA]; see also Chapter 8).

Simple awareness of possible costs to the self is unlikely to deter harmful behavior if the would-be perpetrator perceives the likelihood of incurring such costs to be low (Anderson & Galinsky, 2006 [USA]). In fact, *successfully managing risks can itself sometimes be experienced as rewarding*. Consider a Dutch study by Lammers and Maner (2016) that found that higher occupational status predicted more infidelity among people in a relationship, but not more casual sex among people *not* in a relationship. At first glance, this finding might seem surprising, because you might think that higher-status (versus lower-status) individuals have more to lose if their infidelities are publicly exposed. At the same time, however, higher-status individuals are likely to have more resources available for dealing with reputational risk and other possible negative personal consequences of their violations of trust (see Grover & Hasel, 2015 [France/New Zealand]). In fact, the higher-status cheaters in Lammers and Maner reported the naughtiness of infidelity to be inherently exciting. Irrespective of the actual risk, believing that one has the wherewithal to escape accountability for unethical behavior may allow anxiety to morph into exhilaration—perhaps another manifestation of the "cheater's high" described in Chapter 3 (Ruedy et al., 2013 [UK/USA]; see also Gino & Wiltermuth, 2014 [USA], and the discussion of participation in massacres in Chapter 8).

"Mind over Matter" Triggers

When choosing to engage in evil behavior, according to the MioMa principle, expected costs to victims often must be overlooked or trivialized and expected costs to self must be ignored or managed. The effort necessary to do both doesn't make sense without sufficient reward, so let's turn our attention to payoffs.

At the most basic level, I suggest that the payoff that drives much of people's behavior—including behavior that harms others—is *feeling*, whether the focus is on anticipated experience of a positive state or anticipated relief from a negative state. The sequence looks like this:

If I do A, then B will happen.
If B happens, then I will feel (more of) C.
and/or
If B happens, I will stop feeling (or at least feel less of) D.

Wrapping your head around this sequence will help you make sense out of a lot of behaviors, including any that you might perceive to be "evil." Just remember that the feeling goal may not always be obvious, in part because the actor's intentions may not be articulated consciously (especially the critical link between B and either C or D).

Also, remember that what you as an outside observer regard as personally rewarding or costly often does not match up with an actor's perceptions. For example, I suspect that the idea of going to prison is an extremely unpleasant thought for most people. When dealing with the prospect of homelessness, however, incarceration can be seen by some as a means of securing stable food and housing: "If I (re)offend, I will go (back) to jail, so I will stop feeling hungry and cold" (see Bowpitt, 2015 [UK]). Similarly, the idea of contracting a potentially fatal disease terrifies most people. Nevertheless, many members of a Cuban punk movement called the Frikis injected themselves with HIV-infected blood during the early years of the AIDS outbreak in order to access better living conditions and camaraderie inside state-run sanitariums (see Saeed, 2017). With this as a backdrop, let's consider harm-producing behaviors in the service of either *anticipated positive states* or *anticipated relief from negative states* in the next two sections.

Anticipated positive states

Aron et al. (2013 [USA]) have made a case for a human *self-expansion motive*—that is, that people "seek to enhance their potential efficacy by increasing the resources, perspectives, and identities that facilitate achievement of any goal that might arise. . . . Such resources, perspectives, and identities include knowledge, social status, community, possessions, wealth, physical strength, health, and everything else that can facilitate goal attainment" (p. 91). Self-expansion, then, helps people achieve their goals—and I would argue that "feeling good" (happy, satisfied, moral, vindicated, etc.) is the ultimate goal in many, many instances.

Wherein lies the potential for *evil*, then? In line with the MioMa principle, the key is the extent to which a person pursues a self-expansion agenda *without regard for, or at direct cost to, another's well-being* (see Burris et al., 2013 [Canada]). Consider the story of a married father in India who was having an online affair. In response to his girlfriend's urgings that the two go on a holiday together, the man—a travel agent who was low on cash—came up with a face-saving "solution": He sent his girlfriend a fake airline ticket and then emailed a false bomb threat targeting the departing airport to police. His hoped-for outcome was that the flight would be canceled for security reasons so his girlfriend wouldn't know about the fake ticket and he could still seem like a good guy. Police tracked him down via the Internet café from which he sent the email in question, however, and he subsequently faced charges (Suri, 2017).

The sequence certainly seems to fit the "if I do A . . ." sequence outlined earlier: Based on his confession, the perpetrator made a false report concerning a planned hijacking with the intent of preserving his illicit online relationship (which would presumably feel good) and saving face (which would presumably feel less bad). Certainly, managing relationship expectations and safeguarding one's reputation are motives with which many people can sympathize. At the same time, there is evidence of tunnel vision and apparent negligence in this case: The perpetrator approached his situation as a problem needing to be solved, despite the fact that execution of his plan triggered costly mobilization of security personnel at multiple airports and undoubtedly created unnecessary stress and inconvenience for many travelers and their loved ones. Given that the man was also a married father, the impact of his decision on his own family must be considered as well. Nevertheless, in the true spirit of the MioMa principle, it appeared that this perpetrator perceived his actions to be justifiable, at least at the time.

Now consider the case of a young British man who planted a simulated explosive device on a London tube train. His stated intent was for the device to smoke rather than explode, thereby forcing train stoppage and (it was hoped) news coverage "for a bit of fun" (BBC News, 2017; Ross, 2017). As described, this appears to be an especially clear example of: "If I do A, then B will happen. If B happens, then I will feel C." Here the perpetrator's stated ultimate goal—fun—hinged on creating a newsworthy level of chaos and panic among his unsuspecting victims. Thus, the perpetrator's motivation was arguably sadistic, in that he sought to feel good by making others feel bad (see Chapter 6). Nevertheless, in line with the MioMa principle, the perpetrator apparently perceived this to be a defensible tradeoff.

Sometimes a bit more effort is needed to uncover the link between a course of action and the sought-after feeling state. Consider the case of "A.A.," an American professional contract killer who had amassed over 100 victims in his 30-year career prior to incarceration (Schlesinger, 2001). "When A.A. was asked in court why he had committed the murders he pled guilty to, he responded, 'It was business.' " He showed a marked ability "to encapsulate his emotions so that they did not interfere with his overall functioning: 'I don't think about it. It doesn't bother me. Nothing haunts me—nothing. If I think about it, it would hurt me, so I don't think about it' " (p. 1122). As a career criminal rather than a one-off offender, A.A.'s response seems to suggest considerable energy expenditure to enact the MioMa principle. So what was his (positive feeling) payoff?

According to Schlesinger (2001), A.A. became tearful when speaking about his wife and children, who described him as caring, albeit occasionally explosive and physically abusive. A.A. claimed that he tried to keep his family insulated "from the dirt and scum of the world." Predictably, although he concealed his business from his family, A.A. saw his occupational choice as well justified: "It may not have been the right way, but for me it was the only way. What was I supposed to do, push a yarn truck for the rest of my life? I wouldn't have been able to afford one child, let alone three" (p. 1122). So, A.A. sought to feel good by providing his family a middle-class lifestyle and sending his children to private schools. He just so happened to do so by murdering people for money.

Sometimes other people are perceived to block self-expansion efforts—that is, they are seen as obstacles on the path toward feel-good goal attainment. Anger and its variants are commonly experienced in such instances (see Harmon-Jones & Harmon-Jones, 2016 [USA]). Thus, in keeping with the MioMa principle, harming the other may be undertaken to clear the path.

For example, in the largest study of contract killings in Australia at that time (94 cases, including both attempted and successful, from 1989 to 2001), Mouzos and Venditto (2003) observed that approximately one-third were linked to the dissolution of an intimate relationship. Particularly illustrative were cases involving individuals "who incited or solicited a hit man to eliminate their current partner so that they can be with their lover" as well as those who hired "the services of a contract killer to kill their ex-partner so that they may gain sole custody of the children" (p. 25). In one case, a married father of three conspired with his mistress, making arrangements to kill his wife with the assistance of a hitman involved with the very same mistress. On the specified night, the husband took his children to a video store, leaving the wife at home alone. After the two assailants arrived, the wife was

> punched to the face by [the mistress] and was stabbed seven times by [the hitman] in the chest and once in the back as she fought for her life by striking the hit man with a frying pan. [The mistress] stood by and watched as the hit man carried out instructions. The court later heard at her trial that [the mistress] encouraged the hit man and then laughed about it afterwards. [The mistress] then telephoned [the husband] to tell him the job had been completed at which time [he] returned home and allowed the children to make the horrific discovery. (p. 28, brackets inserted)

A mother was killed, her three children were severely traumatized, and the three offenders—including the husband/father—sustained lengthy prison terms (Mouzos & Venditto, 2003). Nevertheless, applying the MioMa principle, all three offenders apparently decided that the potential rewards of their respective actions outweighed the costs to the victims and any possible costs to themselves. Given the amount of planning necessary for the murder to transpire, this was not an impulsive act. Thus, through some combination of tunnel vision and justifications, all three offenders—each in their own way—must have concluded that this was the best course of action available to them at the time in pursuit of a desired feeling state.

Intense, and potentially harmful, reactions to blocked pursuit of feeling good are observable in many other contexts. For example, in a series of Canadian studies (including one involving a driving simulator), Philippe et al. (2009) showed that motorists perceived to be obstructive evoked anger and aggressive driving among those with an "obsessive passion" for driving. Illustrative of this, Lupton (2002, p. 286) interviewed a self-confessed

Australian road rager who described an incident in which he, driving solo, attempted to flag down a vehicle with four occupants who had thrown a glass bottle that had shattered on the road in front of his car. Paralleling the contract killing case study presented earlier, we see evidence of tunnel vision: Despite having other behavioral options and conceding the risk of injury had a physical altercation actually transpired, the interviewee chose to attempt confrontation because "it's stupid what they did. . . . They know it's going to piss me off and drive me psycho."

Anticipated relief from negative states

In addition to engaging in harmful behavior in pursuit of a positive feeling state, people are often motivated to do whatever they think might offer them relief from a negative state. Remember the sequence: "If I do A, then B will happen. If B happens, then I will stop feeling D."

For example, Mouzos and Venditto (2003) summarized an Australian case in which former in-laws were targeted for a contract killing. Although "certain property settlement issues" may have contributed to the offenders' motive (consistent with goal blockage), in their pitch to a friend to carry out the hit, the offenders focused on the fact that they were annoyed at being "the ones that had to always take their daughter to the doctor when she returned [from her grandparents'—the intended victims'—home] with severe sunburn" (p. 30, brackets inserted). Thus, analogous to swatting a pesky insect, *simple annoyance* appeared to contribute to the offenders' homicidal intent.

Some affective states signal a greater threat or challenge to the self than does simple annoyance, however. Although not inevitable, harming the other is sometimes perceived to be a viable, practical means for reducing such states. I will focus here on three: fear, disgust, and shame (see Horberg et al., 2011 [USA], for an overview of evidence of the domain-specific impact of specific emotions on moral judgments).

Fear

As an emotional response to perceived threat, fear most often motivates escape or avoidance behaviors (e.g., Chawla & Ostafin, 2007 [USA]). When escape or avoidance is seen as unfeasible, however, behavioral strategies may shift toward *eliminating the threat*, often via direct harm. Legal codes typically reflect the lay understanding that harming another who poses a clear and present threat to one's physical well-being is justified, however regrettable. Even when threats are ambiguous or (merely) potential, they can still evoke harmful responses in the presumed service of self-protection, however.

For example, Simunovic et al. (2013; see also Halevy, 2017 [USA]) had pairs of Japanese participants play a "preemptive strike game" in which they were simply presented a button that they could press or not press within a 1-minute span. Participants in each pair were told that both would get the largest possible cash payoff if *neither* chose to press the button. Pressing the button before the other person did, however, would result in a minor cost to self but a major cost to the other, as well as taking away the other's ability to retaliate. Thus, if you assume that the other person wants to get the largest payoff like you presumably would, then your logical choice would be *not* to press the button. In contrast, if you assume that the other person isn't "rational" like you are, then it would make more sense to press the button—that is, to "get them before they get you."

In fact, 50% of participants pressed the button, all within the first second. When told that they could press the button but their partner could not—which eliminated the other's first-strike capability—only 4% pressed the button. Moreover, results from follow-up questions suggested that most of the participants who chose to press the button in the first strike condition did so *to protect themselves* rather than to disadvantage the other.

Of course, lab studies with clear instructions, simple tasks, and comparatively trivial outcomes may at first glance appear to be several steps removed from real-world nastiness. That being said, Simunovic et al. (2013) pointed to previous research (e.g., Wildschut et al., 2003 [UK/USA]) suggesting that fear may drive decision-making more strongly in intergroup versus interpersonal situations (see Böhm et al., 2016 [Germany], who showed that this pattern extends to first strikes). With that in mind, suppose that the press of a button launched a missile: Perhaps this lab study has something of consequence to say about the real world after all.

Disgust

Buckels and Trapnell (2013 [Canada], p. 772) labeled disgust "the rejection emotion." At the physical level, it has been argued that the visceral urgency of the rejection response (e.g., the urge to vomit) functions to protect the body from adverse consequences that can arise from contact with toxins and pathogens (see Tybur et al., 2013 [Netherlands/USA]). At the same time, perceived moral violations that are not logically linked to such consequences are also capable of evoking a rejection response. In Nemeroff and Rozin's (1994 [USA]) provocative study, for example, many interviewees reported considerable discomfort at the thought of donning a sweater previously worn by someone whom they considered to be evil (see also Erskine et al., 2013 [USA]). Moreover, apparently because people's model of evil's contaminating power often straddles the spiritual and the material, Nemeroff and Rozin observed that "physical cleaning manipulations do reduce, very slightly, these symbolic contagion effects" (p. 178).

Consider a pair of studies reported by Ritter and Preston (2011). In both, American Christian participants were asked to complete two supposed "taste tests" and to provide a handwriting sample. Thus, in the initial study, participants first rated how disgusting a diluted lemon juice drink tasted to them, and then hand-copied a passage from the dictionary, the Koran, or an atheist manifesto (the assumption being that both of the latter two writing tasks could be experienced as spiritually contaminating). They subsequently rated a second lemon drink. Although this drink blend was the same as before, participants found it *more* disgusting after having copied from the Koran or the atheist manifesto, but not from the dictionary. The follow-up study (in which control-condition participants copied from the Christian New Testament rather than the dictionary) showed basically the same effect, but this effect was virtually eliminated if participants *cleaned their hands with an antiseptic wipe* before making the second drink rating. Perceiving themselves as "spiritually contaminated" therefore seemed to intensify participants' unrelated disgust judgments, unless they "purified" themselves via a mundane hand sanitizer.

A curious turnabout appeared in the film *Bloody Cartoons* (Hayling & Kjær, 2007), which documented the furor that erupted following a Danish newspaper's publication of a dozen cartoons that were perceived to be blasphemous in parts of the Muslim world. Amidst one street protest in Pakistan against "anything Western," one demonstrator could be observed forcefully plucking and discarding bottles out of a popular-brand soft drink crate. Although other interpretations are plausible, this act could be seen as a disgust-fueled refusal to ingest a (symbolic) contaminant.

So far, the impact of experiencing disgust on harm directed toward others seems hardly straightforward. The impact of individual differences in *disgust sensitivity*—that is, the likelihood of experiencing disgust in response to traditional elicitors such as pathogens, bodily products, and moral violations—appears clearer, however. For example, Pond et al. (2012 [USA]) showed that higher disgust sensitivity predicted lower levels of physical and verbal aggression, including intimate partner violence, across a variety of contexts and samples. Likewise, Richman et al. (2014 [UK]) found that higher disgust sensitivity predicted a decreased desire to retaliate if wronged by a friend, and Meere and Egan (2017 [USA]) reported that higher disgust sensitivity predicted lower sadistic tendencies (see Chapter 6).

Although a definitive demonstration of the mechanism(s) responsible for this set of relationships has yet to appear, researchers have suggested that disgust and aggression may be motivationally incompatible. That is, people who are disgust-sensitive feel *repelled* or *repulsed* by a variety of objects and situations, which implies that disgust triggers a desire to *avoid* those things. In contrast, directly aggressing against a target verbally or physically requires the opposite—that is, *approaching* the target. Consequently, aggressing against targets may simply be seen as "not worth it" if an individual is chronically concerned about becoming physically or spiritually contaminated.

At first glance, then, it would appear that disgust doesn't fit well under the "anticipated relief from negative states" umbrella. Indeed, the flip side of the preceding research is that people who are *less* likely to experience disgust are *more* likely to be verbally abusive, physically violent, or sadistic. But what if an individual links *a specific experience of disgust* to a potential target of aggression? A very different picture emerges.

For example, in Buckels and Trapnell (2013), Canadian university participants were assigned by chance to one of two groups based on their supposed results on a (fake) personality test. After being subsequently exposed to unrelated pictures intended to evoke either disgust, sadness, or neutral emotion, participants were presented with various pairings of photos of either outgroup members or fellow ingroup members with words linked to either humans or animals. Compared to those in the other two conditions, people exposed to the disgust-evoking pictures were more likely to link supposed outgroup members with animal-related words and ingroup members with human-related words. This suggests that feeling disgust can make people more likely to dehumanize outgroup members—even when disgust is triggered by something irrelevant and the "outgroup" label is completely arbitrary.

Importantly, linking a disgust experience to a potential target affects not only how one thinks, but also how one behaves. For example, Molho et al. (2017 [Netherlands]) suggested that anger and disgust have different consequences even though these emotions are often evoked by similar perceived moral violations. Specifically, when oneself is the victim of a moral violation, anger is the predominant emotion and direct (physical and verbal) aggression toward the perceived perpetrator is the result. When someone else is the victim, however, disgust is the predominant emotion and indirect aggression—attempting to socially isolate the perpetrator and damage their reputation—is the result. Public displays of disgust, then, may function as a sort of "coordinated condemnation" of a moral violator (Tybur et al., 2013)—in effect, branding the violator with the Mark of Cain.

If successful, coordinated condemnation efforts can ultimately enlist many perpetrators and entrap many victims. Indeed, based on analysis of the contents of political speeches that preceded large-scale action in several countries, Matsumoto et al. (2015 [USA]) showed that the speakers' verbal and nonverbal expressions of disgust (along with contempt and, to a lesser extent, anger) directed toward an opponent outgroup predicted subsequent violence toward that group.

Thus, linking one's feelings of disgust to a potential target increases the likelihood of attempting to harm that target. Moreover, higher sensitivity to disgust predicts more negative reactions to perceived moral violations (Jones & Fitness, 2008 [Australia]). At the same time, as already noted, individuals most likely to experience disgust are generally less likely to aggress. Pond et al. (2012, p. 185) proposed a compelling resolution to this apparent contradiction: "[A]voidant emotions, such as disgust and fear, provoke anger and aggression when the actor is unable to get out of the threatening situation." Under such circumstances, the experience of disgust may seem intolerable. Eliminating the perceived cause therefore becomes a compelling option, especially if the dirty work can be outsourced, much like one would hire an exterminator to destroy household pests (cf. Matsumoto et al., 2015). Viewed in this way, disgust indeed seems to fit the "anticipated relief from negative states" framework as I have described it.

Shame

If disgust is the "rejection emotion," then shame is the "response to rejection" emotion. Unlike its cousin guilt, shame is focused on the doer, not the behavior. That is, shame is linked to the appraisal that there is something *fundamentally unacceptable about the self* (e.g., Tracy & Robins, 2006 [Canada/USA]). Humiliation goes a step further with the target's perception that shaming and devaluation has become a public spectacle (e.g., Elshout et al., 2016 [Netherlands]).

Shame and humiliation are thus arguably core to Mark of Cain dynamics discussed in Chapter 3 (see Sznycer et al., 2016 [international]). Consequently, if judgments are perceived (rightly or wrongly) by the judged to be about *the doer* rather than the doer's *behavior*, justifications and the like lose their utility as deflection strategies. Instead, harming others (including actual and would-be judges) as an assertion of power and invulnerability may be increasingly considered as a viable self-protective strategy. As Elison et al. (2014 [Italy/USA]) put it, "aggression may be most common when individuals feel completely rejected (stigmatized or shamed), with no chance of regaining social connection" (p. 450; see also Velotti et al., 2014 [Italy/USA]).

According to McCauley (2017 [USA]), the experience of humiliation can be understood as a reaction to shaming that is perceived by the target as unjust. A sense of powerlessness can contribute to a target's initial passivity, further amplifying the experience and often prompting efforts to amass resources to retaliate. Although lone wolf terrorists and mass shooters often fit this pattern well, McCauley noted that his model could apply at the intergroup level as well as the interpersonal level, for humiliation is a recurrent theme in anecdotal analyses of the roots of organized terrorism.

It's worth noting that the fate of terrorists and mass shooters is often death by suicide or military/law enforcement intervention. Thus, to suggest that aggressive responses to the experience of humiliation are dysfunctional from a long-term standpoint is an understatement. Although tragic, such ends make some sense if the targets perceive themselves as beyond acceptance, as Elison et al. (2014) suggested, however.

Websdale's (2010 [USA]) analysis of domestic multiple homicide cases underscores this point even further: "[T]he single most important and consistent theme among the familicide cases is the presence of intense shame in the lives of perpetrators, much of it unacknowledged or bypassed" (p. 46). Across the 200+ incidents from a dozen countries examined, Websdale suggested that most conformed to one of two patterns.

So-called *livid coercive* cases were presaged by a history of controlling behavior, verbal abuse, and physical violence by perpetrators who often appeared romantically obsessed with, and emotionally dependent upon, their partners. Familicide is said to occur when the situation reaches a "tipping point beyond which emotional estrangement [largely precipitated by the perpetrators themselves] convinces eventual perpetrators of the inevitability of being abandoned and their intimate familial arrangements being torn asunder" (p. 165, brackets inserted). Congruent with the negative self-assessment endemic to shame, the majority of perpetrators also attempted or completed suicide after killing family members.

In *civil reputable* cases, prior domestic violence was quite infrequent. Outwardly, perpetrators appeared conventional, motivated by duty, and often fastidious. Religious involvement was common. The trappings of stability often masked secrets that culminated in an impending, gendered sense of failure, however: among men, compromised ability to be a provider; among women, self-perceived inadequacy as a partner or mother. The decision to kill one's family was often framed as altruistic by perpetrators—that is, victims presumably would be spared the burden of disgrace that the perpetrators themselves experienced, and that led to suicide in most cases. Meticulous efforts to deflect public scrutiny until the last possible moment were often manifest in the kills themselves. For example, Websdale (2010) detailed one case in which the perpetrator, facing bankruptcy and mortgage foreclosure, killed his wife and four children. In quick succession afterwards, he canceled milk delivery, a daughter's bus pick-up, and his wife's meet-up with a friend that evening via text from the wife's cell phone. The perpetrator then let the pets out of the house and hung himself.

Triggers Versus Hair Triggers: The Role of Individual Differences

Social psychologists are quick to emphasize the power of the situation: Remember Ariely and Loewenstein's (2006) study that demonstrated that sexual arousal appeared to increase risky "tunnel vision" in pursuit of sexual gratification. *Not all* men's responses evidenced this shift, however. Similarly, although Simunovic et al. (2013) clearly showed that distrust of the other's intentions increased the likelihood of a fear-based first strike directed toward the other, half of the participants in their key condition did *not* choose a first-strike response. Thus, there are clearly *individual differences* in how people respond to the same situations that ought to be taken into account. I previewed this approach when considering disgust sensitivity earlier in this chapter. Let's take it up again now.

The "Dark Triad"

One cluster of personality traits of seemingly obvious relevance is the so-called Dark Triad (a term coined by Paulhus & Williams, 2002 [Canada]): (1) psychopathy (callous, antisocial, and impulsive); (2) Machiavellianism (cynical, manipulative, and strategic); and (3) narcissism (grandiose, entitled, and attention-seeking). How "dark" is the Dark Triad? A sampling of research from a single publication year has linked it to:

- all of the "seven deadly sins" (that is, anger, envy, gluttony, pride, sloth, lust, and greed; Jonason et al., 2017 [USA])
- pro-doping attitudes among competitive athletes (Nicholls et al., 2017 [UK])
- bullying (both traditional and cyber; van Geel et al., 2017 [Netherlands])
- violent delinquency (Wright et al., 2017 [Saudi Arabia])
- psychological abuse of intimate partners (Carton & Egan, 2017 [UK])
- intimate partner cyberstalking (Smoker & March, 2017 [Australia]).

If this is not unsettling enough, see Furnham et al. (2013 [Canada/UK]) and Muris et al. (2017 [Netherlands]) for reviews of earlier research. Indeed, notwithstanding occasional, circumscribed claims of adaptive correlates such as well-being (Aghababaei & Błachnio, 2015 [Iran/Poland]) or creativity (Lebuda et al. 2021 [Poland]), it seems safe to assume that research documenting the nasty correlates of the Dark Triad will continue to mount.

When attempting to account for these disturbing links, it's important first to note that *the Dark Triad traits tend to co-occur*. That is, in statistical terms, correlations among the three (especially psychopathy and Machiavellianism) are moderate to strong. This appears to be the case across diverse groups of respondents and with a variety of Dark Triad measures (mostly questionnaires: see McLarnon & Tarraf, 2017 [Canada/USA]; Muris et al., 2017; Vize et al., 2018 [USA]). Thus, despite the fact that the different components of the Dark Triad sometimes predict different things (lying and cheating under different circumstances, for example; see Jones & Paulhus, 2017 [Canada/USA]), it would be misleading to think about the Dark Triad as referring to *different types of people*, as if someone is either a narcissist *or* a psychopath *or* a Machiavellian. In other words, although it's certainly possible to be a "pure narcissist," someone who is highly narcissistic is more likely than not to have psychopathic and Machiavellian tendencies as well.

In fact, the degree and consistency of overlap among Dark Triad components has prompted researchers to consider what that overlap is—that is, whether there is a "supertrait of malevolence," as Muris et al. (2017, p. 188) put it. Bertl et al. (2017 [international]; see also Dinić et al., 2021 [Croatia/Serbia], and Jones & Figueredo, 2013 [Canada/USA]) suggested that *callousness* and *manipulation* are central. Kajonius et al. (2016 [Sweden]) proposed that the simple statement "*I exploit others*" captures the essence. Perhaps the most ambitious conceptual-empirical analysis to date was undertaken by Moshagen et al. (2018 [Denmark/Germany]), who concluded that the "dark core of personality" embodies the "tendency to maximize one's individual utility—disregarding, accepting, or malevolently provoking disutility for others—accompanied by beliefs that serve as justifications" (p. 684). In other words, someone scoring high on the Dark Triad has taken the MioMa principle and turned it into a lifestyle, a way of moving through the world. It should therefore be no surprise that the Dark Triad is correlated with a variety of specific forms of nastiness. Indeed, Harms et al. (2014 [USA]) suggested that it's more accurate to think about a person's score on the Dark Triad (or other trait measures) as a *summary* of that person's behavior rather than a suggestion of its cause.

So the next question to emerge naturally is: What might move a person to adopt a "dark" lifestyle? The literature has been nearly silent on this issue, leading Jonason and Ferrell (2016) to assert that theirs was perhaps the first investigation of the motivational underpinnings of the Dark Triad. Across four studies involving literally thousands of Australian and American participants, these researchers found that all three Dark Triad components were linked to a greater desire for power or interpersonal dominance, whereas a sense of social connection and belongingness was generally devalued (although the latter was less clear for narcissism viewed separately). As Jonason and Ferrell themselves noted, one limitation of their research—like most simple correlational studies wherein participants complete all measures at the same point in time—is that one cannot confidently state what causes what. Are the motives driving the Dark Triad, or is the reverse true? Or is some unmeasured variable driving both?

One way to begin to untangle the causality question, as Jonason and Ferrell (2016) rightly noted, is to conduct a longitudinal study—that is, to measure the *same* variables of interest among the *same* sample of individuals at *more than one point in time*. My colleagues and I (Rempel et al., 2018) did just that by having a Canadian undergraduate sample complete a Dark Triad measure and two measures tapping the appetite for symbolic self-expansion twice, about a month apart. Higher initial appetite scores (which included themes of greed, insatiability, and the desire to "mark one's [psychological] territory") predicted increased Dark Triad scores over time, whereas initial Dark Triad scores did *not* predict fluctuations in appetite scores. Consistent with Moshagen et al. (2018), these results suggest that "dark" behavior can be understood as a set of *strategies* and *justifications* for trying to satisfy a relentless appetite for "more." Compare chemical dependency: As the disease advances, an afflicted individual's life may revolve increasingly around securing the next dose, even as financial resources and social support become depleted. Manipulating, lying, stealing, and the like that targets loved ones as well as strangers may be embraced eventually in the spirit of "doing what needs to be done."

But supposing that a seemingly insatiable desire for expanding one's psychological territory drives the Dark Triad, what causes the insatiability, the sense of "never having enough"? Research by Brumbach et al. (2009) offered clues: Thousands of American adolescents were initially surveyed and followed up nearly a decade later. Results showed that "social deviance" in young adulthood (which included measures related to psychopathy and Machiavellianism) was predicted by "environmental unpredictability" and "environmental harshness" in adolescence, with the latter two measures focusing on inadequate care by parents/guardians and witnessing or being the victim of lethal violence, respectively. This suggests that early exposure to significant threats may be particularly likely to foster a short-term, survivalist worldview akin to: "Get what you can, however you can, because you're basically on your own and you may be dead tomorrow." Seeking power (Jonason & Ferrell, 2016) and amassing symbolic resources (Rempel et al., 2018) via Dark Triad strategies can therefore perhaps be understood, at least in part, as desperate attempts to ensure one's own *psychological* survival—although the cost to others and self is often considerable.

Shame sensitivity

Earlier in this chapter, I made the case that shame can trigger aggressive responses as a means of (re)asserting one's power in the face of perceived social rejection. Although humans appear hard-wired to experience such rejection as unpleasant (see Chapter 3), some individuals may find it to be especially intolerable, in which case "I will stop feeling D [shame]" becomes a top priority. Schoenleber and Berenbaum (2012 [USA]) suggested that those who are perceived as drawing attention to a person's presumed defectiveness may be subjected to a variety of retaliatory tactics, both direct (verbal aggression, physical aggression) and indirect (undermining/obstruction, reputational damage, and social exclusion).

Some researchers have begun to apply this reasoning as a means of better understanding the link between posttraumatic stress disorder (PTSD) and the (subsequent) perpetration of violence. For example, Lawrence and Taft (2013 [USA], p. 192) concluded that "evidence suggests that individuals with PTSD are at increased risk for experiencing pathological levels of shame" as well as unsatisfying relationships and episodes of aggression (for convergent physiological evidence of the PTSD/shame link, see Freed & D'Andrea, 2015 [USA]). For some, hypervigilance to shame may be an automatic, nonconscious process. For example, Sippel and Marshall (2012) measured how quickly American participants reacted to shame-related words that were presented subliminally (that is, below the level of conscious awareness). Reactions were fastest among participants with more severe PTSD symptoms. This "shame processing bias," in turn, predicted a greater likelihood of having committed acts of domestic violence. Similarly, Hundt and Holohan (2012) found that PTSD predicted more self-reported shame, which in turn predicted more self-reported acts of domestic violence, in a U.S. veteran sample.

Shame has also been linked to problematic outcomes in the context of maladaptive tendencies besides PTSD, most notably borderline personality disorder (BPD) and narcissistic personality disorder (NPD). For example, Peters et al. (2014) found that shame predicted anger and angry rumination, which in turn predicted BPD symptoms such as emotional and relational instability in a non-clinical American sample. Ritter et al. (2014) showed that individuals diagnosed with either BPD or NPD reported greater shame-proneness relative to a non-clinical German sample. Nonconscious sensitivity to shame (relative to anxiety) was especially evident for those diagnosed with NPD, leading those authors to suggest that the self-aggrandizement and interpersonal hostility often associated with the disorder could function as distraction and deflection strategies intended to keep (too much) shame from becoming conscious. Keene and Epps (2016) found that recollection of physical abuse in childhood was linked to shame-proneness and narcissistic tendencies, which in turn predicted aggressive tendencies in an

American university sample (see Baumeister, 1997 [USA], for a related discussion concerning the problematic interpersonal consequences associated with high-but-unstable self-esteem). This sounds a lot like the link between harsh, unpredictable childhood environments and later social deviance in Brumbach et al. (2009) described earlier. Keep in mind that these are only *trends*, however. Thus, although trauma of various kinds increases the likelihood of shame and various forms of interpersonal nastiness, the latter are not *guaranteed* outcomes. In the spirit of individual differences, some who are traumatized choose differently.

Looking Back and Looking Forward

In this chapter I've attempted to present, unpack, and illustrate the central principle that is operative in those instances wherein people choose "evil" behavior. In basic terms, the MioMa or "Mind over Matter" principle suggests that people pursue good feelings and try to escape bad feelings, and that they make specific plans with anticipated feeling outcomes in mind. Whether impulsive or carefully premeditated, such plans are often accompanied by tunnel vision wherein others' well-being is either flat-out ignored, deemed of secondary importance, or deliberately destroyed.

Potential perpetrators often underestimate risks to their own well-being or attempt to deflect negative consequences away from themselves. And *of course* perpetrators will attempt to justify their behavior—first to themselves, then to others as needed—or else posture as if they are under no compunction to do so. Remember that the perceived evilness of intentional, harm-causing behavior depends on whether it is seen as justifiable (Chapter 1). Remember also that the threat of the Mark of Cain is ever-present (see Chapter 3), and so the costs of being labeled an "evildoer" can be considerable (Chapter 2). It is therefore both ironic and tragic that the desire to avoid the Mark of Cain—as manifest in shame sensitivity, for example—can give rise to precisely the kinds of behavior (such as domestic violence) that many would regard as "evil."

In Part 2 of this book, my goal is to show you how the core principles that I've laid out in Part 1 can help you better understand hate (Chapter 5), sadism (Chapter 6), serial killers (Chapter 7), and organized evil such as corporate wrongdoing and genocide (Chapter 8). Why these four? Perhaps because they all capture elements of the myth of pure evil (see Chapter 2), I suspect that many readers would be surprised if a book on evil *didn't* address them somehow. Fair warning: Although the magnitude of harm inflicted by perpetrators onto victims can be massive in the context of each of these phenomena, the motivation isn't exotic. Each is a manifestation of "mind over matter." Thus, it is fitting (albeit unintentional) that the MioMa acronym can be pronounced "me-oma," which sounds a lot like "cancer of the self." For evil to metastasize, all that is needed is diligent prioritization of one's own agenda at others' expense.

References

Aghababaei, N., & Błachnio, A. (2015). Well-being and the Dark Triad. *Personality and Individual Differences, 86*, 365–368. doi:10.1016/j.paid.2015.06.043

Anderson, C., & Galinsky, A. D. (2006). Power, optimism, and risk-taking. *European Journal of Social Psychology, 36*(4), 511–536. doi:10.1002/ejsp.324

Ariely, D., & Loewenstein, G. (2006). The heat of the moment: The effect of sexual arousal on sexual decision making. *Journal of Behavioral Decision Making, 19*(2), 87–98. doi:10.1002/bdm.501

Aron, A., Lewandowski, G. W., Jr., Mashek, D., & Aron, E. N. (2013). The self-expansion model of motivation and cognition in close relationships. In J. A. Simpson & L. Campbell (Eds.), *The Oxford handbook of close relationships* (pp. 90–115). Oxford University Press. doi:10.1093/oxfordhb/9780195398694.013.0005

Associated Press. (2017, April 2). Chicago police arrest boy, 14, in Facebook Live sexual assault. http://www.cbc.ca/news/world/chicago-teen-arrest-sexual-assault-facebook-live-1.4051706

Baumeister, R. F. (1997). *Evil: Inside human cruelty and violence*. W. H. Freeman.

BBC News. (2017, April 26). London Tube bomb accused Damon Smith claims it was a prank. http://www.bbc.com/news/uk-england-london-39721416

Bertl, B., Pietschnig, J., Tran, U. S., Stieger, S., & Voracek, M. (2017). More or less than the sum of its parts? Mapping the Dark Triad of personality onto a single Dark Core. *Personality and Individual Differences, 114*, 140–144. doi:10.1016/j.paid.2017.04.002

Biglan, A. (2011). Corporate externalities: A challenge to the further success of prevention science. *Prevention Science, 12*(1), 1–11. doi:10.1007/s11121-010-0190-5

Blanton, H., & Gerrard, M. (1997). Effect of sexual motivation on men's risk perception for sexually transmitted disease: There must be 50 ways to justify a lover. *Health Psychology, 16*(4), 374–379. doi:10.1037/0278-6133.16.4.374

Böhm, R., Rusch, H., & Gürerk, O. (2016). What makes people go to war? Defensive intentions motivate retaliatory and preemptive intergroup aggression. *Evolution and Human Behavior, 37*(1), 29–34. doi:10.1016/j.evolhumbehav.2015.06.005

Bowpitt, G. (2015, December 29). Homelessness causes offenders to end up back in prison—here's how to break the cycle. http://theconversation.com/homelessness-causes-offenders-to-end-up-back-in-prison-heres-how-to-break-the-cycle-52059

Brumbach, B. H., Figueredo, A. J., & Ellis, B. J. (2009). Effects of harsh and unpredictable environments in adolescence on development of life history strategies: A longitudinal test of an evolutionary model. *Human Nature, 20*, 25–51. doi:10.1007/s12110-009-9059-3

Buckels, E. E., & Trapnell, P. D. (2013). Disgust facilitates outgroup dehumanization. *Group Processes & Intergroup Relations, 16*(6), 771–780. doi:10.1177/1368430212471738

Burris, C. T., Rempel, J. K., Munteanu, A. R., & Therrien, P. A. (2013). More, more, more: The dark side of self-expansion motivation. *Personality and Social Psychology Bulletin, 39*(5), 578–595. doi:10.1177/0146167213479134

Canadian Press. (2017, April 5). Daycare owner admits toddler left 7 hours in hot car after saying she stopped breathing during nap. http://www.cbc.ca/news/canada/toronto/daycare-death-1.4056033

Carton, H., & Egan, V. (2017). The dark triad and intimate partner violence. *Personality and Individual Differences, 105*, 84–88. doi:10.1016/j.paid.2016.09.040

Chawla, N., & Ostafin, B. (2007). Experiential avoidance as a functional dimensional approach to psychopathology: An empirical review. *Journal of Clinical Psychology, 63*(9), 871–890. doi:10.1002/jclp.20400

Dinić, B. M., Wertag, A., Sokolovska, V., & Tomašević, A. (2021). The good, the bad, and the ugly: Revisiting the Dark Core. *Current Psychology*. Advance online publication.

Elison, J., Garofalo, C., & Velotti, P. (2014). Shame and aggression: Theoretical considerations. *Aggression and Violent Behavior, 19*(4), 447–453. doi:10.1016/j.avb.2014.05.002

Elshout, M., Nelissen, R. M. A., & van Beest, I. (2016). Conceptualising humiliation. *Cognition and Emotion, 31*(8), 1581–1594. doi:10.1080/02699931.2016.1249462

Erskine, K. J., Novreske, A., & Richards, M. (2013). Moral contagion effects in everyday interpersonal encounters. *Journal of Experimental Social Psychology, 49*(5), 947–950. doi:10.1016/j.jesp.2013.04.009

Freed, S., & D'Andrea, W. (2015). Autonomic arousal and emotion in victims of interpersonal violence: Shame proneness but not anxiety predicts vagal tone. *Journal of Trauma & Dissociation, 16*(4), 367–383. doi:10.1080/15299732.2015.1004771

Furnham, A., Richards, S. C., & Paulhus, D. L. (2013). The Dark Triad of personality: A 10-year review. *Social and Personality Psychology Compass, 7*(3), 199–216. doi:10.1111/spc3.12018

Gino, F., & Wiltermuth, S. S. (2014). Evil genius? How dishonesty can lead to greater creativity. *Psychological Science, 25*(4), 973–981. doi:10.1177/0956797614520714

Grover, S. L., & Hasel, M. C. (2015). How leaders recover (or not) from publicized sex scandals. *Journal of Business Ethics, 129*, 177–194. doi:10.1007/s10551-014-2146-3

Halevy, N. (2017). Preemptive strikes: Fear, hope, and defensive aggression. *Journal of Personality and Social Psychology, 112*(2), 224–237. doi:10.1037/pspi0000077

Hamilton, V. L., & Sanders, J. (1999). The second face of evil: Wrongdoing in and by the corporation. *Personality and Social Psychology Review, 3*(3), 222–233. doi:10.1207/s15327957pspr0303_5

Harmon-Jones, E., & Harmon-Jones, C. (2016). Anger. In L. F. Barrett, M. Lewis, & J. M. Haviland-Jones (Eds.), *Handbook of emotions* (4th ed., pp. 774–791). Guilford Press.

Harms, P. D., Spain, S. M., & Wood, D. (2014). Mapping personality in dark places. *Industrial and Organizational Psychology, 7*(1), 114–117. doi:10.1111/iops.12117

Hayling, A. (Producer), & Kjær, K. (Director). (2007). *Bloody cartoons* [Motion picture]. STEPS International.

Horberg, E. J., Orveis, C., & Keltner, D. (2011). Emotions as moral amplifiers: An appraisal tendency approach to the influences of distinct emotions upon moral judgment. *Emotion Review, 3*(3), 237–244. doi:10.1177/1754073911402384

Horney, J., & Marshall, I. H. (1992). Risk perceptions among serious offenders: The role of crime and punishment. *Criminology, 30*(4), 575–594. doi:10.1111/j.1745-9125.1992.tb01117.x

Hundt, N. E., & Holohan, D. R. (2012). The role of shame in distinguishing perpetrators of intimate partner violence in U.S. veterans. *Journal of Traumatic Stress, 25*(2), 191–197. doi:10.1002/jts.21688

Jonason, P. K.,.& Ferrell, J. D. (2016). Looking under the hood: The psychogenic motivational foundations of the Dark Triad. *Personality and Individual Differences, 94*, 324–331. doi:10.1016 /j.paid.2016.01.039

Jonason, P. K., Zeigler-Hill, V., & Okan, C. (2017). Good v. evil: Predicting sinning with dark personality traits and moral foundations. *Personality and Individual Differences, 104*, 180–185. doi:10.1016/j.paid.2016.08.002

Jones, A., & Fitness, J. (2008). Moral hypervigilance: The influence of disgust sensitivity in the moral domain. *Emotion, 8*(5), 613–627. doi:10.1037/a0013435

Jones, D. N., & Figueredo, A. J. (2013). The core of darkness: Uncovering the heart of the dark triad. *European Journal of Personality, 27*(6), 521–531. doi:10.1002/per.1893

Jones, D. N., & Paulhus, D. L. (2017). Duplicity among the Dark Triad: Three faces of deceit. *Journal of Personality and Social Psychology, 113*(2), 329–342. doi:10.1037/pspp0000139

Kajonius, P. J., Persson, B. N., Rosenberg, P., & Garcia, D. (2016). The (mis)measurement of the Dark Triad Dirty Dozen: Exploitation at the core of the scale. *PeerJ, 4*, e1748. doi:10.7717/peerj.1748

Keene, A. C., & Epps, J. (2016). Childhood physical abuse and aggression: Shame and narcissistic vulnerability. *Child Abuse & Neglect, 51*, 276–283. doi:10.1016/j.chiabu.2015.09.012

Lammers, J., & Maner, J. (2016). Power and attraction to the counternormative aspects of infidelity. *Journal of Sex Research, 53*(1), 54–63. doi:10.1080/00224499.2014.989483

Lawrence, A. E., & Taft, C. T. (2013). Shame, posttraumatic stress disorder, and intimate partner violence perpetration. *Aggression and Violent Behavior, 18*(2), 191–194. doi:10.1016/j.avb.2012.10.002

Lebuda, I., Figura, B., & Karkowski, M. (2021). Creativity and the Dark Triad: A meta-analysis. *Journal of Research in Personality, 92*, 104088. doi:10.1016/j.jrp.2021.104088

Litowitz, D. (2003-2004). Are corporations evil? *University of Miami Law Review, 58*, 811–841.

Lupton, D. (2002). Road rage: Drivers' understandings and experiences. *Journal of Sociology, 38*(3), 275–290. doi:10.1177/144078302128756660

Matsumoto, D., Frank, M. G., & Hwang, H. C. (2015). The role of intergroup emotions in political violence. *Current Directions in Psychological Science, 24*(5), 369–373. doi:10.1177/0963721415595023

McCauley, C. (2017). Toward a psychology of humiliation in asymmetric conflict. *American Psychologist, 72*(3), 255–265. doi:10.1037/amp0000063

McLarnon, M. J. W., & Tarraf, R. C. (2017). The Dark Triad: Specific or general sources of variance? A bifactor exploratory structural equation modeling approach. *Personality and Individual Differences, 112*, 67–73. doi:10.1016/j.paid.2017.02.049

Meere, M., & Egan, V. (2017). Everyday sadism, the Dark Triad, personality, and disgust sensitivity. *Personality and Individual Differences, 112*, 157–161. doi:10.1016/j.paid.2017.02.056

Molho, C., Tybur, J. M., Güler, E., Balliet, D., & Hofmann, W. (2017). Disgust and anger relate to different aggressive responses to moral violations. *Psychological Science, 28*(5), 609–619. doi:10.1177/0956797617692000

Moshagen, M., Hilbig, B. E., & Zettler, I. (2018). The dark core of personality. *Psychological Review, 125*(5), 656–688. doi:10.1037/rev0000111

Mouzos, J., & Venditto, J. (2003). *Contract killings in Australia* (*Australian Institute of Criminology Research and Public Policy Series No. 53*). Australian Institute of Criminology.

Muris, P., Merckelbach, H., Otgaar, H., & Meijer, E. (2017). The malevolent side of human nature: A meta-analysis and critical review of the literature on the Dark Triad (narcissism, Machiavellianism, and psychopathy). *Perspectives on Psychological Science, 12*, 183–204. doi:10.1177/1745691616666070

Nemeroff, C., & Rozin, P. (1994). The contagion concept in adult thinking in the United States: Transmission of germs and of interpersonal influence. *Ethos, 22*(2), 158–186. doi:10.1525/eth.1994.22.2.02a00020

Nicholls, A. R., Madigan, D. J., Backhouse, S. H., & Levy, A. R. (2017). Personality traits and performance enhancing drugs: The Dark Triad and doping attitudes among competitive athletes. *Personality and Individual Differences, 112*, 113–116. doi:10.1016/j.paid.2017.02.062

Paulhus, D. L., & Williams, K. M. (2002). The Dark Triad of personality: Narcissism, Machiavellianism, and psychopathy. *Journal of Research in Personality, 36*(6), 556–563. https://doi.org/10.1016/S0092-6566(02)00505-6

Peck, M. S. (1983). *People of the lie: The hope for healing human evil.* Simon and Schuster.

Peters, J. R., Geiger, P. J., Smart, L. M., & Baer, R. A. (2014). Shame and borderline personality features: The potential mediating role of anger and anger rumination. *Personality Disorders: Theory, Research, and Treatment, 5*(1), 1–9. doi:10.1037/per0000022

Philippe, F. L., Vallerand, R. J., Richer, I., Vallières, É., & Bergeron, J. (2009). Passion for driving and aggressive driving behavior: A look at their relationship. *Journal of Applied Social Psychology, 39*(12), 3020–3043. doi:10.1111/j.1559-1816.2009.00559.x

Pond, R. S., Jr., DeWall, C. N., Lambert, N. M., Deckman, T., Bonser, I. M., & Fincham, F. D. (2012). Repulsed by violence: Disgust sensitivity buffers trait, behavioral, and daily aggression. *Journal of Personality and Social Psychology, 102*(1), 175–188. doi:10.1037/a0024296

Rempel, J. K., Cheng, S. K., & Burris, C. T. (2018, March). *Greed drives the Dark Triad.* Poster presented at the Annual Meeting of the Society for Personality and Social Psychology, Atlanta, Georgia.

Richman, S. B., DeWall, C. N., Pond, R. S., Lambert, N. M., & Fincham, F. D. (2014). Disgusted by vengeance: Disgust sensitivity predicts lower vengeance. *Journal of Social and Clinical Psychology, 33*(9), 831–846. doi:10.1521/jscp.2014.33.9.831

Ritter, K., Vater, A., Rüsch, N., Schröder-Abé, M., Schütz, A., Fydrich, T., Lammers, C.-H., & Roepke, S. (2014). Shame in patients with narcissistic personality disorder. *Psychiatry Research, 215*(2), 429–437. doi:10.1016/j.psychres.2013.11.019

Ritter, R. S., & Preston, J. L. (2011). Gross gods and icky atheism: Disgust responses to rejected religious beliefs. *Journal of Experimental Social Psychology, 47*(6), 1225–1230. doi:10.1016/j.jesp.2011.05.006

Ross, A. (2017, May 3). Devon student guilty of planting homemade bomb on London tube. https://www.theguardian.com/uk-news/2017/may/03/devon-student-damon-smith-guilty-homemade-bomb-london-tube-underground

Ruedy, N. E., Moore, C., Gino, F., & Schweitzer, M. E. (2013). The cheater's high: The unexpected affective benefits of unethical behavior. *Journal of Personality and Social Psychology, 105*(4), 531–548. doi:10.1037/a0034231

Saeed, A. (2017, February 1). Why a community of punks chose to infect themselves with HIV in Castro's Cuba. https://www.vice.com/en_ca/article/qkzvxm/why-a-community-of-punks-chose-to-infect-themselves-with-hiv-in-castros-cuba

Schlesinger, L. B. (2001). The contract murderer: Patterns, characteristics, and dynamics. *Journal of Forensic Sciences, 46*(5), 1119–1123. doi:10.1520/JFS15108J

Schoenleber, M., & Berenbaum, H. (2012). Shame regulation in personality pathology. *Journal of Abnormal Psychology, 121*(2), 433–446. doi:10.1037/a0025281

Sezer, O., Gino, F., & Bazerman, M. H. (2015). Ethical blind spots: Explaining unintentional unethical behavior. *Current Opinion in Psychology, 6*, 77–81. doi:10.1016/j.copsyc.2015.03.030

Simunovic, D., Mifune, N., & Yamagishi, T. (2013). Preemptive strike: An experimental study of fear-based aggression. *Journal of Experimental Social Psychology, 49*(6), 1120–1123. doi:10.1016/j.jesp.2013.08.003

Sippel, L. M., & Marshall, A. D. (2012). Posttraumatic stress disorder symptoms, intimate partner violence perpetration, and the mediating role of shame processing bias. *Journal of Anxiety Disorders, 25*(7), 903–910. doi:10.1016/j.janxdis.2011.05.002

Skakoon-Sparling, S., Cramer, K. M., & Shuper, P. A. (2016). The impact of sexual arousal on sexual risk-taking and decision-making in men and women. *Archives of Sexual Behavior, 45*, 33–42. doi:10.1007/s10508-015-0589-y

Smoker, M., & March, E. (2017). Predicting perpetration of intimate partner cyberstalking: Gender and the Dark Tetrad. *Computers in Human Behavior, 72*, 390–396. doi:10.1016/j.chb.2017.03.012

Suri, M. (2017, April 21). Married man sends hijack hoax email to avoid trip with girlfriend. http://www.cnn.com/2017/04/21/asia/india-married-man-hijack-hoax-trnd/index.html

Svensson, R. (2015). An examination of the interaction between morality and deterrence in offending: A research note. *Crime and Delinquency, 61*(1), 3–18. doi:10.1177/0011128713486068

Sznycer, D., Tooby, J., Cosmides, L., Porat, R., Shalvi, S., & Halperin, E. (2016). Shame closely tracks the threat of devaluation by others, even across cultures. *Proceedings of the National Academy of Sciences USA, 113*(10), 2625–2630. doi:10.1073/pnas.1514699113

Tracy, J. L., & Robins, R. W. (2006). Appraisal antecedents of shame and guilt: Support for a theoretical model. *Personality and Social Psychology Bulletin, 32*(10), 1339–1351. doi:10.1177/0146167206290212

Tybur, J. M., Lieberman, D., Kurzban, R., & DeScioli, P. (2013). Disgust: Evolved function and structure. *Psychological Review, 120*(1), 65–84. doi:10.1037/a0030778

van Geel, M., Goemans, A., Toprak, F., & Vedder, P. (2017). Which personality traits are related to traditional bullying and cyberbullying? A study with the Big Five, Dark Triad and sadism. *Personality and Individual Differences, 106*, 231–235. doi:10.1016/j.paid.2016.10.063

Velotti, P., Elison, J., & Garofalo, C. (2014). Shame and aggression: Different trajectories and implications. *Aggression and Violent Behavior, 19*(4), 454–461. doi:10.1016/j.avb.2014.04.011

Vize, C. E., Lynam, D. R., Collison, K. L., & Miller, J. D. (2018). Differences among dark triad components: A meta-analytic investigation. *Personality Disorders: Theory, Research, and Treatment, 9*(2), 101–111. doi:10.1037/per0000222

Websdale, N. (2010). *Familicidal hearts: The emotional style of 211 killers.* Oxford University Press.

Wikström, P.-O. H., Tseloni, A., & Karlis, D. (2011). Do people comply with the law because they fear getting caught? *European Journal of Criminology, 8*(5), 401–420. doi:10.1177/1477370811416415

Wildschut, T., Pinter, B., Vevea, J. L., Insko, C. A., & Schopler, J. (2003). Beyond the group mind: A quantitative review of the interindividual–intergroup discontinuity effect. *Psychological Bulletin, 129*(5), 698–722. doi:10.1037/0033-2909.129.5.698

Wright, J. P., Morgan, M. A., Almeida, P. R., Almosaed, N. F., Moghrabi, S. S., & Bashatah, F. S. (2017). Malevolent forces: Self-control, the Dark Triad, and crime. *Youth Violence and Juvenile Justice, 15*(2), 191–215. doi:10.1177/1541204016667995

PART 2
A PANTHEON OF EVIL

5
Hate

Has anyone ever hated you? What did they do or say to give you that impression?

Have you ever hated anyone? What did you do or say, and think or feel, that makes you sure it was hate?

Some of you may be feeling as uncomfortable with these questions as you were with the "Are you evil?" question in Chapter 4. There I suggested that your discomfort was linked to the Mark of Cain. Might Mark of Cain dynamics apply to hate here as well?

Hate and Evil: Are They Linked?

The easiest way to make a case for this would be to assemble evidence that people intuitively link "hate" and "evil." Does such evidence exist? A bit, yes.

First, anecdotal evidence that laypeople see a connection is easy to find. For example, consider the August 2017 incident in Charlottesville, Virginia, in which an individual attending a white supremacist demonstration drove a car into a crowd of counter-demonstrators, killing one and injuring many. Most regarded the incident as a "hate crime" inspired by "hate groups"—an interpretation reinforced by U.S. Republican Senators Cory Gardner and Orrin Hatch, who insisted that people should "call evil by its name" (Cilizza, 2017 [USA]).

Social scientists likewise often utter "hate" and "evil" in the same breath. Consider these three titles: "Roots of evil, violence, and hate" (Baumeister & Butz, 2005 [USA]); " 'Hate torts' to fight hate crimes: Punishing the organizational roots of evil" (Koenig & Rustad, 2007 [USA]); and "Making a virtue of evil: A five-step social identity model of the development of collective hate" (Reicher et al., 2008 [UK]).

Second, remember the Burris and Rempel (2011 [Canada]) study that showed that exposure to "evil" symbols such as "666" and the Nazi swastika (vs. religious or neutral symbols) increased the extent to which people

Evil in Mind. Christopher T. Burris, Oxford University Press. © Oxford University Press 2022.
DOI: 10.1093/oso/9780197637180.003.0005

endorsed the "myth of pure evil" (MOPE; see Chapter 2)? I also conducted a (currently unpublished) study in which 136 Canadian student participants first completed the evil, religious, or neutral symbols matching task followed by a word completion task in which a series of fragments could each be filled in with a letter to make either a target word or one or more alternative words. The first fragment that participants encountered was "HA_E," which could be completed as either the target word "HATE" or any of several alternatives such as "HAVE." In the neutral and religious symbols conditions, just over one-fourth of participants (27% and 29%, respectively) completed the fragment as "HATE." In the evil symbols condition, the "HATE" completion rate nearly doubled (49%). Thus, symbols of evil not only tend to bring the MOPE mentally online—they also appear to make the concept of hate more internally accessible.

Third, over three-fourths of Halperin's (2008) Israeli interviewees described a target of hate as "evil and dispositionally bad" (p. 718). A follow-up experiment that made use of actual group-based conflict narratives provided by these interviewees revealed a similar pattern: When a story protagonist deemed a target to be "evil" (vs. did not), participants were much more likely to say that the protagonist experienced hate for the target. Anger showed a similar pattern, but the effect was weaker; fear did not show this pattern at all. Similarly, Goodvin (2019 [USA]) found that solicited hate experiences—compared to experiences of anger, contempt, or dislike—were much more likely to involve perceiving the target to be "evil." These findings suggest that *those who are seen as evil are hated.*

Fourth, it is probably also the case that *those who hate are (often) seen as evil.* This suggestion is based largely on people's apparent reluctance to attribute hate to themselves or to those whom they regard as members of their ingroup. For example, Waytz et al. (2014 [USA]) showed in both Israeli/Palestinian and (U.S.) Republican/Democratic contexts that people tend to see the behavior of the "other side" as motivated primarily by hate, whereas they see themselves as motivated primarily by love (for their ingroup; see also Halperin, 2008, footnote 1). When Burris and Rempel's (2006) Canadian participants were presented with a specific definition of hate (to be discussed later) and then asked if they had ever hated someone, the denial rate was a stunning 50% (107 of 213). When Aumer et al. (2015) asked their American survey participants a similar question without an accompanying definition of hate, the denial rate was 24% (35 of 148).

Should we take every individual's denial at face value? Probably not. For example, Aumer et al. (2015) noted that a number of deniers seemed to balk at "hate," saying that the word was "'too strong,' but they do 'extremely dislike' someone" (p. 4). Likewise, a number of Burris and Rempel's (2006) participants seemed squeamish at the thought of labeling an experience of theirs as "hate": Again, "hate" was "too strong," or else it was incompatible with their self-image. Alternatively, some claimed a loophole related to specific elements of the hate definition that they were presented, or else *described an experience that matched the definition* but denied that the "hate" label applied.

Moreover, in another (currently unpublished) study, about half of my 148 Canadian participants were simply asked if they had ever hated anyone; the other half were asked the same question from the perspective of their "Hidden Observer"—an imaginary part of the mind that knows a person's innermost secrets and can readily disclose them (see Burris & Mathes, 2011 [Canada]). Among those who were simply asked the question, the denial rate was 29%—fairly close to Aumer et al. (2015). In the "Hidden Observer" condition, however, the denial rate was more than cut in half (down to 13%). It would appear that admitting that one has hated is a sensitive matter (for a broad discussion of the challenges in securing accurate reports in such domains, see Tourangeau & Yan, 2007 [USA]).

Do people see a link between hate and evil? Although the evidence is fragmentary and some remains unpublished as I write this, the tentative answer seems to be "yes." Assuming that such a link exists, the next logical question is "Why?" A convincing answer should be able to account for both "those who are seen as evil are hated" and "those who hate are (often) seen as evil" and hinges on a proper understanding of what hate *is*.

Hate Is . . .

I suspect that most people have a sense of what hate is until they are asked to define it. Based on what we were able to locate up to that point, a colleague and I (Rempel & Burris, 2005 [Canada]) noted a number of commonalities and lack of consensus across the social scientific literature on hate. With respect to commonalities, he and I observed that scholars often (1) refer to hate as an emotion that (2) tends to be durable and (3) has motivational implications.

That is, hate is something that people *feel*, it's hard to shake off, and it makes people *want to do* things. The lack of consensus is most evident among those who assume that emotion is hate's conceptual core (e.g., Sternberg, 2020 [international]), as there seems to be little agreement as to whether hate is a distinct emotion or is instead a subtype or hybrid of other emotions: Anger, contempt, disgust, and fear have all been implicated across various analyses. With that in mind, my colleague and I opted to focus on the more agreed-upon "motivational implications," and proposed that hate is best understood as "*a motive associated with the goal of destroying or diminishing the object's well-being*" (p. 300, italics in original). Stated simply, "hate" means *wanting a target to experience harm*.

A motivational approach to hate sets aside debates concerning the specifics of hate's emotional core: *Any* emotion that provokes the desire for target harm is, by definition, related to hate. A motivational approach also provides a framework for thinking about different hate trajectories. For example, if the desire for target harm is a *means* to some other end, then hate can possibly be defused if the hater is made aware of *some other means* of obtaining that goal. In contrast, if harming the target is *an end itself*, an ultimate goal, then the hater is likely to accept no substitutes. Thus, hate is likely to persist until the target is completely annihilated. Such instances may help account for claims of hate's durability, for when people choose not to act on their desire to harm a hated target, the hate motive may stay switched on.

So what evidence is there for a motivational understanding of hate? Although a simple online search for hate scholarship yields thousands of hits, the vast majority focus on the legal concepts of "hate speech" (e.g., Bilewicz & Soral, 2020 [Poland]; Gelber & McNamara, 2016 [Australia]; Reichelmann et al., 2021 [international]) and "hate crimes" (e.g., Cheng et al., 2013 [Taiwan/USA]; Paterson et al., 2019 [USA]; Williams et al., 2020 [UK]) wherein one or more individuals are targeted for harm because they are linked to an identifiable group (e.g., ethnic, religious, sexual orientation). Note that although intended harm is part of legal definitions, "hate" therein is based on a perpetrator's criteria for choosing targets.

In contrast to the voluminous hate speech/hate crime literature, studies that directly address (rather than assume) the nature of hate appear to be extremely rare so far. One noteworthy exception (Zeki & Romaya, 2008 [UK]) attempted to locate regions of brain activity that are active during a hate experience by performing functional magnetic resonance imaging (fMRI) on participants' brains as they looked at a picture of someone they hated. They found evidence of activation in a brain network that has components "considered to be important in (a) generating aggressive behavior and (b) translating this behavior into motor action through motor planning" (p. 4). This seems entirely consistent with a motivational understanding of hate: Exposure to a hated target appears to trigger the intention to hurt that target.

The work of Halperin and colleagues is also suggestive. For example, Halperin (2008, Study 3) asked Israeli Jews first to think about a "least liked" Palestinian political group. They subsequently read a short passage that accused that group of undermining or attacking Israel's security. Participants then indicated how much hate, anger, and fear they felt in response to that group. Hate stood out as the best (indeed, nearly unique) predictor of reactions such as "removal or destruction of outgroup" and "physical and violent action [toward the outgroup]." Hate did *not* predict trying to avoid the outgroup or change the outgroup's attitudes, but it did predict *decreased* endorsement of "live and let live: create a safe environment [for the outgroup]." In a similar context, Halperin et al. (2011) showed that an "anger-inducing" article that portrayed Palestinians as uncooperative and untrustworthy moved Israeli Jews who hated them to want to cooperate with them even less; in contrast, when hate for Palestinians was low, this same article provoked *increased* desire to cooperate.

Halperin et al. (2012) attempted to differentiate between what they labeled "immediate hatred" and "chronic hatred" toward a political outgroup. Labels aside, it's important to examine the items used to measure these two constructs. Of the six "immediate hatred" items, the three most central were: "To feel a desire to take action in order to take revenge on members of the [selected outgroup] and its leaders;" "To imagine a violent action against members of the [selected outgroup];" and "Thoughts of a desire to get rid of or destroy members of the [selected outgroup] in any kind of manner." Clearly, these are consistent with Rempel and Burris's (2005) motivational definition of hate. In contrast, the themes of items anchoring the "chronic hatred" measure included not wanting to get to know members of the outgroup, having "negative feelings" toward the outgroup, and assuming that outgroup behaviors are the result of " 'bad' internal character": None directly tapped a desire for the outgroup to experience harm. When the two measures were pitted against each other to predict Israeli Jews' political behavior leading up to an election, the results suggested that "immediate haters do not thoroughly consider all potential alternatives, but mainly more extreme ones" (p. 2245)—that is, supporting factions that are likely to treat hated political outgroups more harshly. So-called chronic hatred—which actually seems more like a negative attitude toward, rather than hate for, the outgroup—did *not* predict these extremist tendencies.

Across four broad-based Israeli surveys, Halperin et al. (2009) found that hate toward outgroups predicted the desire to marginalize them politically, as indexed by denying them parliamentary representation, voting rights, and mass media platforms—and even by simply outlawing them. Moreover, although anger and fear also predicted the desire to harm political outgroups by disenfranchising them, hate fully explained those links. So, for example, fear predicted the desire to politically marginalize outgroups only because fear was related to hate and hate directly predicted marginalization. Thus, although limited to an Israeli context, the studies by Halperin and colleagues reviewed here all seem consistent with the idea that the core of hate is the desire for a target to experience harm—whether at the hands of oneself or someone else.

Perhaps the most direct support for Rempel and Burris's (2005) motivational understanding of hate comes from a series of studies reported by Rempel et al. (2019 [Canada/USA]; see also Goodvin, 2019). In the first, over 200 Canadian student participants were asked to write down what the word "hate" meant to them; a total of 52 distinct statements about hate were extracted from their responses. A second group of participants then rated how well each of these statements captured the essence of hate, and their ratings could be sorted into three big themes: the desire that the target be harmed (e.g., "wishing death upon the target," "desire to hurt"), strong emotions ("detesting," "loathing"), and weak emotions ("agitation," "frustration"). The desire to harm was seen as best capturing the essence of hate, followed by strong emotions, followed by weak emotions.

In the second study, Rempel et al. (2019) presented Canadian student participants with a set of "thought quotes" directed toward a target and asked them to rate the extent to which they considered each thought to be hate. Thoughts containing the desire for harm were rated as better examples of hate than thoughts wherein the desire for harm was absent. For example, the highest-rated statement was "I want him to hurt. *Period.*" In contrast, disliking the target intensely, thinking that he is an extremely bad person, and wanting to smash things when thinking about him were much less likely to be seen as hate, for all were accompanied by the qualifying phrase "but I don't want him to be hurt."

Canadian student participants in Rempel et al.'s (2019) third study were presented either of two paragraphs again portrayed as someone's thoughts directed toward a target. In one, the desire for harm was extreme—for example, "I sometimes felt that if every reminder that they ever existed were destroyed, the world would be a better place." In the other, the desire for harm was framed as being in the service of justice—for example, "The world is a better place if they are held accountable and suffer consequences for what they did." Participants were asked whether or not they considered the thoughts to be expressions of hate, and then explained why. For both sets of thoughts, those who said "yes, this is hate" were more likely to make mention of intended harm in their explanations compared to those who said "no, this isn't hate."

In the final study, conducted in Botswana, Rempel et al. (2019) presented student participants with a series of brief stories wherein a person expressed thoughts regarding a target experiencing harm. Specifically, that person framed the harm either as *undesirable but necessary* to accomplish some other goal, as *necessary and acceptable/desirable* for goal attainment, or as the *preferred option* for goal attainment. Framing harm as the preferred option or as necessary and acceptable/desirable resulted in comparably higher hate ratings compared to when hate was framed as undesirable but necessary—so, again, a greater desire for harm was seen as evidence of more hate.

Thus, although research that directly addresses the nature of hate is limited, the story it tells seems remarkably consistent. That is, regardless of whatever add-ons may be present, the core of what people label "hate" appears to be motivational—simply, *the desire for a target to experience harm*. You may have heard someone's mother say that "You can be angry with someone, but you're not supposed to hate them." This is probably the reason why: People seem to have an intuitive sense that hate can create victims in ways that anger and other emotions by themselves cannot.

Hate and the Mark of Cain

At the outset of this chapter, I asked whether you had ever hated anyone. I raised the possibility that any discomfort that you experienced considering this question could be linked to Mark of Cain dynamics. Since then, we've looked at evidence suggesting that: (1) hate and evil are cognitively linked; (2) people often appear reluctant to admit that they hate someone;

and (3) the core of hate is the desire for a target to be harmed. This is a nice setup for suggesting that hate is indeed in Mark of Cain territory, because *hate as defined here recalls two of the three prototypic features of evil—that is, intent (desire) and harm*. Therefore, if "hate" is detected, it needs to be justified, or else the hater risks being perceived as evil. With that in mind, let's consider how some of the strategies for deflecting the Mark of Cain play out in the context of dealing with the prospect of being a hater. Specifically, we will focus on *justified denial, justified admission*, and *normalized admission* (see also Chapter 3).

Justified denial

Based on the motivational definition presented in this chapter, hate is simply the desire for a target to suffer harm. Thus, all it takes to be a hater is to experience this desire. A person wishing to avoid the stigma of being (seen as) a hater by engaging in justified denial has two options. Specifically, they can *redefine* hate by insisting that "true" hate requires something more or something different than the desire for a target to suffer harm. Alternatively, they can *divert attention* away from the experience itself. The goal in either case is to be able to say, with reasonable conviction, that one's own experience *isn't* "hate." So what might these forms of justified denial look like?

One redefinition strategy is to equate hate with behavior rather than motivation, so "it's not hate if I don't act on it." In fact, the limited relevant data suggest that—all else being equal—inaction or thwarted action may actually fuel hate. For example, Rempel and Burris (2015 [Canada], as summarized in Rempel & Sutherland, 2016 [Canada]) reported two studies involving several hundred participants who wrote about one of their own hate-related experiences. They were subsequently asked to list what they *thought about* saying and doing, as well as what they *actually* said and did, during that experience, and these were coded for whether or not harm themes were evident. Finally, participants rated how resolved they felt that experience to be. Both studies showed a similar pattern: If harm-related thoughts were not proportionally accompanied by harmful actions, people tended to see their hate experience as unresolved.

Moreover, in a third study reported by Rempel and Burris (2015), participants were given an opportunity to write a letter expressing their "true thoughts, feelings, and wishes" regarding a convicted sex offender whom they believed could soon be released into their community. Some were told that the target audience was the researchers running the study, whereas others were told that it was the offender himself. In either case, when participants finished their letter and hit "send," some read that the letter was in fact sent successfully, whereas others read that it was one of a number of randomly chosen letters *not* to be sent. All participants subsequently completed a measure of hate for (i.e., desire to harm) the offender. The pattern of results was quite clear: Compared to the other three conditions, hate for the offender was highest among those who wrote to the offender but believed that their letter would not be sent—that is, among those whose opportunity to attack the offender verbally was taken away from them. Thus, although it may be comforting to deny that one is a hater because one has never actually tried to harm a target, this doesn't seem to reflect the reality of how people experience hate.

Another redefinition strategy is to restrict hate to the very sort of prolonged, intense experiences that moved many theorists to point out hate's durability (see Rempel & Burris, 2005). Thus, some individuals who want to avoid seeing themselves, or being seen by others, as haters may assert that an experience involving harm directed toward another wasn't hate "because I acted on impulse" or "because I felt guilty and remorseful afterwards." The idea here is that "real" hate involves rumination, both before and after any harm-producing episodes.

Again, although this redefinition strategy may offer some comfort, research suggests that it may not let the hater off the hook in others' eyes: Rempel et al. (2010 [Canada], as summarized in Rempel & Sutherland, 2016) presented Botswanan participants with a story about a student who verbally assaulted and physically intimidated a striking university staff member who was publicly derogating students. The student's behavior was framed as either impulsive (that is, that he "lost it" and acted without thinking) or deliberate (that is, that he thought through his actions and then returned to the scene to carry them out). Participants were asked to rate how intentional they thought that the student's actions were, as well as how much hate for the staff member they thought that the student experienced before, during, and after the episode. Although perceived hate was lower *before* and *after* the episode when the student's behavior was framed as impulsive, hate ratings in the impulsive and deliberate conditions were highest and not significantly different from each other *during* the episode. Moreover, hate ratings and intentionality ratings were linked. Thus, even brief, reactive behavior that causes harm appears to be seen as hate-driven by others if they conclude that the harm was intentional.

An alternative strategy for bolstering justified denial involves diverting attention away from the hate experience proper, most typically by focusing on one's ultimate goal. Drawing on a distinction used in classic motivation research, Rempel and Burris (2005) suggested that a target suffering harm can be sought not only as an end in itself, but also as a means to some other end. Thus, a person might deny being a hater because "what I *really* wanted was [insert nice-sounding ultimate goal]." This may not be as easy as it sounds: Recall that Rempel et al. (2019) showed that outside observers perceived less hate *only* when harm was framed as *undesirable but necessary* to accomplish some other goal, and that harm framed as *necessary and acceptable* was seen as just as hate-driven as when it was the *preferred option* for goal attainment. Nevertheless, noble-sounding ultimate goals may sometimes effectively distract both hater and judges from the hater's hate. For example, in the first "thought quotes" study reported by Rempel et al., although "I want him to be hurt, *because society would be better off*" and "I want him to be hurt, *because justice requires it*" were rated above the hate midpoint, neither was rated as far toward the "definitely hate" end of the spectrum as was "I want him to hurt. *Period.*"

Consider also the results of Rempel et al.'s (2019) second "thought quotes" study wherein the desire for target harm was framed as either an end in itself or a means of balancing the scales of justice. Recall that participants were asked whether or not they considered the thoughts to be expressions of hate, and then were asked to explain their answers. When the desire for harm was framed as an end in itself, 62% mentioned this desire in their explanations; when framed as a means to a just end, only 15% did so. More importantly, participants who read the "end in itself" description were less likely to see that experience as hate if their explanations did not mention harmful intentions (compared to those who did). The pattern was the same but stronger for the "means of justice" participants, such that those who failed to mention harmful intentions actually rated the experience toward the "not hate" end of the spectrum on average. This strongly suggests that noble-sounding ends can sometimes interfere with the detection of hate.

At the extreme are instances in which hate-driven behavior directed toward a target is attributed not to hate but to *love*. Rempel and Burris (2005) labeled one form of this as "tethering": Fueled by fear of abandonment, an individual may be moved to do whatever is necessary to disable the "loved" one to keep them from leaving. One of the most chilling fictional portrayals of this—and a stunning illustration of the MioMa principle (see Chapter 4)—appeared in the film adaptation (Nicolaides et al., 1990 [USA]) of Steven King's *Misery*: Although "#1 fan" Annie rescued her writer/crush Paul from a car accident, his healing would guarantee his departure. Thus, Annie hobbled him. That is, she shattered Paul's ankles with a sledgehammer, after which she whispered/exclaimed: "God, *I love you*!"

Although fictional, key elements of Annie's portrayal—idealization of a "loved" target coupled with desperate, often aggressive, attempts to maintain a sense of closeness with that person—overlap considerably with what has been termed borderline personality organization (BPO; see Kivisto, 2014 [USA]). BPO has been shown to be a strong predictor of violence directed toward intimate partners (for a review, see Jackson et al., 2015 [USA]) whether the focal perpetrators are adult men (e.g., Dutton, 2007 [Canada]), women (e.g., Clift & Dutton, 2011 [Canada]), or teens (e.g., Reuter et al., 2015 [USA]). BPO also predicts an array of subtler coercive and manipulative strategies that include monopolizing the partner's time and putting them down when communicating with perceived rivals. Collectively referred to as "costly mate retention tactics," these strategies tend to have a negative impact on both the partner's well-being and the relationship (Tragesser & Benfeld, 2012 [USA]).

Thus, there's certainly evidence that some people in relationships willingly subject their partners to physical and psychological harm in a dysfunctional attempt to keep them close. Is there any evidence that abusers interpret their behavior like *Misery*'s "Annie" did? Yes. For example, Henton et al. (1983 [USA]; see also Roscoe & Callahan, 1985 [USA]) asked high school students who had been involved in one or more physically violent dating relationships how they made sense out of the violence that had occurred. Although the sample was somewhat small (78, most of whom self-identified as both victims and perpetrators), the pattern of results was unsettling: When explaining their own abusive behavior, 54% said that they were "angry" and 60% said that they were "confused," but *31% attributed their behavior to "love."* In contrast, *only 3% attributed their behavior to "hate."* Strikingly, victims' explanations closely matched perpetrators': 71% said that the perpetrator was "angry" and 59% said that the perpetrator was "confused," but *27% attributed the perpetrator's behavior to "love."* In contrast, *only 4% mentioned "hate."*

On the surface, such findings may seem as perplexing as they are disturbing. Although no single explanation can fully account for them, the existing literature does point to a few likely contributors. For example, Puente and Cohen (2003) found that U.S. participants across multiple studies reported less-negative reactions to depictions of spousal abuse when the perpetrator claimed it was motivated by jealousy. Likewise, Black and Weisz (2005) found that a "jealousy is love" assumption is sometimes used to justify violence among young Mexican American dating couples.

Dunn (1999) showed that the trappings of romance sometimes blur the lines between unwanted interaction and "love." Over 250 American university sorority women were asked to imagine how they would feel if a hypothetical ex-partner, *with whom they desired no further contact*, left multiple messages for them or showed up in person to see them. Overall, the women expected to feel less annoyed and frightened, and more flattered, if these "forcible interaction" behaviors were accompanied by gifts or flowers. Many seemed ambivalent, reporting that they would feel both frightened *and* flattered. Moreover, based on her review of well over 100 domestic violence stalking cases, Dunn observed that "36 percent of victims reported that the men charged with stalking intermingled declarations of love with their threats to commit mayhem" (p. 443). Conflicting reactions of the pursued therefore seem to mirror conflicting behaviors of the pursuers.

Although a number of Borochowitz and Eisikovits's (2002) married Israeli interviewees attempted to trivialize or otherwise distance themselves from their experience of domestic violence, a few insisted that violence served a positive function. It's not surprising that perpetrators made such claims in an attempt to justify their behavior: "When I'm violent, *it's not because I hate her*, it's because, like I told you, another serious mistake she's made and she doesn't try to correct" (p. 486, italics added). More surprising, perhaps, is the fact that some victims expressed similar ideas: "If he beats his wife, then he cares, he loves his wife, he wants everything to be all right. . . . If a man beats his wife, it's a sign that *he loves and cares about her*, he wants her to behave right . . . that's one of the signs" (p. 487, italics added). In both instances, note that the stated ultimate goal of domestic violence is not just *any* noble-sounding end—rather, it's for the *targeted spouse's own good.* Of course, people outside violent relationships can quite rightly dispute the truthfulness or rationality of such claims: Would the Hidden Observers (see earlier in this chapter) of either perpetrators or victims *really* believe that intimate partner violence benefits the target (cf. Liargovas & Burris, 2015 [Canada])?

Justified admission

Justified denial—in its extreme, making the case that what looks like hate is actually "love"—can require a fair bit of mental gymnastics. By comparison, justified admission is more straightforward: One can say "I hate X" and still sidestep the Mark of Cain—that is, being seen as evil—IF one can offer adequate justifications for hating. The least subtle way of doing this is to *portray the target as an unjustified hater who is therefore evil.*

Some of Halperin's (2008) findings, briefly mentioned earlier, are consistent with this possibility (see also Waytz et al., 2014). For example, when "asked to recall an incident in which he or she thought that a certain person felt hatred toward a certain social group" (p. 737), over 80% of Halperin's Israeli interviewees confessed to wanting bad things to happen to members of the targeted group. Why? Nearly two-thirds indicated that the targeted group had intentionally done something that was unfair, and 73% linked hate to the perception that members of the targeted group were evil. In a large follow-up experiment, Halperin had participants read several stories involving an outgroup member engaging in harmful behavior. Of the key elements of the stories that were varied systematically across participants, the two that had the biggest impact on reported hate were whether the outgroup member was (1) portrayed as intending the harm and (2) (especially) portrayed as evil. For anger, the effects of both of these story variations were weaker; for fear, the effects were negligible. Thus, although these results do not offer direct evidence of Mark of Cain dynamics, they do suggest that thinking of a target as "evil" is a particularly powerful way to decrease people's reluctance to admitting hate (see also Goodvin, 2019).

Normalized admission

Finally, recall my suggestion in Chapter 3 that people sometimes deal with the threat of the Mark of Cain by attempting to normalize expressed sentiments and behaviors that others might find questionable. Hopefully you are reasonably convinced by now that "I hate . . ." gets into Mark of Cain territory. The only data of which I'm aware that directly speak to this, however, come from an unpublished online study that my colleague John Rempel and I conducted some years ago. We had nearly 200 Canadian undergraduates imagine either themselves or an acquaintance engaging in morally questionable behaviors (that is, not doing their fair share on a group project, gossiping about a friend, falsifying a résumé). They were subsequently asked to rate how likely they would use each of 20 justifications when explaining these behaviors. Three of the justifications explicitly involved normalizing: "As if other people don't do this all the time—I don't deserve to be singled out or disadvantaged;" "This isn't a big deal—most people do a lot worse;" and "People are hypocrites; they like to pretend that they are better than everyone else, but they all do the same kind of thing."

Now here's the twist: Participants were randomly assigned to one of four possible subliminal priming conditions. That is, prior to rating each justification, the words "I hate," "I dislike," "I am angry," or (the neutral) "People are walking" appeared—fast enough to register outside of awareness, but not consciously. (People reported, at most, seeing a flash or the occasional word.)

Compared to participants exposed to the other three primes, those exposed to the "I hate" prime were more likely to say that they'd try to normalize their questionable behaviors (based on their responses to the three justification items just described). Importantly, this pattern did not emerge when people imagined an acquaintance engaging in questionable behavior. Moreover, the effect of the subliminal "I hate" prime appeared to be specific to normalizing, as the prime did not appear to boost other types of justifications. Thus, a not-quite-conscious sense that one is a hater appeared sufficient to trigger motivation to portray oneself as not standing out from others in a bad way. It's only one study, of course, but the results do seem to suggest that people have a gut understanding that hating makes them vulnerable to being branded with the Mark of Cain.

Real Hate

In this chapter I've tried to make the case that *real* hate should be equated with *wanting a target to experience harm*. To be sure, the "hate speech" and "hate crimes" that are the focus of most current hate scholarship contain this motivational core, probably without exception. Nevertheless, hate can exist *even if the hater says or does nothing about it*.

Thus, although a simple "I HATE you!" can cut quite deeply, haters can hate without "dropping the H bomb." Haters can also hate without lifting a finger against their target of choice. Keep in mind that, in addition to making oneself socioemotionally vulnerable to the Mark of Cain, acting on one's desire to harm someone can come with a whole host of practical consequences such as retaliation or incarceration. "Lucky" haters who delay action may see their hated targets suffer harm as the result of circumstances, others' deeds, and possibly even the hated targets' own missteps (see Chapter 6 for a discussion of schadenfreude).

And although the concepts of "hate speech" and "hate crimes" rightly underscore the ugly fact that many people are targeted for harmful intentions simply because of their actual or assumed group memberships, hate elicitors are much more diverse than these legal designations imply. Consider two examples of solicited experiences from the first hate study I ever conducted.

Respondent 1 wrote about a classmate whose voice they found to be particularly irritating. When prompted to write about things that they wanted to say or do as part of their experience, Respondent 1 toyed with the idea of pushing the classmate off a rooftop. Is this *real* hate? Imagine that Respondent 1 actually pushed their classmate off.

Respondent 2, who was the victim of persistent school bullying, confessed to fantasizing about a bomb that would annihilate the tormentors. Is this *real* hate? Imagine that Respondent 2 built, placed, and detonated that bomb.

Why did these individuals hate? Why do "hate groups" hate? Why does anyone hate? Bringing back a central theme of Chapter 4, I suggest that *hate occurs in pursuit of a feeling*: If you suffer harm—be it the result of my doing or someone else's—then I will experience more good feeling and/or less bad feeling. The hoped-for outcomes may well appear to be much more varied across specific situations—for example, ethnic pride, relationship security, divine approval, justice, or a more serene tomorrow at school. Nevertheless, if the chosen path toward any of these outcomes requires holding hands with harm befalling others, there is hate.

Of course, sometimes others' suffering simply seems to make people flat-out feel good. Thus, we'll take a look at sadism in Chapter 6.

References

Aumer, K., Bahn, A. C. K., & Harris, S. (2015). Through the looking glass, darkly: Perceptions of hate in interpersonal relationships. *Journal of Relationships Research*, 6, 1–7. doi:10.1017/jrr.2014.14

Baumeister, R. F., & Butz, D. A. (2005). Roots of evil, violence, and hate. In R. J. Sternberg (Ed.), *The psychology of hate* (pp. 87–102). American Psychological Association. doi:10.1037/10930-005

Bilewicz, M., & Soral, W. (2020). Hate speech epidemic: The dynamic effects of derogatory language on intergroup relations and political radicalization. *Advances in Political Psychology, 41(S1)*, 3–33. doi:10.1111/pops.12670

Black, B. M., & Weisz, A. N. (2005). Dating violence: A qualitative analysis of Mexican American youths' views. *Journal of Ethnic & Cultural Diversity in Social Work, 13*(3), 69–90. doi:10.1300/J051v13n03_04

Borochowitz, D. Y., & Eisikovits, Z. (2002). To love violently: Strategies for reconciling love and violence. *Violence Against Women, 8*(4), 476–494. doi:10.1177/10778010222183170

Burris, C. T., & Mathes, S. (2011). Digging in my secret garden: Disinhibitory effects of the "Hidden Observer" on reported sexual fantasies. *Canadian Journal of Human Sexuality, 20*(4), 143–150.

Burris, C. T., & Rempel, J. K. (2006, January). "You're worthless": The role of devaluation in *the experience of hate.* Poster presented at the Annual Meeting of the Society for Personality and Social Psychology, Palm Springs, CA.

Burris, C. T., & Rempel, J. K. (2011). "Just look at him": Punitive responses cued by "evil" symbols. *Basic and Applied Social Psychology, 33*(1), 69–80. doi:10.1080/01973533.2010.539961

Cheng, W., Ickes, W., & Kenworthy, J. B. (2013). The phenomenon of hate crimes in the United States. *Journal of Applied Social Psychology, 43*(4), 761–794. doi:10.1111/jasp.12004

Cilizza, C. (2017, August 14). 9 times Republicans denounced Trump but came back to him. http://www.cnn.com/2017/08/14/politics/trump-republicans-criticism/index.html

Clift, R. J. W., & Dutton, D. G. (2011). The abusive personality in women in dating relationships. *Partner Abuse, 2*(2), 166–188. doi:10.1891/1946-6560.2.2.166

Dunn, J. L. (1999). What love has to do with it: The cultural construction of emotion and sorority women's responses to forcible interaction. *Social Problems, 46*(3), 440–459. doi:10.2307/3097109

Dutton, D. G. (2007). *The abusive personality: Violence and control in intimate relationships.* Guilford Press.

Gelber, K., & McNamara, L. (2016). Evidencing the harms of hate speech. *Social Identities, 22*(3), 324–341. doi:10.1080/13504630.2015.1128810

Goodvin, A. (2019). *Is hate a distinct emotion?* Unpublished master's thesis. State University of New Jersey—Rutgers.

Halperin, E. (2008). Group-based hatred in intractable conflict in Israel. *Journal of Conflict Resolution, 52*(5), 713–736. doi:10.1177/0022002708314665

Halperin, E., Canetti, D., & Kimhi, S. (2012). In love with hatred: Rethinking the role hatred plays in shaping political behavior. *Journal of Applied Social Psychology, 42*(9), 2231–2256. doi:10.1111/j.1559-1816.2012.00938.x

Halperin, E., Canetti-Nisim, D., & Hirsch-Hoefler, S. (2009). The central role of group-based hatred as an emotional antecedent of political intolerance: Evidence from Israel. *Political Psychology, 30*(1), 93–123. doi:10.1111/j.1467-9221.2008.00682.x

Halperin, E., Russell, A. G., Dweck, C. S., & Gross, J. J. (2011). Anger, hatred, and the quest for peace: Anger can be constructive in the absence of hatred. *Journal of Conflict Resolution, 55*(2), 274–291. doi:10.1177/0022002710383670

Henton, J., Cate, R., Koval, J., Lloyd, S., & Christopher, S. (1983). Romance and violence in dating relationships. *Journal of Family Issues, 4*(3), 467–482. doi:10.1177/019251383004003004

Jackson, M. A., Sippel, L. M., Mota, N., Whalen, D., & Schumacher, J. A. (2015). Borderline personality disorder and related constructs as risk factors for intimate partner violence perpetration. *Aggression and Violent Behavior, 24*, 95–106. doi:10.1016/j.avb.2015.04.015

Kivisto, A. J. (2014). Abandonment and engulfment: A bimodal classification of anxiety in domestic violence perpetrators. *Aggression and Violent Behavior, 19*(3), 200–206. doi:10.1016/j.avb.2014.04.005

Koenig, T. H., & Rustad, M. L. (2007). "Hate torts" to fight hate crimes: Punishing the organizational roots of evil. *American Behavioral Scientist, 51*(2), 302–318. doi:10.1177/0002764207306061

Liargovas, A., & Burris, C. T. (2015, February). *Letting the beloved count the ways: Positive relationship illusions and partner narcissism*. Poster presented at the Annual Meeting of the Society for Personality and Social Psychology, Long Beach, CA.

Nicolaides, S., Reiner, R., Scheinman, A., & Stott, J. (Producers), & Reiner, R. (Director). (1990). *Misery* [Motion Picture]. Columbia Pictures.

Paterson, J. L., Brown, R., & Walters, M. A. (2019). The shorter- and longer-term impacts of hate crimes experienced directly, indirectly, and through the media. *Personality and Social Psychology Bulletin, 45*(7), 994–1010. doi:10.1177/0146167218802835

Puente, S., & Cohen, D. (2003). Jealousy and the meaning (or nonmeaning) of violence. *Personality and Social Psychology Bulletin, 29*(4), 449–460. doi:10.1177/0146167202250912

Reichelmann, A., Hawdon, J., Costello, M., Ryan, J., Blaya, C., Llorent, V., Oksanen, A., Räsänen, P., & Zych, I. (2021). Hate knows no boundaries: Online hate in six nations. *Deviant Behavior, 42*(9), 1100–1111. doi:10.1080/01639625.2020.1722337

Reicher, S., Haslam, S. A., & Rath, R. (2008). Making a virtue of evil: A five-step social identity model of the development of collective hate. *Social and Personality Psychology Compass, 2*(3), 1313–1344. doi:10.1111/j.1751-9004.2008.00113.x

Rempel, J. K., & Burris, C. T. (2005). Let me count the ways: An integrative theory of love and hate. *Personal Relationships, 12*(2), 297–313. doi:10.1111/j.1350-4126.2005.00116.x

Rempel, J. K., & Burris, C. T. (2015, July). *A poison tree: The dark side of regulating hate.* Paper presented at the International Association for Relationship Research Conference, Amsterdam, The Netherlands.

Rempel, J. K., Burris, C. T., & Fathi, D. (2019). Hate: Evidence for a motivational conceptualization. *Motivation and Emotion, 43*(1), 179–190. doi:10.1007/s11031-018-9714-2

Rempel, J. K., Hertz, S., & Burris, C. T. (2010, July). *But I didn't mean it: The role of intention in defining hate*. Paper presented at the International Association for Relationship Research Conference, Hertzliya, Israel.

Rempel, J. K., & Sutherland, S. (2016). Hate: Theory and implications for intimate relationships. In K. Aumer (Ed.), *The psychology of love and hate in intimate relationships* (pp. 105–129). Springer International. doi:10.1007/978-3-319-39277-6_7

Reuter, T. R., Sharp, C., Temple, J. R., & Babcock, J. C. (2015). The relation between borderline personality disorder features and teen dating violence. *Psychology of Violence, 5*(2), 163–173. doi:10.1037/a0037891

Roscoe, B., & Callahan, J. (1985). Adolescents' self-report of violence in families and dating relations. *Adolescence, 20*(79), 545–553.

Sternberg, R. J. (Ed.). (2020). *Perspectives on hate: How it originates, develops, manifests, and spreads*. American Psychological Association. doi:10.1037/0000180-000

Tourangeau, R., & Yan, T. (2007). Sensitive questions in surveys. *Psychological Bulletin, 133*(5), 859–883. doi:10.1037/0033-2909.133.5.859

Tragesser, S. L., & Benfeld, J. (2012). Borderline personality disorder features and mate retention tactics. *Journal of Personality Disorders*, *26*(3), 334–344. doi:10.1521/pedi.2012.26.3.334

Waytz, A., Young, L. L., & Ginges, J. (2014). Motive attribution asymmetry for love vs. hate drives intractable conflict. *Proceedings of the National Academy of Sciences USA*, *111*(44), 15687–15692. doi:10.1073/pnas.1414146111

Williams, M. L., Burnap, P., Javed, A., Liu, H., & Ozalp, S. (2020). Hate in the machine: Anti-black and Anti-Muslim social media posts as predictors of offline racially and religiously aggravated crime. *British Journal of Criminology*, *60*(1), 93–117. doi:10.1093/bjc/azz049

Zeki, S., & Romaya, J. P. (2008). Neural correlates of hate. *PLoS ONE*, *3*(10), e3556. doi:10.1371/journal.pone.0003556

6
Sadism

What comes to mind when you read the word "sadist"?

I suspect that most people would agree that a sadist is someone who enjoys hurting others. Until quite recently, psychological investigations of sadism have focused mostly on individuals who inflict *extreme harm* on others—harm that is therefore often criminal, and that is sometimes also eroticized by the perpetrator (see Bulut, 2017 [Serbia], Foulkes, 2019 [UK], and Paulhus & Dutton, 2016 [Canada]; see also Burris & Leitch, 2016 [Canada]). Probably due in part to this historical focus on those who engage in multiple acts of flagrant, severe harm, some psychologists (e.g., Baumeister, 1997 [USA]) have suggested that sadism is actually quite rare—that is, that the vast majority of people really don't like hurting others. In this chapter I will argue that sadistic outcomes are much more likely to be measured than excessive, and covert or justified rather than flaunted. Viewed through this lens, sadism is not rare but common.

What Is Sadism?

There's a reason why a chapter on sadism appears immediately following the chapter on hate: My colleagues and I (Burris & Leitch, 2016; Rempel & Burris, 2005 [Canada]) have argued elsewhere that sadism is, in fact, a form of hate. Remember from Chapter 5 that hate is best understood in motivational terms—that, at its core, hate is the desire for a target to experience harm. In the case of sadism, or sadistic motivation, target harm is desired because it is seen as a path toward positive emotional payoff. That is, one seeks either to make other beings (human or non-human) suffer, or to be assured of such suffering secondhand, in hopes of experiencing pleasure, satisfaction, arousal, etc., as a result.

The sequence just outlined puts us in a good position to understand when it is, and when it is not, reasonable to infer sadistic motivation: The *desired/anticipated* outcome, not the actual outcome, is key. Thus, if an individual

Evil in Mind. Christopher T. Burris, Oxford University Press. © Oxford University Press 2022.
DOI: 10.1093/oso/9780197637180.003.0006

desires to do harm in hopes of a good-feeling payoff, the motivation is sadistic even if it does not result in harmful behavior. After all, not doing something doesn't mean that the person doesn't *want* to do it. Likewise, suppose a person desires to do harm in hopes of a good-feeling payoff and acts on this desire, but the anticipated good-feeling payoff doesn't materialize: The *intent* is still there, so the motivation is sadistic. (Note that the emphasis on desired/anticipated outcome differs from the focus on *actual* behavioral or feeling outcomes, as in O'Meara & Hammond, 2016 [Ireland], and Paulhus & Dutton, 2016 [Canada]).

In contrast, suppose an individual wants to harm someone, but positive emotional payoff is *not* anticipated (even if it occurs): The motivation certainly qualifies as hate, but it is *not* sadistic. Likewise, suppose that, while under coercion or duress, an individual attempts to harm someone: Sadistic motivation is a "luxury" that is most probably *not* relevant for understanding that person's behavior. Finally, suppose an individual "harms" a target other in order to gratify or benefit that target, as in some forms of consensual sexual power play (see Miller & Devon, 1995 [USA]): The motivation is *not* sadistic. Indeed, gratifying or benefiting the other would actually block a true sadist's goal pursuit (see Burris & Leitch, 2016).

Is Sadism "Evil"?

Is sadism "evil"? The short answer is that a lot of people apparently think so. In fact, as noted in Chapter 2, sadistic motivation is part of the "myth of pure evil" (MOPE) as originally articulated by Baumeister (1997).

Why? You should be able to anticipate the answer by now based on the core principles I presented in Part 1: The label "evil" is applied when harm is perceived to be both intentional and unjustifiable, and the ultimate goal of sadistic motivation is arguably the *least acceptable justification that could possibly be offered* for intentionally harming someone (cf. Trémolière & Djeriouat, 2016 [France]). So if someone says: "I publicly humiliated them because I thought it would be hilarious," they're clearly making no effort whatsoever to sugarcoat their actions. The motivation is brazenly unambiguous: The speaker inflicted psychological suffering on others for personal amusement's sake. The goal is simple, self-absorbed, and a particularly flagrant illustration of the MioMa principle (see Chapter 4). *Of course* those whose motivation is seen as sadistic will be labeled "evil" (see Gromet et al.,

2016 [USA]). *Of course* sadism is part of the MOPE. Frankly, you and I should be shocked were that *not* the case.

As a clear candidate for the "evil" label and the Mark of Cain dynamics that go along with it, appearing sadistically motivated is risky. Consequently, forthright admissions of sadistic motivation for severe victim harm should only be expected among individuals attempting to display their personal power as a means of bolstering the claim that they are immune to the Mark of Cain (see Chapter 3). Otherwise, I would suggest that sadistically motivated actors are likely to resort to some combination of: (1) minimizing harm severity to bring it down below the "unacceptable" threshold; and (2) claiming a motivation other than sadism—that is, one that seems inherently more justifiable (e.g., Tortoriello et al., 2019 [USA]). Both of these strategies can take additional aim at the target.

Consider pranking as a context. In response to victims' claims about the severity of physical or psychological suffering that they are experiencing, a sadistic prankster may assert that the victims are overreacting or "can't take a joke." Another may insist that the victims deserve to be pranked based on their gullibility or past misdeeds. Others may claim that their ultimate goal is neither self-focused nor sinister, but rather victim-focused and benign. For example, the prank may be positioned as shared fun or as a way for a "victim" to be more connected to a social group (see Marsh, 2015 [USA], whose pro-prank apologetic is rife with examples of the strategies just described).

As I pointed out elsewhere (Burris & Leitch, 2016), there appears to be a curious gap among perpetrators willing to admit to harming a target because it makes them (the perpetrators) feel good. Sexual sadists, animal abusers, hazing practitioners, Internet trolls, and pranksters will all confess—at least sometimes—to harming others in pursuit of positive feelings. Such confessions appear rare among perpetrators of intimate partner violence (IPV), however, for sadistic motivation "(i.e., pleasure, satisfaction as a desired end) was nowhere mentioned in an up-to-the minute, comprehensive review of research concerning abusers' stated motives" (p. 98).

Based on the same review by Neal and Edwards (2017 [USA]), IPV victims didn't point to sadism when assessing the perpetrator's motives, either. In fact, in a small sample of American respondents who had experienced IPV, Arriaga (2002, p. 605) found that those highly committed to their relationship were more likely than those less committed to report "'jokingly' being beat up, assaulted with a weapon, and kicked—behaviors that objectively do not occur in a joking context." Arriaga apparently did not determine whether such "joking" explanations were offered by perpetrators and accepted by victims, or instead generated by the victims themselves. Whichever, the fact that "joking violence" was more readily embraced as plausible by victims who were highly committed to their relationship suggests that they were trying to deflect harmful intentions away from their abusive partners.

Why does that make sense? Think about how this sounds: "On many occasions my partner has made me suffer simply because that makes them feel good. No other reason." Remember that raw sadistic motivation is part of the MOPE. Thus, if detected and labeled as such, sadism is probably a relationship deal-breaker. Consequently, perpetrators and victims who want to stay in a relationship have every reason to steer away from sadism as an explanation for harm-causing behavior.

Do Be Bitter: Sadism as an Individual Difference

A growing body of research suggests that sadistic tendencies differ across individuals. Such research relies heavily on questionnaires containing straightforward items such as "Being mean to others can be exciting" (Plouffe et al., 2017 [Canada]) and "I enjoy seeing people hurt" (O'Meara et al., 2011 [Ireland]). Some researchers have made the case that dispositional sadism is a fourth "dark" personality trait (e.g., Buckels et al., 2013 [Canada/USA]) that should be considered—along with psychopathy, Machiavellianism, and narcissism—as part of a the "Dark Tetrad."

With that in mind, I raise the same caution here that I did before considering research relating to the Dark Triad in Chapter 4: Higher scores on a self-report measure of dispositional sadism are the result of individuals introspecting and admitting sadistic tendencies. It should not be surprising that freely identifying oneself as someone who takes pleasure in others' suffering predicts a variety of nasty interpersonal outcomes—but it's arguably a step too far to say that a "sadistic trait" *causes* these nasty outcomes. Nevertheless, it seems worthwhile to provide an overview of some of the predictor–outcome links that have been documented in recent research. Some seem obvious, but not all of them.

Paralleling the Dark Triad, higher sadism scores predict a wide range of harmful behaviors and harm-congruent attitudes. For example, Paulhus and Dutton (2016) reported that individual differences in sadism predicted "reports of animal abuse, fire setting, vandalism, and dominance via threats, including partner abuse" (p. 113; see also Pfattheicher et al., 2019 [Germany/Serbia]). Russell and King (2016) found that (especially physical) sadism predicted sexual aggression in a community sample of American men. Dispositional sadism also predicts both traditional bullying and cyberbullying (van Geel et al., 2017 [Netherlands]) as well as trolling—that is, making intentionally offensive or controversial online comments in order to enjoy the outbursts of negative emotions in others that such comments create (e.g., Buckels et al., 2014 [Canada/USA]; Craker & March, 2016 [Australia]; see also Hardaker, 2010 [UK]). It's also been linked to mistreating coworkers (Min et al., 2019 [USA]) and insensitive reactions to bereaved individuals (Lee, 2019 [USA]).

Non-humans as well as humans can be targeted: In Buckels et al. (2013), Canadian students were given a choice of several presumably unpleasant tasks that included cleaning a dirty toilet, enduring an ice bath, or grinding up live bugs. Those who chose to grind up live bugs had the highest sadism scores. Moreover, higher sadism scorers reported enjoying the bug-grinding task more than the other tasks, whereas lower sadism scorers did not show this pattern. (Note: Participants who chose the toilet or the ice didn't have to follow through, and the grinder was rigged so that, unbeknownst to participants, no bugs were actually killed. Psychologists—at least most of them, I hope—aren't that sadistic.)

In Buckels et al.'s (2013) other study, participants were led to believe that they were competing in a game with a participant in another room, and when they "won" they could send a blast of noise to the other participant—although sometimes they were instructed that they had to work for it by completing an additional tedious task. The supposed other participant never sent noise when winning the game, so any noise that the actual participants worked for and sent could be interpreted as unprovoked, gratuitous aggression. Higher sadism (along with higher psychopathy and narcissism) predicted choosing to send longer, louder blasts of noise. Moreover, higher sadism uniquely predicted a willingness to work for the opportunity to do so. In other words, higher sadism scorers appeared motivated to hurt the supposed other participant "just because."

Sadistic tendencies have been linked also to greater frequency of violent video game play, whether assessed at the same point in time (Greitemeyer, 2015 [Austria]) or with a 6-month gap in between (Greitemeyer & Sagioglou, 2017 [Austria]). There are two seemingly obvious implications of these results. First, it would appear that pretend-but-realistic virtual violence can gratify sadistic impulses, at least somewhat (see Greitemeyer et al., 2019 [Austria]). Second, because violent game play also predicted sadism 6 months later in Greitemeyer and Sagioglou's study, persistent exposure to such virtual violence can possibly amplify sadistic tendencies. Given that many such games involve multiple players and real-time communication, it's worth asking whether gratification of sadistic impulses is most likely when real others can be taunted, tricked, and verbally abused as part of "normal" game play (see Achterbosch et al., 2017 [Australia]). Because neither set of results reported in the Austrian studies distinguished between solo and multi-player game play, this hypothesis awaits further research.

What Does Sadism *Feel* Like?

Recall my argument in Chapter 4 that we're all ultimately chasing feelings, so a key question is what we're willing to do, and to whom, in hopes of securing more of the good, less of the bad. As defined in the current chapter, sadism means putting the suffering of other beings explicitly in the service of one's pursuit of a positive emotional experience. That others experience harm is not optional. Neither is it regrettable, at least in the moment. It is *required.* With this in mind, it's worth digging deeper into research concerning how those with sadistic tendencies experience positive and negative states. So let's look at some relevant research.

Schumpe and Lafrenière (2016 [Canada/Germany]) reported the results of two online studies involving American participants who completed a measure of dispositional sadism. In the first, participants learned about a competitive cyclist's accident that not only caused him to lose a race narrowly, but also resulted in either a minor or potentially career-ending injury. The outcome measure was schadenfreude, or positive (sadistic) feelings—that is, participants indicated how much learning about the accident was enjoyable and satisfying. High sadism scorers reacted more positively to the accident than did low sadism scorers, *especially when the cyclist's injury was severe*. The second study found a similar effect that was most pronounced when the race was framed as an important one—that is, those with sadistic tendencies were most enthused when the cyclist's suffering was maximized by the combination of a severe physical injury and an especially crushing defeat. As a pair, these studies offer unambiguous evidence that those with sadistic tendencies derive pleasure from others' suffering, especially when that suffering is intense. Moreover, note that people with sadistic tendencies feel pleasure even when the victim is someone with whom they have had no prior interaction: This eliminates the possibility that grudges against the victim are the fuel for sadists' positive reactions.

Across three online studies involving hundreds of participants, Trémolière and Djeriouat (2016) documented evidence of "impaired moral judgment" among people with sadistic tendencies, even when taking into account overlap with the Dark Triad: Sadistic individuals were more lenient in their judgments of perpetrators who intentionally harmed someone (or at least tried to). Moreover, their leniency appeared to be driven, at least in part, by positive emotional reactions (such as "joyful" and "enthusiastic") to the harm attempts. In contrast, among less sadistic individuals, negative emotional reactions seemed to drive moral condemnation of harm attempts. These results certainly illustrate the link between people's emotional reactions to a situation and their moral judgments of those involved in it. (Indeed, people appear somewhat willing to express schadenfreude when a habitual moral violator finally gets their just deserts: see Berndsen & Tiggemann, 2020 [Australia].) At the same time, the outcomes also hint at self-protective processes among people with sadistic tendencies in particular: Were they to condemn a perpetrator whose actions make them feel good, they would also arguably be condemning themselves. As I hope should be obvious to you by this point in the book, people are not generally inclined to do that.

For people with sadistic tendencies, the evidence is mounting that *nasty feels good*, but it also may be the case that *nice feels bad*, at least some of the time. For example, Međedović (2017 [Serbia]) found that higher scores on a dispositional sadism measure were linked not only to more positive emotional reactions to violent images (like a boot stomping on bare feet), but also to *more negative emotional reactions to peaceful/joyful ones* (like two individuals engaged in a warm handshake).

How deep is this apparent "feeling inversion" among people with sadistic tendencies? In two studies involving large American community samples, Sagioglou and Greitemeyer (2016) observed a link between dispositional sadism and bitter taste preferences. This is noteworthy because Sagioglou and Greitemeyer (2014 [Austria]) showed that exposure to a bitter taste increased feelings of hostility, aggressive intentions, and unprovoked as well as provoked aggressive behavior. Given that much of the behavior spawned by sadistic motivation can be considered unprovoked aggression, is it possible that regularly satisfying one's "bitter tooth" might amp up an individual's sadistic tendencies? To my knowledge, this question has yet to be answered (but see Burris & Hood, 2020 [Canada], later in this chapter).

Some research also exists concerning how sadists deal with emotions in general. For example, Paulhus and Dutton (2016) reported that dispositional sadism was unrelated to scores on a neuroticism measure, which taps emotional instability and a tendency toward negative emotional states in particular. Likewise, Zeigler-Hill and Vonk (2015 [USA]) found no relationship between dispositional sadism and emotion dysregulation, which includes "a lack of acceptance of one's own emotional experiences, difficulties performing tasks or controlling impulses when upset, a lack of awareness or understanding of one's own emotions, or limited strategies for regulating emotions" (p. 693).

Thus, although the absence of significant statistical relationships should often be interpreted more cautiously than their presence, nothing so far suggests that sadistic tendencies are linked to emotional outbursts or a sense that one's emotions are uncontrollable. This is potentially quite important, because sadistically motivated acts are often preceded by meticulous planning and execution accompanied by savoring and anticipation. Uncontrolled emotions could easily disrupt this process (cf. Duan et al., 2021 [China]).

Why Does Sadism Exist?

Nell (2006 [South Africa], p. 211) asserted that "there is no motivational or neurobiological explanation for cruelty's prevalence or the fascination it holds" as a prelude to hypothesizing that positive reactions to cruelty are a genetic carryover of the rewards associated with successfully hunting and killing (animals) for food. Paulhus and Dutton (2016, p. 115) summarized hypothesized mating advantages as well: "Given that power can be maintained via sadistic behavior and power confers more sexual opportunities, then sadism may have been selected as one reproductive strategy." Of course, convincing support for the ancient origins of *any* modern human phenomenon can be difficult to assemble. This is further complicated here by the fact that the combined emphasis on hunting and mating opportunities seems very much focused on *biological males* and *violent behavior*.

As defined in the present chapter, contemporary sadistic motivation can involve a wide range of perpetrators, contexts, techniques, targets, and consequences, however. It doesn't have to involve men. It doesn't have to involve violence. Indeed, if it's an unexpressed motive, it doesn't even have to involve behavior. A theory of sadism should be able to account for key commonalities across these variable manifestations. In particular, *with* feeling good as the apparent goal, and *without* apparent provocation, the heart of sadism is the desire that other beings suffer—whether the suffering is physical or psychological, and whether it is perpetrated directly or enjoyed vicariously. In addition, at least some of the time, people are willing to act on their sadistic motivation *despite the risk of the Mark of Cain* (recalling that sadistically motivated behavior is seen as evil).

In Burris and Leitch (2016), I sketched out a theory that I think makes sense of the key commonalities I've just described. Let's work through them in backwards order. First, if people see a clear connection between sadism and evil, why would they risk the Mark of Cain by engaging in sadistic acts? I would suggest that some individuals may already feel "under the gun" in terms of how they perceive others regard them—that is, they feel *disrespected*, which can fuel *anger* (cf. Pfattheicher et al.'s, 2020 [international], conceptual analysis of boredom, which was linked to deficits in meaning and perceived constraints on one's autonomy and shown to facilitate sadistically motivated behavior). Second, the unprovoked aggression fueled by sadistic motivation can be understood as *displaced* aggression: The idea here is that, rather than retaliating directly against those whom they perceive to have disrespected them, angered individuals redirect their wish to see suffering onto a different target. Third, although I maintain that feeling good is the *conscious* ultimate goal of sadistically motivated individuals, good feelings are ultimately an indicator that something else has been achieved: The disrespected self has been elevated, at least in the eyes of the perpetrators themselves. Importantly, the goal of reinflating a squashed self is not necessarily consciously articulated. That is, although a sadistically motivated person may seek out others' suffering because doing so feels good, that person may not necessarily "connect the dots" as to *why* it feels good.

Before looking at some of my own research that was built on this model, let's first look at other work that points to its plausibility. For example, across a series of six studies involving hundreds of American participants, Chester and DeWall (2017) found consistent evidence that people who feel rejected strike back at those whom they believe rejected them. They strike back, at least in part, because they think that doing so will make them (the rejected) feel better. And it does, to some extent. In one study, participants were first led to believe that another supposed participant was deliberately either including them in or excluding them from an online game. Actual participants were subsequently given an opportunity to aggress symbolically against the person that excluded them by sticking "pins" in a virtual "voodoo doll." (Odd as it sounds, sticking more pins has been shown to predict real-world aggression.) Among participants who believed that acting aggressively *wouldn't* make them feel better, being excluded or included didn't affect the number of stuck pins. Among participants who believed that acting aggressively *would* make them feel better, however, rejection/exclusion resulted in more stuck pins (that is, more aggression) than did inclusion. Chester and DeWall were careful to note that their results were focused on retaliatory aggression, and that the implications for *displaced* aggression (which is the focus here) remained to be tested.

Nevertheless, the results of two Dutch student studies by van Dijk et al. (2011) suggested that another's misfortune can make people who feel bad about themselves feel better even if they did nothing to bring about that person's misfortune. In one study, participants reacted to news that a student got negative feedback from a supervisor; in the other, they read about a student who accidentally drove a rented car into a canal. Compared to positive or no feedback, participants who received negative performance feedback on a task that supposedly assessed their intellectual abilities reported greater schadenfreude (i.e., sadistic positive affect) in response to both stories. Thus, the misfortunes of previously unknown others generated good feelings among people who were deflated by negative feedback about themselves. The results do not speak to whether the good feelings generated specifically include *feeling better about oneself*, however.

It has been well documented that aggression can be displaced—that is, shifted away from the source of provocation onto some other target (see Marcus-Newhall et al., 2000 [USA]; Miller et al., 2003 [USA]). In the model that I have outlined, anger in conjunction with feeling disrespected can trigger sadistic motivation. In turn, sadistic motivation can result in attempts to harm targets who are not necessarily the perceived source of disrespect. In this sense, sadistically motivated harm can be understood as a form of displaced aggression. Several lines of research offer convergent support for this possibility.

For example, Pfattheicher and Schindler (2015) asked about 100 German university students to write either about the prospect of their own death—a task that is often experienced as a profound threat to the self—or a neutral topic, after which they played a carefully constructed economic game. After thinking about their own death (versus a neutral topic), participants with higher levels of dispositional sadism were more likely to engage in *antisocial punishment*. That is, they were more likely to "screw over" those who were playing the game in a sharing/cooperative fashion, even though doing so actually cost higher sadism scorers more money in the game. Thinking about death seemed to have amped up a sense of powerlessness: Striking out at a non-provoking other, even at personal financial cost, may have been a way for people with sadistic tendencies to reduce a sense of personal vulnerability and restore a sense of control.

Krizan and Zohar (2015) presented four studies, involving several hundred American student and community participants, focused on what clinicians have referred to as "narcissistic rage"—often explosively aggressive responses to perceived self-esteem threats among individuals with narcissistic tendencies. Notwithstanding narcissism's common core of entitlement and self-absorption, these authors suggested that its manifestations "vary from arrogance, exhibitionism, and exploitativeness (i.e., grandiosity), to hypersensitivity, resentfulness, and victimization (i.e., vulnerability)" (p. 796). They found that vulnerable (but not grandiose) narcissism predicted angry rumination, which in turn predicted both retaliatory and displaced aggression. To be clear, no measures that directly tapped sadistic tendencies, motivation, or emotion were included in this set of studies. Nevertheless, the results do suggest that individuals who are sensitized to being disrespected tend to stew over anger-evoking episodes, and that the latter tendency increases the likelihood of aggression that targets innocent others.

Across seven studies involving thousands of participants, Greitemeyer and Sagioglou (2016 [Austria]) found that a sense of "social deprivation" (feeling socioeconomically disadvantaged compared to others) was a reliable predictor of aggression. This included not only (retaliatory) aggression directed toward those who amped up an individual's sense of social deprivation, but also (displaced) aggression directed toward those who had nothing to do with it. The one study that included a measure of dispositional sadism found it to be unrelated to a sense of social deprivation, however.

At first glance, the latter finding might seem to pose a problem for the model I have proposed: If sadism is triggered by feeling disrespected, shouldn't a sense of social deprivation predict it? Not necessarily, for reactions to a sense of social deprivation can be diverse. My model suggests that a tendency to ruminate over anger-evoking episodes may be critical for generating sadistic motivation (Burris & Leitch, 2016; see also Miller et al., 2003), and whereas some may respond to a sense of social deprivation with seething anger, others may not. Indeed, in a Canadian student sample, Balakrishnan et al. (2017) showed that people with sadistic tendencies tended to value interpersonal control and being respected by others. The flip side is that *those who didn't prioritize respect and control tended to be less sadistic*. Strikingly, although sadism predicted decreased endorsement of many values, it did *not* predict greater endorsement of any other value on the extensive menu presented to participants. Thus, sadists appeared to have quite narrowly focused priorities: respect and control.

Research by Scott et al. (2015) also seems consistent with the suggestion that sadistic motivation is associated with displaced harmful intentions rather than retaliatory ones: About 200 American undergraduates did an increasingly frustrating timed arithmetic task and were told that they didn't do well regardless of their actual performance. This was intended to put study participants in a foul mood, and probably also temporarily led them to feel not-too-good about themselves. Participants were instructed either to focus on the positive and treat the task like a game while completing it or simply to try to mask any emotional reactions they experienced while completing it. Then, making use of an aggression measure that has been used in many other lab studies, Scott et al. gave participants an opportunity to dispense hot sauce that would allegedly have to be consumed by a participant in another study. Those instructed to suppress their emotional expression doled out more hot sauce than did those not so instructed.

Responding to a frustrating failure experience by doling out lots of hot sauce to an unsuspecting stranger seems like a textbook example of displaced aggression. Moreover, it seems reasonable to conclude that the motivation for such an unprovoked, gratuitous act was probably sadistic—that is, that the idea of making someone else suffer *felt good* at the time. If my assumptions here are correct, then expressive suppression can facilitate the displacement process that fuels sadistic motivation. (For other research linking sadistic tendencies to expressive suppression via schizotypy, see Henry et al., 2009 [Australia], and Međedović, 2017).

How might this work? Expressive suppression can reduce the intensity of negative emotional experiences, but does not eliminate them (see Gross, 2014 [USA]). Thus, Scott et al.'s (2015) participants who were instructed to try to contain the emotions that they experienced following "failure" may have continued to feel bad in general, and bad about themselves in particular.

Especially among those who believe that harming someone can make themselves feel better, sadistically motivated behavior becomes a viable option for doing just that (see Chester & DeWall, 2017; Chester et al., 2019 [USA]). In other words, acting on sadistic motivation may allow some people to rebound emotionally—off the backs of innocent victims.

In a direct test of the sadism model I have outlined (Burris & Hood, 2020), about 150 Canadian undergraduates completed several premeasures, including two that assessed feeling sensitized to the prospect of being disrespected by others and the tendency to hold onto (ruminate about) anger-provoking events, respectively (see McDonald, 2008 [USA], and Sukhodolsky et al., 2001 [USA]; cf. Krizan & Zohar, 2015). These two measures—disrespect sensitivity (DS) and anger rumination (AR)—were moderately positively correlated, so people who scored high on one tended to score high on the other. After the scores were standardized so that they would be on the same metric, they were averaged to create a single DSAR index: We expected that simultaneously feeling put down and simmering with anger would increase the likelihood that sadistic motivation would manifest if conditions were right.

We then set up different conditions by randomly assigning participants to swish plain water (neutral), stevia solution (sweet), or wormwood tea (bitter) in their mouths for 20 seconds. (Ethical disclosure: I tried the wormwood myself, and "bitter" is a polite descriptor.) Most were told that their taste and "swish duration" had been assigned by a previous study participant, although a few were told that their bitter swish was computer-assigned by chance. We expected that the bitter-swish-assigned-by-a-person group would be the most reactive. To assess this, we had participants subsequently rate their reactions to their taste assignment. Finally, to assess displaced aggression, we asked participants to make six taste duration recommendations that would allegedly affect the next participant's experience: Bitter, hot, and sour were combined into an aggressive index, and sweet, salty, and neutral were combined into a non-aggressive index.

Higher DSAR scorers appeared to be hypersensitive to being "screwed over": They reacted negatively when assigned not only the bitter wormwood (whether by person or computer), but also the plain water! Feeling "screwed over" when assigned the bitter taste by a supposed other person, in turn, predicted more aggressive (but not non-aggressive) taste dosage recommendations. Simply put, the disrespect sensitivity/anger rumination combo indeed seemed to work like a hair-trigger mechanism for displaced aggression: (Literal?!) distaste for the 20 seconds of misery that some random person visited upon them was all it took for higher DSAR scorers to decide to lash out in kind against an innocent (cf. Sagioglou & Greitemeyer, 2014). But were higher DSAR scorers chasing positive feelings when they thought they were doling out wormwood, hot sauce, and vinegar to unsuspecting others? Maybe this wasn't sadistic motivation, but instead a case of misery loving company. More data are needed—so let's look at some.

Testing the Sadism Model in a Novel Context: Pranking

As I noted at the outset of this chapter, the majority of laypeople and social scientists seem to have assumed—at least, until very recently—that *real* sadism is rare and takes the form of extremely harmful behavior that is very often criminal, and also often sexualized. In contrast, others (e.g., Buckels et al., 2013), including myself (Burris & Leitch, 2016), have argued that manifestations of sadism are often both less exotic and less extreme. One simply needs to look for the motivational core: Harming others, or appreciating their harm from a distance, is in the service of good feelings (pleasure, satisfaction, etc.). From this perspective, pranking seems like an obvious, accessible context in which to study sadistic dynamics.

Other than a passing mention by O'Meara and Hammond (2016), pranking seems to have escaped psychological attention, however. But think about why a focus on pranks makes sense: Pranks are premeditated, often carefully orchestrated acts intended to cause unsuspecting others physical or psychological discomfort for the stated purpose of amusement (the prankster's and/or an audience's). "Failed" pranks result when the intended victims' foreknowledge allows them to foil the prankster's gotcha and escape the planned unpleasantness. Understood in these terms, the sadistic motivational structure of pranking seems clear (see also Dundes, 1988 [USA]; Hobbs & Grafe, 2015 [Germany/USA]; Plester, 2013 [New Zealand]; Wiggins, 2014 [USA]).

A student collaborator and I conducted two pranking studies inspired by this perspective that together involved over 300 Canadian undergraduates (Burris & Leitch, 2018). In both, participants completed a measure of dispositional sadism along with the DSAR index described earlier. With these background measures in place, the first study asked participants whether they had ever pranked someone. Those who had were asked to recall the all-time favorite prank that they had performed and to answer questions about their thoughts and emotions both during the planning stage and during/after the prank proper. Finally, the pranksters were asked to rate their overall experience of that prank and to justify their rating.

The DSAR index was moderately positively correlated with dispositional sadism. Thus, although the data can't confirm what causes what, they did show that sadistic tendencies are more common among people who feel chronically angry and disrespected. Moreover, people with sadistic tendencies were more likely to admit having pranked someone. So far, so good.

Turning to pranksters' recollections of a favorite prank, dispositional sadism predicted a set of thoughts across the course of the prank that seemed like good indicators of sadistic motivation (e.g., "I thought it would be fun," "This is awesome," and "I can't wait to do another prank"), as well as justifications for pranking (e.g., "I had the opportunity" and "The individual[s] being pranked deserved it"). Dispositional sadism also predicted an array of positive emotions (e.g., excitement, happiness, pride, satisfaction)—but not negative emotions (e.g., nervousness, guilt) or misgivings—across the course of the prank. Remember that pranks are about subjecting an unsuspecting other to physical or psychological discomfort, so the fact that people who admit sadistic tendencies reported feeling rather pumped up throughout again seems to suggest that pranking is an outlet for sadistic motivation.

So what about the DSAR index? DSAR not only predicted everything that dispositional sadism did—it was a *better* (that is, stronger) predictor. So, for example, when the overlap between DSAR and dispositional sadism was taken into account, dispositional sadism was no longer significantly related to positive (sadistic) emotion during the prank experience, but DSAR was. The same pattern held for sadistic thoughts and justifications for the prank. Moreover, among those who reported a positive overall evaluation of their prank experience, higher (versus lower) DSAR scores predicted asserting that the prank only had benign outcomes—that is, that it was all in good fun and no one *really* got hurt. This doesn't make sense if sadistic gratification hinges upon real harm (cf. Schumpe & Lafrenière, 2016). Minimizing perceived harm after the fact would be a convenient way for a prankster to reduce a sense of moral culpability, however (see Buckels et al., 2019 [Canada]).

The second study reported by Burris and Leitch (2018) focused on people's reactions to two prank videos: an adolescent male tricked into tossing a log onto a shovel head while blindfolded, which caused the shovel handle to strike his groin forcefully; and a woman terrorized by ghouls in a parking garage. Because the prank victims were complete strangers, any viewer assertion that they deserved what happened to them could not be based on a grudge or revenge. Moreover, in order to get a better sense of whether the "no harm done" justification offered for positive prank evaluations in the first study reflected actual perceptions, some participants in the second study read a brief commentary intended to draw their attention to the possibility that the victims in the prank videos suffered significant long-term harm (pain and fertility problems in the first instance; posttraumatic stress disorder in the second). Others read that the possibility of long-term harm was minimal. People then indicated their reactions to the pranksters, the pranks, and the victims. As in the first study, dispositional sadism and the DSAR index (which were again correlated with each other) were examined as predictors of these outcomes.

Higher DSAR scores predicted reactions suggestive of sadistic motivation (e.g., enjoyment and the desire to be involved in executing the prank), but *only* when participants were reminded that the prank victims could have suffered long-term physical or psychological harm. Likewise, higher DSAR scores predicted boosting oneself at the victim's expense (e.g., the victim was really stupid, deserved what happened, and completely overreacted; the viewer would not have fallen for the prank and actually could have executed it better than the prankster), but *only* following reminders of the prospect of significant victim harm. The dispositional sadism measure also predicted sadistic motivation and boosting the self at the victims' expense, but did so irrespective of whether the prospect of long-term harm was emphasized or downplayed. Thus, DSAR seems to have done a better job of predicting bona fide sadistic outcomes than a more straightforward sadism measure, perhaps because DSAR more closely taps the driving force behind sadistic motivation.

Indeed, DSAR predicted a cluster of variables across both pranking studies that seem consistent with the sadism model described earlier. That is, whether executing or simply viewing pranks, higher DSAR scorers reported engagement and positive feelings, and they appeared to see prank victims as stupid and themselves as smart. There was no evidence of guilt or regret—in fact, higher DSAR pranksters really wanted to prank again. Moreover, although they were quick to minimize the impact of pranks and appeared willing to chide victims for overreacting, the results of the second study in particular suggested that higher DSAR scorers were in fact more enthused when victims faced the real prospect of long-term suffering. Thus, among those who simultaneously hold onto their anger and feel disrespected by others, "harmless fun" isn't fun, but *harmful fun is.*

It's Probably *Not* "Just a Prank": Disconnected Sadism

In light of Burris and Leitch's (2018) findings, pro-prank assertions such as "[p]lay is fun, and that's all the reason people need to do it" (Marsh, 2015, p. 151) seem increasingly difficult to defend. There are at least two key problems. The first is a disconnect between the conscious ultimate goal of sadistic motivation and the means of obtaining it. An experience typified by excitement, a sense of spontaneity, happiness, and satisfaction (all part of the "positive emotion" cluster in Burris and Leitch's first study) sounds lovely—one worth seeking out and reveling in. And pranksters certainly do.

Unfortunately, this can contribute to tunnel vision (see Chapter 4) capable of producing an unanticipated degree of harm that exceeds that which is "necessary" for sadistic gratification (cf. Lui et al., 2020 [Denmark/Germany], who showed that higher sadism scorers reported less schadenfreude when explicitly instructed to imagine what a victim must have experienced). Consider these two coincidentally themed postings from the hapless confessional website *fmylife.com*: "Today my girlfriend decided it would be hilarious if she pulled a prank on me, so she did the classic 'bucket of water on a door' one. I ended up getting stitches and a concussion on my birthday" (3 July 2012). "Today, my friends got me a cake for my birthday. As I blew out the candles, they shoved my head into it and I was knocked out for 3 minutes before an ambulance took me to the hospital. I got a concussion from a cake" (8 September 2017). Although the perpetrators clearly intended to inflict some level of discomfort on their victims, it is doubtful that serious head injuries were part of the plan. They happened, anyway.

The second problem with attempts to minimize the harmfulness of pranks involves anticipated rather than unanticipated consequences, and centers on a disconnect between the positive feelings that pranks can produce and what appears to be triggering the sadistic motive that underlies pranks in the first place. That is, although executing or watching pranks may make some people feel good, they don't necessarily know why this is the case. I have argued that these good feelings are a signal that the underlying goal of boosting a downtrodden sense of self is being met. Nevertheless, with good feelings as the focus, people may simply not be aware of the displaced hostility that makes causing others pain or humiliation seem like a reasonable tradeoff for feeling good themselves. They simply "know" that harming the other is worth the payoff (cf. Chapter 4's MioMa principle).

An illustrative case concerns the now-defunct YouTube channel DaddyOFive that featured videos of a husband/wife duo's pranks on their children. One that drew much attention featured the couple falsely accusing and verbally abusing their youngest child for spilling ink on his bedroom carpet, which led to the child becoming increasingly indignant and distraught. Inspection of many other DaddyOFive videos led to growing public concern regarding the children's well-being. Eventually, despite the parents' eventual claims of staged/"fake" content in their videos, psychological evaluation revealed evidence of "mental injury" in two of the five children. Those two children were put into the custody of their biological mother. Pursuant to a plea agreement, the couple was given 5 years of probation for child neglect. When commenting on the case, Frederick County (Maryland, USA) Assistant State's Attorney Lindy Angel characterized the couple's actions as "insensitive" and "cruel," but stated that "there was no real intention behind it" (Nashrulla, 2017; see also Tait, 2017). Given that *cruelty is intentional*, the self-contradiction is fascinating.

As noted earlier in this chapter, making others suffer for one's own pleasure and satisfaction is arguably one of the easiest contexts for spotting "evil." Consequently, it's safe to assume that perpetrators will do their best to minimize perceived harm and/or offer a spate of more acceptable justifications for it. Statements such as Ms. Angel's above suggest that such strategies can sometimes convince audiences—and, perhaps, the perpetrators themselves—that harm is the result not of sadism, but of a motive more benign. That being said, the possibility remains that at least some sadists may not be aware of the extent to which simmering anger and the sense of being disrespected fuels the harming-others-feels-good dynamic. This raises the provocative possibility that connecting those dots and dealing with the underlying respect and anger issues could, in fact, defuse sadistic motivation.

It's possible that you the reader now think that I've strayed far off topic. You thought that this was supposed to be a book about evil, and I've just spent a fair bit of time writing about something as "trivial" as pranks. If that is indeed your reaction, there are a couple of points I'd like you to consider. First, be mindful that the consequences of pranks—even if unanticipated—are sometimes severe. Consider the grievous case of a UK nurse who fielded a call from two Australian radio personalities impersonating Queen Elizabeth and Prince Charles and inquiring about the medical status of the Duchess of Cambridge, who had been admitted to the hospital. Ashamed at having been duped and for breaching hospital protocol, the nurse—who had no known history of mental illness—hung herself (Davies, 2014). Second, whether life-altering or comparatively minor, and whether in a torture chamber or an office cubicle, if intentional victim harm is in the direct service of securing good feelings for the perpetrator, the structure of the motivation is the same. It is sadistic.

Of course, sometimes intended harm doesn't simply alter lives. Sometimes it ends them. So let's examine serial killers next.

References

Achterbosch, L., Miller, C., & Vamplew, P. (2017). A taxonomy of griefer type by motivation in massively multiplayer online role-playing games. *Behaviour & Information Technology, 36*(8), 846–860. doi:10.1080/0144929X.2017.1306109

Arriaga, X. B. (2002). Joking violence among highly committed individuals. *Journal of Interpersonal Violence, 17*(6), 591–610. doi:10.1177/0886260502017006001

Balakrishnan, A., Plouffe, R. A., & Saklofske, D. H. (2017). What do sadists value? Is honesty-humility an intermediary? Replicating and extending findings on the link between values and "dark" personalities. *Personality and Individual Differences, 109*, 142–147. doi:10.1016/j.paid.2016.12.055

Baumeister, R. F. (1997). *Evil: Inside human cruelty and violence.* W. H. Freeman.

Berndsen, M., & Tiggemann, M. (2020). Multiple versus single immoral acts: An immoral person evokes more schadenfreude than an immoral action. *Motivation and Emotion, 44*(4), 738–754. doi:10.1007/s11031-020-09843-5

Buckels, E. E., Jones, D. N., & Paulhus, D. L. (2013). Behavioral confirmation of everyday sadism. *Psychological Science, 24*(11), 2201–2209. doi:10.1177/0956797613490749

Buckels, E. E., Trapnell, P. D., Andjelovic, T., & Paulhus, D. L. (2019). Internet trolling and everyday sadism: Parallel effects on pain perception and moral judgment. *Journal of Personality, 87*(2), 328–340. doi:10.1111/jopy.12393

Buckels, E. E., Trapnell, P. D., & Paulhus, D. L. (2014). Trolls just want to have fun. *Personality and Individual Differences, 67*, 97–102. doi:10.1016/j.paid.2014.01.016

Bulut, T. (2017). The concept of sadism in the current empirical literature. *Zbornik Instituta za kriminološka i sociološka istraživanja, 36*, 23–41.

Burris, C. T., & Hood, T. W. (2020, June). *Bitter taste in YOUR mouth: Aversive flavour experiences assigned by ostensible others evoke sadistic aggression.* Poster to be presented at Conference of the Consortium of European Research on Emotion (CERE), Granada, Spain. (*Postponed due to COVID-19 pandemic).

Burris, C. T., & Leitch, R. (2016). Your pain, my gain: The interpersonal context of sadism. In K. Aumer (Ed.), *The psychology of love and hate in intimate relationships* (pp. 85–103). Springer International Publishing.

Burris, C. T., & Leitch, R. (2018). Harmful fun: Pranks and sadistic motivation. *Motivation and Emotion, 42*(7), 90–102. doi:10.1007/s11031-017-9651-5

Chester, D. S., & DeWall, C. N. (2017). Combating the sting of rejection with the pleasure of revenge: A new look at how emotion shapes aggression. *Journal of Personality and Social Psychology, 112*(3), 413–430. doi:10.1037/pspi0000080

Chester, D. S., DeWall, C. N., & Enjaian, B. (2019). Sadism and aggressive behavior: Inflicting pain to feel pleasure. *Personality and Social Psychology Bulletin, 45*(8), 1252–1268. doi:10.1177/0146167218816327

Craker, N., & March, E. (2016). The dark side of Facebook®: The Dark Tetrad, negative social potency, and trolling behaviours. *Personality and Individual Differences, 102*, 79–84. doi:10.1016/j.paid.2016.06.043

Davies, C. (2014, September 12). Duchess of Cambridge hoax call nurse blamed herself, inquest told. https://www.theguardian.com/uk-news/2014/sep/12/duchess-cambridge-hoax-call-nurse-inquest

Duan, J., Yang, Z., Zhang, F., Zhou, Y., & Yin, J. (2021). Aggressive behaviors in highly sadistic and highly impulsive individuals. *Personality and Individual Differences, 178*, 110875. doi:10.1016/j.paid.2021.110875

Dundes, A. (1988). April Fool and April Fish: Towards a theory of ritual pranks. *Etnofoor, 1*(1), 4–14.

Foulkes, L. (2019). Sadism: Review of an elusive construct. *Personality and Individual Differences, 151*, 109500. doi:10.1016/j.paid.2019.07.010

Greitemeyer, T. (2015). Everyday sadism predicts violent video game preferences. *Personality and Individual Differences, 75*, 19–23. doi:10.1016/j.paid.2014.10.049

Greitemeyer, T., & Sagioglou, C. (2016). Subjective socioeconomic status causes aggression: A test of the theory of social deprivation. *Journal of Personality and Social Psychology, 111*(2), 178–194. doi:10.1037/pspi0000058

Greitemeyer, T., & Sagioglou, C. (2017). The longitudinal relationship between everyday sadism and the amount of violent video game play. *Personality and Individual Differences, 104*, 238–242. doi:10.1016/j.paid.2016.08.021

Greitemeyer, T., Weiß, N., & Heuberger, T. (2019). Are everyday sadists specifically attracted to violent video games and do they emotionally benefit from playing those games? *Aggressive Behavior, 45*(2), 206–213. doi:10.1002/ab.21810

Gromet, D. M., Goodwin, G. P., & Goodman, R. A. (2016). Pleasure from another's pain: The influence of a target's hedonic states on attributions of immorality and evil. *Personality and Social Psychology Bulletin, 42*(8), 1077–1091. doi:10.1177/0146167216651408

Gross, J. J. (2014). Emotion regulation: Conceptual and empirical foundations. In J. J. Gross (Ed.), *Handbook of emotion regulation* (2nd ed., pp. 3–20). Guilford Press.

Hardaker, C. (2010). Trolling in asynchronous computer-mediated communication: From user discussions to academic definitions. *Journal of Politeness Research, 6*(2), 215–242. doi:10.1515/JPLR.2010.011

Henry, J. D., Green, M. J., Restuccia, C., de Lucia, A., Rendell, P. G., McDonald, S., & Grisham, J. R. (2009). Emotion dysregulation and schizotypy. *Psychiatry Research, 166*(2–3), 116–124. doi:10.1016/j.psychres.2008.01.007

Hobbs, R., & Grafe, S. (2015). YouTube pranking across cultures. *First Monday, 20*(7). doi:10.5210/fm.v20i7.5981

Krizan, Z., & Zohar, O. (2015). Narcissistic rage revisited. *Journal of Personality and Social Psychology, 108*(5), 784–801. doi:10.1037/pspp0000013

Lee, S. A. (2019). The Dark Tetrad and callous reactions to mourner grief: Patterns of annoyance, boredom, entitlement, schadenfreude, and humor. *Personality and Individual Differences, 137*, 97–100. doi:10.1016/j.paid.2018.08.019

Lui, L. F., Sassenrath, C., & Pfattheicher, S. (2020). When is your pain my gain? The use of perspective taking by everyday sadists. *Personality and Individual Differences, 167*, 110213. doi:10.1016/j.paid.2020.110213

Marcus-Newhall, A., Pedersen, W. C., Carlson, M., & Miller, N. (2000). Displaced aggression is alive and well: A meta-analytic review. *Journal of Personality and Social Psychology, 78*(4), 670–689. doi:10.1037/0022-3514.78.4.670

Marsh, M. (2015). *Practically joking*. Utah State University Press.

McDonald, K. L. (2008). *Interpretations and beliefs associated with children's revenge goals in conflict situations* [Unpublished doctoral dissertation]. Duke University.

Međedović, J. (2017). Aberrations in emotional processing of violence-dependent stimuli are the core features of sadism. *Motivation and Emotion, 41*(2), 273–283. doi:10.1007/s11031-016-9596-0

Miller, N., Pedersen, W. C., Earleywine, M., & Pollock, V. E. (2003). A theoretical model of triggered displaced aggression. *Personality and Social Psychology Review, 7*(1), 75–97. doi:10.1207/S15327957PSPR0701_5

Miller, P., & Devon, M. (1995). *Screw the roses, send me the thorns: The romance and sexual sorcery of sadomasochism*. Mystic Rose Books.

Min, H., Pavisic, I., Howald, N., Highhouse, S., & Zickar, M. J. (2019). A systematic comparison of three sadism measures and their ability to explain workplace mistreatment over and above the dark triad. *Journal of Research in Personality, 82*, 103862. doi:10.1016/j.jrp.2019.103862

Nashrulla, T. (2017, September 12). Parents who "pranked" their kids on YouTube sentenced to five years' probation for child neglect. https://www.buzzfeed.com/tasneemnashrulla/parents-who-pranked-their-kids-on-youtube-sentenced-to-five?bftw&utm_term=.ld6rZDeR7#.buPd3RGZn

Neal, A. M., & Edwards, K. M. (2017). Perpetrators' and victims' attributions for IPV: A critical review of the literature. *Trauma, Violence, & Abuse, 18*(3), 239–267. doi:10.1177/1524838015603551

Nell, V. (2006). Cruelty's rewards: The gratifications of perpetrators and spectators. *Behavioral and Brain Sciences, 29*(3), 211–224. doi:10.1017/S0140525X06009058

O'Meara, A., Davies, J., & Hammond, S. (2011). The psychometric properties and utility of the Short Sadistic Impulse Scale (SSIS). *Psychological Assessment, 23*(2), 523–531. doi:10.1037/a0022400

O'Meara, A., & Hammond, S. (2016). The sadistic impulse and relating to others. In J. Birtchnell, M. Newberry, & A. Kalaitzaki (Eds.), *Relating theory: Clinical and forensic applications* (pp. 277–291). Palgrave MacMillan. doi:10.1057/978-1-137-50459-3_21

Paulhus, D. L., & Dutton, D. G. (2016). Everyday sadism. In V. Zeigler-Hill & D. K. Marcus (Eds.), *The dark side of personality: Science and practice in social, personality, and clinical psychology* (pp. 109–120). American Psychological Association. doi:10.1037/14854-006

Pfattheicher, S., Keller, J., & Knezevic, G. (2019). Destroying things for pleasure: On the relation of sadism and vandalism. *Personality and Individual Differences, 140*, 52–56. doi:10.1016/j.paid.2018.03.049

Pfattheicher, S., Lazarević, L. B., Westgate, E. C., & Schindler, S. (2020). On the relation of boredom and sadistic aggression. *Journal of Personality and Social Psychology*. Advance online publication. doi:10.1037/pspi0000335

Pfattheicher, S., & Schindler, S. (2015). Understanding the dark side of costly punishment: The impact of individual differences in everyday sadism and existential threat. *European Journal of Personality, 29*(4), 498–505. doi:10.1002/per.2003

Plester, B. (2013, December). *When is a joke not a joke? The dark side of organizational humour*. Paper presented at the 27th Australia and New Zealand Academy of Management Conference, Hobart, Australia.

Plouffe, R. A., Saklofske, D. H., & Smith, M. M. (2017). The assessment of sadistic personality: Preliminary psychometric evidence for a new measure. *Personality and Individual Differences, 104*, 166–171. doi:10.1016/j.paid.2016.07.043

Rempel, J. K., & Burris, C. T. (2005). Let me count the ways: An integrative theory of love and hate. *Personal Relationships, 12*(2), 297–313. doi:10.1111/j.1350-4126.2005.00116.x

Russell, T. D., & King, A. R. (2016). Anxious, hostile, and sadistic: Maternal attachment and everyday sadism predict hostile masculine beliefs and male sexual violence. *Personality and Individual Differences, 99*, 340–345. doi:10.1016/j.paid.2016.05.029

Sagioglou, C., & Greitemeyer, T. (2014). Bitter taste causes hostility. *Personality and Social Psychology Bulletin, 40*(12), 1589–1597. doi:10.1177/0146167214552792

Sagioglou, C., & Greitemeyer, T. (2016). Individual differences in bitter taste preferences are associated with antisocial personality traits. *Appetite, 26*, 299–308. doi:10.1016/j.appet.2015.09.031

Schumpe, B. M., & Lafrenière, M.-A. K. (2016). Malicious joy: Sadism moderates the relationship between schadenfreude and the severity of others' misfortune. *Personality and Individual Differences, 94*, 32–37. doi:10.1016/j.paid.2016.01.005

Scott, J. P., DiLillo, D., Maldonado, R. C., & Watkins, L. E. (2015). Negative urgency and emotion regulation strategy use: Associations with displaced aggression. *Aggressive Behavior, 41*(5), 502–512. doi:10.1002/ab.21588

Sukhodolsky, D. G., Golub, A., & Cromwell, E. N. (2001). Development and validation of the Anger Rumination Scale. *Personality and Individual Differences, 31*(5), 689–700. doi:10.1016/S0191-8869(00)00171-9

Tait, A. (2017, April 21). "It's just a prank, bro": Inside YouTube's most twisted genre. http://www.newstatesman.com/science-tech/internet/2017/04/its-just-prank-bro-inside-youtube-s-most-twisted-genre

Tortoriello, G. K., Hart, W., & Richardson, K. (2019). Predicting perceived harmful intent from the Dark Tetrad: A novel cognitive account of interpersonal harm. *Personality and Individual Differences, 147*, 43–52. doi:10.1016/j.paid.2019.04.020

Trémolière, B., & Djeriouat, H. (2016). The sadistic trait predicts minimization of intention and causal responsibility in moral judgment. *Cognition, 146*, 158–171. doi:10.1016/j.cognition.2015.09.014

van Dijk, W. W., Ouwerkerk, J. W., Wesseling, Y. M., & van Koningsbruggen, G. M. (2011). Towards understanding pleasure at the misfortunes of others: The impact of self-evaluation threat on schadenfreude. *Cognition and Emotion, 25*(2), 360–368. doi:10.1080/02699931.2010.487365

van Geel, M., Goemans, A., Toprak, T., & Vedder, P. (2017). Which personality traits are related to traditional bullying and cyberbullying? A study with the Big Five, Dark

Triad and sadism. *Personality and Individual Differences, 106*, 231–235. doi:10.1016/j.paid.2016.10.063

Wiggins, B. A. (2014). The culture industry, new media, and the shift from creation to curation; or, enlightenment as a kick in the nuts. *Television & New Media, 15*(5), 395–412. doi:10.1177/1527476412474696

Zeigler-Hill, V., & Vonk, J. (2015). Dark personality features and emotion dysregulation. *Journal of Social and Clinical Psychology, 34*(8), 692–704. doi:10.1521/jscp.2015.34.8.692

7
Serial Killers

What would it take for you to kill someone?

Remember the basic principle, introduced in Chapter 4, that much of our behavior as humans is the result of chasing feelings: "If I do A, then B will happen. If B happens, I will feel more of C and/or less of D." For most people, the decision to kill another person is geared toward feeling "*less of D*"—that is, less negative emotion. Often this is about *eliminating a perceived threat*. As I've noted elsewhere (Burris & Rempel, 2010 [Canada]), perceived threats generally come in one of three forms: physical, social, or symbolic. Thus, someone may be moved to kill someone else in order to prevent bodily injury or death (physical threat), to defend one's honor or reputation (social threat), or to preserve a preferred way of life (symbolic threat).

But there's more to it than that. Think about when a parent says: "When my child died, I felt like *part of me* died." This language reflects the psychological reality that our sense of self stretches beyond our sense of existence as separate individuals. That is, each of us has an extended sense of self that can include loved ones, ingroups such as those based on shared nationality or faith, and even elements of our physical environment such as cherished places and possessions. This means that threats to any of these can sometimes nudge an individual toward the decision to kill. Such was the case for an American father who in 2014 fatally shot his daughter's sexual abuser (Buncombe, 2017).

Although that father's homicidal act was in retaliation for offenses that occurred over a decade prior, the "chasing less of D" principle still applies. Why? Obviously, sustaining physical, social, or symbolic injury can be a source of negative feelings. The perceived threat, I would suggest, stems from a sense that these negative feelings will persist indefinitely. Thus, whether framed as "revenge" or "justice" or "closure," fatally striking back is ultimately about trying to *feel less bad* (cf. Chester & DeWall, 2017 [USA]).

But if eliminating threat or "trying to feel less bad" was the sole factor that accounted for why an average person might choose to kill someone, we'd have good reason to expect a higher body count. There's obviously something missing, and it is this: *Most people choose to kill when they perceive*

Evil in Mind. Christopher T. Burris, Oxford University Press. © Oxford University Press 2022.
DOI: 10.1093/oso/9780197637180.003.0007

that the alternatives for dealing with threat are inadequate or exhausted. In fact, the more imminent the threat, the more likely it is that alternatives will not be perceived at all. Thus, a criminal seeks to silence an eyewitness permanently. Or a domestic violence victim wants to ensure that their partner doesn't follow through on homicidal utterances. Or a combat soldier aims to protect homeland, family, comrades, and self. Or a father is convinced that his daughter's abuser hasn't suffered enough within legal system (as in the American case I just described). This is how killing works for most people.

But serial killers are *not* "most people."

By definition (to be discussed soon), serial killing is *repetitive* killing. Moreover, it is often routinized, even ritualized. Repetition pushes interpretation of the killing in a different direction. Sure, a person may kill when faced with the prospect—or the aftermath—of being victimized, but victimization makes less and less sense as an explanation when the body count rises. Indeed, one might expect a trauma survivor who killed someone to try to avoid ever being in another situation where killing seemed necessary.

Consequently, I would suggest that serial homicide is not so much about feeling "less of D" as it is feeling "more of C." That is, it's about the pursuit of a positive emotional payoff: *Killing is repeated because it is rewarding.* This was evident in Kraemer et al.'s (2004 [USA]) comparison of 147 multiple-offense versus 197 single-offense killers: Single-offense motives were more likely to be classified as "emotion-based" (e.g., argument-triggered anger: negative), whereas multiple-offense motives were much more likely to be classified as sexual (positive).

Before unpacking this idea further, I want to make sure that you have a clear sense of where this chapter will and won't go. My intent is to demystify serial killers by showing you that the motives and mechanisms that give rise to their destructive behaviors are more mundane than exotic. In the process, I am purposely steering away from voyeurism and ghoulishness. There's already an abundance of "true crime" accounts of serial killers (for a compendium, see Aamodt & Moyse, 2012 [USA]; see also Hodgkinson et al., 2017 [UK]) and probably even more pulp fiction derivatives. The basic story is a simple, tragic one: A perpetrator chooses to take the lives of other human beings. In many cases, the victims' suffering before death is intense and prolonged. In all cases, those who cared for the victims suffer thereafter (see Williams, 2020 [USA]). A lurid, case-by-case recounting of details does nothing to enhance your understanding of this chapter's key points. So I won't go there. In fact, minus one illustrative case, I won't even mention perpetrators by name. I suspect that this is a token gesture at best, but I've zero desire to stoke serial killers' sacred fire of celebrity.

Now that you've read the fine print, let's proceed by first considering the most fundamental question: What, exactly, is a serial killer?

Serial Killer: A (Less Than Obvious) Definition

You might think that defining the term "serial killer" would be a simple task with an obvious outcome, but you'd be wrong. In fact, fairly recently Reid (2017a [Canada], p. 291) stated: "To this date, there exists no universally agreed upon definition for serial murder."

One of the main functions of a good definition is to specify what things belong together, as well as what things do not: "All of THESE are *that*, but THOSE *aren't* that." Why is this useful? Consider a medical analogy: Over time, specific combinations of signs and symptoms have been assembled to help determine whether a specific disease or disorder is present while also ruling out others. This matters because—ideally, at least—diagnosis implies cause and cause implies treatment. Likewise, if we are even to begin to attempt to understand what motivates a serial killer, we ought to have a clear understanding of when the label should and should not apply.

Reflecting on their own attempt to dispel the serial killer stereotypes that are sometimes evident among scholars as well as laypeople, Hodgkinson et al. (2017, p. 288) declared:

> Contrary to popular belief the serial killer comes in many forms; they may be female, black, elderly, they may act alone or in pairs or groups, they may kill for a variety of motivations (and this may vary over time), and they may even be someone the victim knows (sometimes even a partner, trusted nurse or doctor, or family member). Mental disorder may or may not be present, and although a label of "personality disorder" or "psychopathy" may be all too readily applied to these individuals, in many cases these may merely cloud our understanding further.

Defusing such stereotypes could be aided by a sufficiently broad definition of serial murder. Adjorlolo and Chan (2014 [China], p. 490) based their offering on three interlaced elements: "(1) Two or more forensic linked murders with or without a revealed intention of committing additional murder,

(2) the murders are committed as discrete event(s) by the same person(s) over a period of time, and (3) where the primary motive is personal gratification." Reid (2017a) required not only two motivationally distinct kills perpetrated by the same individual, but also evidence of at least plans for a third. She concurred with Adjorlolo and Chan's specification of the ultimate goal as personal gratification, and noted that this would exclude kills "based in systems of payment, loyalty, revenge, or self-preservation" (p. 298). The idea here is that role-based killings (*because* one is a professional assassin, a soldier, or a gang member, for example) don't fit because the driving force is arguably more external than internal to the perpetrator. Threat-based killings such as those I considered at the outset of this chapter are likewise excluded. Perplexingly, although Reid attempted to emphasize the voluntary nature of qualifying homicidal acts by excluding those committed during psychotic states, she also asserted that "serial murderers experience a *compulsive drive* or impulse to kill" (p. 297, emphasis added), which seems to undercut her emphasis on voluntary control.

Both of the above definitions have merit. From a practical standpoint, it makes sense to restrict the formal "qualifications" of a serial killer to a minimum of two verifiable homicides. In the spirit of "once is a mistake, twice is a choice," this minimum begins to differentiate serial killers as a group from other groups such as individuals who have committed a single murder. Keep in mind that the two-kill minimum isn't perfect, however: A perpetrator whose second murder is foiled for whatever reason might not be formally classified as a serial killer but would arguably be motivationally indistinguishable from a perpetrator who successfully carried out a second kill (for a particularly acrimonious debate concerning the merits of a two-kill versus a three-kill threshold, see Fridel & Fox, 2019 [USA], and Yaksic, 2018 [USA]). Taking this logic a step further, a "proto-serial killer" may have murdered multiple individuals *in fantasy*—the "most critical factor common to serial killers" (Hickey, 2016 [USA], p. 208)—but not yet acted on these fantasies in real life. Again, obviously, the motivational overlap with officially designated serial killers is considerable.

The specification that each of the two minimum kills is a motivationally distinct event makes it clear that the individual perpetrator views homicide as a behavior rewarding enough to be worth repeating. This differentiates the serial killer not only from single-victim murderers, but also from mass murderers (who kill multiple victims in one location as part of a single event; see Gill et al., 2017 [UK/USA]).

Building on the reward theme, specifying personal gratification as the motive makes sense (cf. DeHart & Mahoney, 1994 [USA]). How to delimit gratification remains a somewhat open question, however. For example, based on his review of 64 American female "serial killers" from 1826 to 2004, Hickey (2016) concluded that there was evidence that nearly three-fourths were motivated by money "only" (26%) or "sometimes" (47%). It is doubtful that money was an end in itself, but rather a means of obtaining pleasure, comfort, and security. Does this qualify as "personal gratification" or not? Should it make a difference whether the victims are spouses and children targeted by the killers themselves rather than chosen by others, as would be the case for contract killers (cf. Reid's, 2017a, "systems of payment" exclusion above)? Suppose money is completely irrelevant. Instead, what if a killer is urged on by the "voice of God" (cf. Reid's, 2017a, psychotic exclusion)—is it fair to assume that the perpetrator would *not* feel gratified in being "chosen to do God's work"?

Clearly, the question of whether a specific perpetrator's motivation should be regarded as a variation of "personal gratification" can be difficult to answer. But there are even more complicating factors. Motives are oftentimes neither singular nor "pure." For example, hired killers may feel a surge of personal power as well as the anticipation of getting paid when carrying out a hit (see Miller, 2014a [USA], and Schlesinger, 2001 [USA]). Moreover, stated motives often do not correspond with actual motives. For example, Leyton (2001) described the well-elaborated claims of demonic influence initially offered by an American shooter as justification for the eight incidents attributed to him—a justification that he subsequently retracted. Thus, "personal gratification" would not necessarily have to be ruled out as a contributing motive in either example.

Serial Killers: Protagonists or Persons?

Clearly, unresolved definitional issues constrain how confident we can be about certain serial killer "facts," for definition drives classification—that is, who should (and should *not*) be considered a serial killer. Obviously, if a trend or relationship is evident in the data despite modest variations in the classification process, we have good reason to be more confident in it. But there are many obstacles to getting "good" data about serial killers (see Yaksic, 2015 [USA], for a similar discussion). Let's take a look at three.

Adequacy of sample

To ensure that any statistical trends observed in a study are likely to apply to the entire population of interest, the ideal is to aim for as large of a sample from the population as is practically possible. But serial killers are rare—and they've gotten rarer in the past 30 years (a trend observed despite variations in the serial killer definition employed; see Yaksic, 2015, and Yaksic et al., 2019 [international]). For example, according to Aamodt (2016), the peak year for U.S. serial killers was 1987: 189 were documented in a population of approximately 242.3 million. That's 0.000078%. Most often, serial killers are incarcerated in maximum-security institutions and are thus difficult to access for research purposes. Some of those who are accessed refuse to participate in research. Others have yet to be apprehended. Still others are dead. Every one of these issues limits how rich and representative a serial killer database can be. Together, they make assumptions such as "(most) serial killers stop killing only if apprehended or dead" (see Miller, 2014a) virtually impossible to prove or disprove.

Accuracy of data

A key question that has preoccupied researchers as well as laypeople concerns serial killers' motivation—that is, what moves them to take multiple human lives? In many other contexts, motivational questions can often be addressed via experiments. Here's a made-up example: Suppose you want to test the idea that people are more likely to offer help to someone in need under warmer versus cooler lighting conditions. You could simply set up a helping opportunity under each of these conditions and then determine whether one group is statistically more likely to help than the other group. Provided that sufficient safeguards are built into the study (ensuring that people don't know the true purpose of the study while participating, for example), you could come away with a reasonably confident conclusion concerning whether lighting has an effect on helping. Importantly, conclusions can be drawn *even if the participants themselves are not aware that lighting affected their motivation to help.*

Within certain ethical and practical limits, experiments can be conducted to identify the triggers of harmful as well as helpful behavior. I discuss many throughout this book. But serial killing goes far, far beyond the ethical and practical limits of experimentation. Without experimentation as a tool for understanding motivation, researchers must look elsewhere, and many rely heavily on *interviews* (cf. Skrapec, 2001b [USA]). If you want to know why people did what they did, why not ask them, right? Unfortunately, the quality of *any* interview—even one conducted in response to a good-faith request for help (by someone seeking counseling, for example)—is constrained by the interviewee's *insight* and *truthfulness*. That is, how well does the interviewee understand the causes of their behavior, and how willing are they to disclose this "as is" to an interviewer?

Recall my suggestion in Chapter 6 that there may be a disconnect between the positive emotional payoffs of acting on sadistic motivation and the underlying negative experience (i.e., feeling disrespected and angry) that may have triggered the motivation in the first place. I will subsequently argue that the majority—perhaps the great majority—of serial killers are sadistically motivated. It's therefore probably unrealistic to expect most to be able to "connect the dots" between a destructive act and its ultimate psychological origin. Moreover, it's hard to imagine an interpersonal behavior more vulnerable to the Mark of Cain than *killing repeatedly because it is rewarding*. Even Cain himself only committed a single homicide. We should therefore expect the full range of strategies for deflecting the Mark of Cain (see Chapter 3) among serial killers when confronted with their crimes. Indeed, acceptance of responsibility has ranged across the spectrum from complete denial to exaggerated claims concerning the number of victims amassed (e.g., Gudjonsson, 1999 [UK]). Thus, although interviews can tap into aspects of a serial killer's experience in a way that other research methods cannot (see Skrapec, 2001b), questions concerning a perpetrator's insight and truthfulness must be kept in mind always.

Attitudes toward serial killers

A third obstacle to understanding is that *serial killers are often mythologized*: Going beyond stereotypic assumptions concerning demographic characteristics such as gender or ethnicity, the serial killer is transformed into either a bogeyman or an antihero (cf. Donnelly, 2012 [USA]). Although the terminology used to refer to serial killers in early media coverage leaned toward the supernatural (Reid, 2017a), "monster" emerged more recently as the most common descriptor in Wiest's (2016) content analysis of U.K. and U.S. outlets (see also Felton, 2021 [USA], for an extended historical perspective). This should not be surprising: In the popular imagination, serial killers combine "destructive aggression" with "sadistic enjoyment of inflicting pain on victims" (Knight, 2007 [South Africa], p. 21). As such, they embody the myth of pure evil (MOPE; see Chapter 2). Moreover, Soothill (1993 [UK]) argued that perpetuation of serial killer mythologies can benefit multiple stakeholders in a "serial killer industry."

At the same time, at least for the general public, there are clear downsides associated with portrayals of serial killers as larger-than-life bogeymen. For example, Lee and DeHart (2007 [USA]) showed that the implied local presence of a serial killer intensified people's overall fear of crime at a magnitude that far exceeded the actual risk posed by the killer himself (see also Custers & Van den Bulck, 2012, for a similar analysis in a Belgian context). Similarly, Wiest (2016, p. 338) made the case that sensationalized media coverage of serial killers can distract from more deadly problems. In particular, she highlighted an article that "proclaims 'Hospital Serial Killers are Big Threat,' yet the 2,100 patients worldwide it claims were murdered by doctors and nurses from 1970 to 2006 pales in comparison to the 98,000 deaths per year in the United States alone that the article attributes to medical mistakes."

But the terror evoked by mythic serial killers is often either supplemented or supplanted by intrigue, at times coupled with outright adulation (see Barnes, 2019 [Canada]). That is, at least for some, serial killers are not "monsters" but "fantastic monsters" (Wiest, 2016), winsome rogues (Donnelly, 2012), and celebrities (Schmid, 2005 [USA]). This apparent enchantment is not restricted to laypeople, but occasionally evident among individuals with academic credentials as well. For example, when promoting his own book concerning people's "love" for serial killers, Bonn (Interview with Dr. Scott Bonn, n.d. [USA]) promised "shocking facts and anecdotes for true crime enthusiasts" and flippantly asserted that "serial killers are for adults what monster movies are for children—that is, scary fun!" Such statements convey a stunning lack of empathy for real victims and those close to them.

To be fair, objectivity is almost always an ideal not-quite-achieved when trying to make sense of emotionally charged phenomena. Having said that, mythologizing serial killers—whether they are demonized or glorified—greatly amplifies the risk of unnecessarily making the motives and mechanisms associated with their destructive behaviors seem mysterious. Skrapec (2001b, p. 47) alluded to this when she juxtaposed "understandable" motives such as rage, greed, and passion typically associated with single homicides against the "senseless" motives assumed to drive serial killers.

If one judges serial killers' motives to be *incomprehensible*, it's not unreasonable to assume that they are *insane* (Hodgkinson et al., 2017, make a similar point). Emotion-driven circular reasoning could certainly support such a conclusion: "There *has to be something wrong* with anybody who would do such a thing, so people who do such things *must be* maladjusted or psychologically disordered." The rest is details—if an existing diagnostic label (like antisocial personality disorder, for example) applies to serial killers, fine. If not, then a new disorder or syndrome needs to be created.

The available data paint a much less clear picture, however. Consider "insanity" in the legal sense of not appreciating the wrongfulness of an offense when in the act of committing it. By well into the 1990s, only 4% of serial killers facing charges attempted an insanity defense, and that defense was actually successful for only 1% of that 4% (Castle & Hensley, 2002 [USA]). But perhaps the legal definition of insanity is too stringent: How do serial killers fare when evaluated against diagnostic criteria for a broad range of psychological disorders? In one study that examined historical documentation of 64 female serial killers in the United States, *less than 40%* showed evidence of "severe mental illness," with only 3 meeting the criteria for antisocial personality disorder (Harrison et al., 2015). Culhane et al. (2016; see also Culhane et al., 2019) took a different approach by having 60 male American serial murderers complete a well-validated screening instrument for psychological disorders. Although two-thirds met the criteria for one or more non–personality-related diagnoses (involving anxiety or substance abuse, for example), only 55% were above the diagnostic threshold for a personality disorder (further, only 10% were antisocial).

Without a doubt, the specific percentages reported could be questioned based on the very real methodological limitations of each study. For example, Harrison et al.'s (2015) sample included cases dating back into the early 1800s, well before formal diagnostic procedures and categories were established. Some extrapolation and interpretation therefore seemed unavoidable. Likewise, for various reasons beyond Culhane et al.'s (2016) control, only about 11% of those initially invited to participate were willing and able to return usable data. Mindful of such limitations, Culhane et al. nevertheless concluded that "[t]he average profile did not show a psychologically disturbed individual, contrary to anecdotal expectations" (p. 282).

Such a conclusion will most likely upend those who, in White's (2014 [USA], p. 99) words, have the "expectations of a monster" when trying to make sense of a serial killer. Indeed, this was a dominant theme that emerged from her qualitative analysis of documents concerning 21 serial killers: "Repeatedly in the data there was insistence that someone capable of such crimes could not or would not be able to maintain an intimate relationship—especially for several years, as in some cases— or a steady career or social life without others knowing about their crimes" (p. 100).

The idea that serial killers engage in behavior that is often mundane and sometimes prosocial in between the planning and execution of their offenses may be especially difficult for many people to grasp (cf. the "evil through-and-through" effect documented by Kular, 2021 [Canada], and summarized in Chapter 2). Winter (2006 [UK]) offered two examples: An English offender, "a friend of whose had been helped by a blind stranger, transcribed books into Braille for Schools for the Blind for 20 of his years in prison" (p. 170). After rattling off his own moral credentials, including stints as a soldier and police officer and his aversion to seeing "*hunger, unemployment, oppression, war, aggression, ignorance, illiteracy, etc.*," a Scottish offender interrupted himself by exclaiming: "STOP. THIS ALL COUNTS FOR NOTHING when I can kill fifteen men (without any reason) and attempt to kill about nine others—in my home and under friendly circumstances" (p. 171, emphases in original).

We'll revisit this issue shortly in the context of understanding the basic mechanisms that allow a serial killer to move through the world, often for quite some time. For now, the fact that not all serial killer behavior is "evil" behavior represents a serious challenge to the serial-killer-as-bogeyman myth.

So . . . Why?

For most readers, I suspect that tackling the "Why?" question is the heart of this chapter. What pieces must be in place for an individual to become a serial killer? Toward the end of their survey of possible risk factors, Allely et al. (2014 [Sweden/UK], p. 297) conceded that the "gaps in our understanding about the actual mechanisms of development toward these most negative of outcomes are enormous, and it is difficult to imagine how conventional research techniques could fill these." There are at least two reasons why this is the case.

First, the more removed in time possible risk factors are from the specific behavior to be explained, the less predictive any one risk factor is likely to be. For example, based on their review of over 200 cases, Allely et al. concluded that more than 10% of serial killers and mass murderers have suffered significant head trauma. This proportion is certainly higher than is evident in the general population, but: (1) The huge majority of people who have suffered significant head trauma *do not* become serial killers; and (2) about 90% of serial killers as defined in that review *have not* experienced significant head trauma. Faced with numbers like these, it is not surprising that scholars such as Reid (2017b) doubt that a surefire biological marker of serial killing propensity will ever be identified. The same can be said for psychosocial risk factors.

Second, harking back to the importance of definitions, serial killers are a varied group. For example, sexual violation is not a part of all kills. Neither is violence (as when victims are drugged or poisoned rather than bludgeoned or strangled, for example). This is especially true for female perpetrators, estimated to represent around 15% of the known serial killer population (see Aamodt, 2016; Harrison et al. 2015; Hickey, 2016). Consequently, predictors of sexual or aggressive dysregulation—even if they were more reliable than they appear to be (e.g., Reid et al., 2019 [Canada/Russia])—would, at most, be applicable to only a subset of serial killers.

The Most Extreme Expression of Sadism?

Rather than focusing on risk factors that are several steps removed from the homicidal acts of a serial killer, perhaps we can get more clarity by focusing on the more immediate—that is, the perpetrator's state of mind and stated motivation(s). Recall my suggestion at the outset of this chapter that *most* people choose to kill when they perceive that the alternatives for dealing with threat are inadequate or exhausted, but that serial killers are not "most people." That is, for the vast majority of serial killers, a sense of imminent threat is not an issue—most certainly not in the same way that would move an average person to kill in self-defense. Thus, taking someone's life is instead elective, not compulsory: Of all the things that *could* be done, a person chooses to *kill*, and to do so more than once.

Clearly, the "mind over matter" (MioMa) principle (see Chapter 4) is operative here. That is, whatever the specific goal(s) being pursued, a serial killer regards the taking of multiple human lives as part of this pursuit to be *worth it*. This is not a new idea: Miller (2014b [USA], p. 13) noted that criminology scholars across time "have recognized that it is a singular lack of conscience combined with an inflated sense of entitlement that characterizes those sadistic criminals that cross over the line into actual predation on other people." In context, Miller's use of the "sadistic" descriptor suggests that he was focused on *sexually motivated* serial killers. In Chapter 6, I argued that sadism is best understood as a willingness to inflict harm in pursuit of any of a broader menu of positive feelings—that is, not only sexual gratification, but also generic excitement, pleasure, or satisfaction. It therefore seems logical to ask to what extent *serial killing can be understood as an extreme behavioral outcome of sadistic motivation* in this broader sense.

"Killing for fun" is not solely the domain of serial killers. For example, Myers et al. (2006 [USA]) noted the existence of game preserves in at least 28 U.S. states that offer "canned hunts" in which "a hunter pays a fee to shoot a captive [and often tame] animal for amusement" (p. 904, brackets inserted). Patterson (1999 [South Africa]) pointed to a number of unsettling parallels between trophy hunters luxuriating in the thrill of the hunt and keeping body parts as evocative souvenirs and those serial killers who do the same. Reminiscent of the sexual motivation that often drives the latter behaviors, Kalof et al. (2004 [USA]) found considerable evidence of the eroticization of trophy hunting across multiple issues of an international bowhunting magazine.

Gunn and Caissie (2006 [Canada]; see also Williams, 2017a, 2017b [USA]) argued that many instances of serial killing can be understood as examples of "deviant leisure." Freely chosen activities that focus on harming others for the express purpose of enjoyment, deviant leisure is the embodiment of sadistically motivated behavior. Perhaps not surprisingly, serial killers themselves have alluded to a killing-as-leisure perspective on occasion. For example, Winter (2006, p. 158) quoted one German perpetrator who flatly stated: "Every man has his passion. Some prefer whist. I prefer killing people." An American perpetrator compared killing humans to fishing and smugly spoke about having planned a murder to coincide with the festivities of a public holiday. Like any dedicated hobbyist, the latter perpetrator developed an action plan for improving his skills. This included performing grip-strengthening exercises after discovering that manual strangulation was a physically demanding task (Williams, 2017b).

It's quite easy to find obvious examples of sadistic motivation such as those just mentioned, but how common is sadistic motivation across the serial killer population? While not forgetting the limitations associated with data collection and interpretation addressed earlier in this chapter, one way of deriving a ballpark estimate is to examine previous attempts to classify serial killers based on their motivation. One of the most frequently used serial killer classification frameworks, proposed by Holmes and Holmes (1998 [USA]), specifies four main types: hedonistic, power/control, mission, and visionary. For the hedonistic type, harming and killing others yields pleasure that is most often linked to either (sexual) excitement or material benefits. For the power/control type, harming and killing others yields satisfaction. Mission killers target a specific type of victim and may take pride in seeing themselves as a "clean-up crew." Often regarded as psychotic and/or legally insane, visionaries claim voices or visions that command them to kill.

To what extent does sadistic motivation manifest within Holmes and Holmes's (1998) typology? Obviously, hedonistic killers who are directly motivated by thrills or sexual arousal qualify. Hedonistic killers seeking material benefits could also be seen as sadistically motivated, however. Material gain is seldom an end in itself, but is instead framed as a necessary extra step in the pursuit of pleasure. In terms of the motivational layout, this differs little from an individual who kills to procure bodies to dissect or sexually violate. This, too, involves an extra step, but it fits the expedient-harm-yields-positive-emotion pattern that typifies sadism. Power/control killers also arguably fit well under the sadism umbrella given the themes of self-elevation and satisfaction.

So what to make of so-called mission and visionary killers? The central issue here is whether the stated motivation should be taken at face value or should instead be regarded as *justifications* offered by perpetrators. Recall that sadistic motivation is part of the MOPE (Chapter 2) and arguably the most unpalatable explanation that perpetrators of harm could offer for their behavior (Chapter 6). There is, therefore, good reason to suspect that even serial killers sometimes may balk at the brazen admission that they killed simply because they found it fun or satisfying. Indeed, the stated rationales are at times astonishingly contorted, as when a Pakistani perpetrator claimed to have sexually abused and killed 100 street children to highlight the plight of runaways (McCarthy, 2000). Thus, perhaps the pride and satisfaction that mission killers derive from their "work" is, in fact, what motivates them. If so, mission killers' motivation is *also* arguably sadistic. This leaves only visionary killers as failing to exemplify sadistic motivation, provided that they are, in fact, experiencing a sense of bona fide compulsion to kill by external forces as a result of identifiable mental illness (see Williams et al., 2020 [Canada/USA], for a similar analysis from the perspective of leisure science).

With that as a backdrop, consider one study that used Holmes and Holmes's (1998) typology to classify 262 male American serial killers (Lester & White, 2014). Using the most conservative criteria for sadistic motivation—that is, the hedonism/sexual and power/control categories *only*—yields a figure of 72%. Adding the "hedonism/other" category raises the total to 89%. Finally, adding the mission category—that is, excluding only visionary killers—raises the total to 96%. In Harrison et al. (2015), 70% of the 64 female American serial killers analyzed were classified as either hedonistic or power/control-oriented in their motivation; adding mission killers raised the total to 73%. Possibly suggesting that different classification rules were utilized compared to Lester and White, Harrison et al. reported that 24% of cases did not fit well within the Holmes and Holmes typology. Nevertheless, the data from both of these studies suggest that the majority—and, probably, the great majority—of serial killers show evidence of sadistic motivation.

Recall that the model presented in Chapter 6 proposed that sadistic motivation manifests as displaced hostility provoked by a sense of having been disrespected coupled with simmering anger. Thus, whether or not a would-be perpetrator is aware of the underlying dynamics, the prospect of harming innocent others is *compensatory*. That is, inflicting harm *feels good* because it functions to *elevate the self* (cf. Arndt et al., 2004 [USA]). Is there any evidence of displacement dynamics among serial killers? Yes—anecdotally, at least.

For example, Skrapec (2001a) concluded that her five American serial murderer interviewees viewed their killings as a means of boosting their own sense of power, control, and vitality—fueled by a sense that it was their prerogative to do so. Further, across the seven male American sexual serial killers interviewed by Beasley (2004), phrases such as the following appeared: "a need to exact revenge on 'all the people who ruined my life'" (p. 402); "generalized anger" (p. 403); "his desire to exact revenge for the pain and suffering he had endured throughout his life" (p. 404); "he could not experience sexual gratification unless his sexual activities were accompanied by violence and pain inflicted on others" (p. 405); and "[h]e said he felt that his victims all 'looked like my wife'" (p. 407). Murray (2017) identified similar dynamics in her content analysis of recorded statements of three American mass/spree killers: Rejection (specific incidents of perceived romantic rejection, in particular) appeared to fuel hate toward all members of a target group—such as "unattainable, perfect" women (p. 741). This hate manifested as grandiose, sadistic fantasies, and—eventually—the deaths of multiple victims.

The "Red Surge" and "the Laughter": Sadism in the Elizabeth Wettlaufer Case

Elizabeth Wettlaufer is from Woodstock, Ontario, Canada. At this writing, she is 54 years old and is a former registered nurse. She is also a serial killer. She pled guilty to eight counts of first-degree murder, four counts of attempted murder, and two counts of aggravated assault. The offenses of which she was convicted spanned across a decade (from 2007 to 2016) and several health care providers who employed her. Most of her victims were elderly; all were sufficiently infirm so as not to be able to stave off her chosen method of inflicting harm: injecting high doses of insulin. Although court documents (R. v. Wettlaufer, 2017a [Canada]) indicate that Wettlaufer disclosed one or more of her offenses to acquaintances at least as far back as 2013, authorities did not become involved until she confessed during her 2016 self-initiated stay at a psychiatric facility. At that time, she reported feeling suicidal, having resigning from her job upon learning that she was being reassigned to monitor insulin levels of school-age children, as she claimed that she couldn't trust herself *not* to harm them as well.

With respect to Wettlaufer's motivation, consider the following quotes from the court's statement of facts (tagged by paragraph number, brackets inserted):

> (19) she felt overwhelmingly angry about her career, responsibilities, and her life in general
>
> (36) anger and pressure was building inside her . . . related generally to her job, life and relationship
>
> (38) [post-injection] "it felt like a pressure had been relieved from me"
>
> (57) she described feeling a "surging"
>
> (63) she got that "red surging feeling that she [i.e., the next victim] was going to be the one"
>
> (75) she got a feeling "in my chest area and after I did it, I got that laughter"
>
> (87) [she] once again felt angry in general
>
> (88) [post-injection] she got "that feeling inside and the laughter"
>
> (95) something "snapped inside" and the "red surge" came back and she thought to herself, "Okay, you *will* die."
>
> (122) she felt angry, frustrated and vindictive. She decided "enough was enough"
>
> (134) she felt frustrated again with her job

(142) [she felt] frustrated and angry with her job and all the people she had to care for . . . [she] felt the same "surge" that evokes her urge to overdose people

Note how uncannily well the dynamics described here map onto the sadistic motivation model presented in Chapter 6. First, note Wettlaufer's repeated reference to a "surge" → harm → "laughter" sequence. Second, although not articulated specifically in terms of feeling disrespected, she conveyed a clear sense of feeling put upon, and it is probably significant that her first offense occurred around the time that her husband of 10 years divorced her. Third, she shows clear evidence of chronic angry rumination. Finally, she described feeling provoked by her victims on a couple of occasions but never threatened, so the magnitude of harm that she inflicted seems consistent with displaced, rather than retaliatory, aggression.

Notwithstanding her admissions of free-floating frustration and anger, Wettlaufer also offered justifications for some of her specific acts of victimization:

(20) "[I] had this sense inside me that she might be a person that God wanted back with him" . . . [but] she did not feel like she was doing the right thing for any of the victims.
(36) she felt it was "his time to go" because of the way he acted
(57) [she] thought "now this must be God because this man is not enjoying his life at all"
(63) [the red surge was] God telling me "*this is the one*"
(134) [she] "sensed" [the victim] did not want to be there anymore

Note the lack of consistency across her justifications: Claims of mercy, retribution, and divine guidance exist alongside a professed sense of wrongdoing. Indeed, after her third victim's death, Wettlaufer claimed that she felt "absolutely awful" and "ashamed" (38), especially when the victim's family expressed appreciation for her nursing care. Setting aside questions concerning the authenticity and depth of this negative emotional experience, the facts clearly show that it was not sufficient to deter subsequent acts of victimization.

Wettlaufer's 2016 psychiatric assessment revealed no evidence of psychosis such as hallucinations—she was not a "visionary" killer (R. v. Wettlaufer, 2017b). Rather, she was judged as having good insight into her own actions and seemed to be well aware of the consequences, including the probability of arrest and incarceration following her hospital discharge. She also expressed concern about the impact of publicity on her family and her victims' families. During the week before self-admitting to the psychiatric hospital, inspection of Wettlaufer's computer revealed online searches for names and obituaries of a number of her victims, how painful deaths due to insulin overdose are, and at least two articles on nurses who kill their patients (R. v. Wettlaufer, 2017a, 156). Note the gaps between offenses—often months, occasionally years—as well as her claim that she quit her job because she couldn't trust herself not to hurt children. These elements speak to her capacity for self-control.

Wettlaufer's interaction with her victims' families also deserves comment. For example, the morning after injecting a patient who died after a 12-hour span that included seizures, she hugged one survivor and expressed how sorry she was for the family's loss (R. v. Wettlaufer, 2017a, 100). Was she glib and cynical, or was there some spark of genuine remorse in her response? Whichever is closer to the truth, it's clear that her victims didn't matter *enough* for her to incorporate alternate strategies for dealing with her emotions across a decade. Instead, out of all possible ways of coping with job frustrations or generalized anger, she chose to kill, again and again.

Wettlaufer does not appear to be an outlier: Of the 64 cases of female serial killers compiled by Harrison et al. (2015), nearly 40% were in a direct health care role, and 25% specifically targeted the elderly and infirm. Moreover, the typical perpetrator profile constructed by Harrison et al. (p. 400) matches Wettlaufer's characteristics in many respects, including: identification with a religious tradition, a history of substance abuse, conflict with the family of origin and in significant adult relationship(s), and issues surrounding sexual expression. Sadistic motivation and lethality (i.e., a relatively high number of victims) are also common among health care providers who kill, according to Yorker et al. (2006 [international]).

One more anecdote seems worth mentioning here: While an inpatient, Wettlaufer reportedly told the nurses that she had thought about playing "a game" with them by swapping nametags on patients' medications (R. v. Wettlaufer, 2017b). In context, this postscript seems hardly coincidental: The "red surge" of sadistic motivation seemed to inspire thoughts of a prank with potentially serious consequences (see Chapter 6).

So . . . How?

Besides motivation (which centers on Chapter 4's MioMa principle), the other big question that needs to be addressed is: How does a serial killer go through with it—again and again? The short answer is: Go back and read Chapter 3. Whether harm is comparatively minor, life-changing, or life-ending (as here), a perpetrator's menu of strategies for dealing with the prospect of the Mark of Cain is pretty much the same (see also Henson & Olson, 2010 [USA], James & Gossett, 2018 [USA], Pettigrew, 2020 [UK], and Tang, 2020 [Canada]).

By definition, a serial killer has committed multiple murders, so even if they can "minimize perceived harm" by concealing their crimes from others, they obviously cannot deny to themselves that they have committed great harm. "Decreasing perceived intent" is a more flexible strategy, however: Whether or not they can be linked directly to mental illness, claims that one is being commanded to kill by an invisible entity fit here. More commonly, however, "invoking justifications" is a go-to strategy for serial killers. For example, so-called mission killers may insist that they're doing society a favor by helping to eliminate members of some "undesirable" target group. Alternatively, serial-killers-to-be may set up narratives of themselves as victims who deserve compensation: They have been abused and humiliated, so—note the leap of logic—*someone* (even an innocent stranger or a helpless dependent) *has to die*.

The two other strategies for dealing with the prospect of the Mark of Cain outlined in Chapter 3 also apply to serial killers, and perhaps especially so. First, serial killers may attempt to blend in with their moral surroundings. This goes beyond simple pretense—concealing a secret world filled with destructive acts by appearing "normal" maps onto "minimizing perceived harm" just described. Instead, an extreme version of moral licensing (Merritt et al., 2010 [USA]) may come into play, as suggested by this American serial killer's assertion: "*You know, normally I'm a pretty nice guy. I'm sorry, but I am. You know, you know, I've raised kids, I had a wife, and, you know, president of the church, been in Scouts . . .*" (Williams, 2017b, p. 31, italics in original). Such an assertion—that one has done (a few) bad things, but also some good things—may sound feeble and absurd coming from a serial killer. Nevertheless, the fact that some serial killers feel motivated to insist that they are not really that different from anyone else speaks to what a core motivator the Mark of Cain is.

Second, some serial killers may vigorously insist that others' judgments cannot hurt them—that they are, in effect, immune to the Mark of Cain. On the surface, this may ring true: They take multiple human lives while sometimes offering no justification other than that they wanted to. Some elude capture for long periods while taunting authorities and the general public. Such actions seem like the ultimate declaration of defiant autonomy.

But recall my argument that a great deal of serial killers' motivation is sadistic—which is, in turn, triggered in part by feeling angry and disrespected. Consider also Wiest's (2016) argument concerning connections between serial murder and cultural values in the United States—a country with less than one-twentieth of the world's population but two-thirds of the world's known serial killers (Aamodt, 2016). Specifically, she implicates not only the value of individualism, but also "competition, recognition, and personal achievement" (p. 329). These are all linked to *favorable comparisons with others*—as was evident in an American perpetrator's assertion that "serial killing allowed him to become 'the only successful member of [his] family'" (Winter, 2006, p. 157). Thus, despite protesting otherwise, serial killers may be quite sensitized to the impact of others' evaluations of them.

Early in this chapter, I flatly stated that serial killers are not like "most people." Thankfully, in terms of the choices that they make that result in the suffering and death of innocent others, that statement remains valid. But it's an uncomfortable truth that the *dissimilarity* between serial killers and most people stops there. For example, most people want affection from others. If not affection, at least approval. If not approval, at least acknowledgment. What separates serial killers from most people, then, is not what they want—but what they are willing to do, and to whom—in the hopes of getting it.

Decision-making that promotes self-interest at the expense of others gets a bit more complex when we embed individuals in organizational contexts such as businesses, nations, or even families. The basic principles—which are hopefully becoming familiar to you by now—remain the same, however. We'll take a look at specifics in Chapter 8.

References

Aamodt, M. G. (2016, September 4). Serial killer statistics. http://maamodt.asp.radford.edu/Serial%20Killer%20Information%20Center/Serial%20Killer%20Statistics.pdf

Aamodt, M. G., & Moyse, C. (2012). Researching the multiple murderer: A comprehensive bibliography of books on specific serial, mass, and spree killers. http://maamodt.asp.radford.edu/Psyc%20405/Teaching%20Corner/Serial%20Killer%20Books.pdf

Adjorlolo, S., & Chan, H. C. (O.) (2014). The controversy of defining serial murder: Revisited. *Aggression and Violent Behavior*, *19*(5), 486–491. doi:10.1016/j.avb.2014.07.003

Allely, C. S., Minnis, H., Thompson, L., Wilson, P., & Gillberg, C. (2014). Neurodevelopmental and psychosocial risk factors in serial killers and mass murderers. *Aggression and Violent Behavior*, *19*(3), 288–301. doi:10.1016/j.avb.2014.04.004

Arndt, W. B., Hietpas, T., & Kim, J. (2004). Critical characteristics of male serial murderers. *American Journal of Criminal Justice*, *29*, 117–131. doi:10.1007/BF02885707

Barnes, N. (2019). Killer folklore: Identity issues in the True Crime Community. *Ethnologies*, *41*(1), 153–172. doi:10.7202/1069850ar

Beasley, J. O., II. (2004). Serial murder in America: Case studies of seven offenders. *Behavioral Sciences & the Law*, *22*(3), 395–414. doi:10.1002/bsl.595

Buncombe, A. (2017, January 9). Thousands call for release of man who shot dead his daughter's rapist. https://www.independent.co.uk/news/world/americas/father-pardon-jay-manor-shot-dead-daughter-sex-attacker-raymond-earl-brooks-release-alabama-jailed-40-years-prison-sentence-a7517576.html

Burris, C. T., & Rempel, J. K. (2010). If I only had a membrane: A review of Amoebic Self Theory. *Social and Personality Psychology Compass*, *4*(9), 756–766. doi:10.1111/j.1751-9004.2010.00291.x

Castle, T., & Hensley, C. (2002). Serial killers with military experience: Applying learning theory to serial murder. *International Journal of Offender Therapy and Comparative Criminology*, *46*(4), 453–465. doi:10.1177.0306624x02464007

Chester, D. S., & DeWall, C. N. (2017). Combating the sting of rejection with the pleasure of revenge: A new look at how emotion shapes aggression. *Journal of Personality and Social Psychology*, *112*(3), 413–430. doi:10.1037/pspi0000080

Culhane, S. E., Hildebrand, M. M., Mullings, A., & Klemm, J. (2016). Self-reported disorders among serial homicide offenders: Data from the Millon Clinical Multiaxial Inventory–III. *Journal of Forensic Psychology Practice*, *16*(4), 268–286. doi:10.1080/15228932.2016.1196099

Culhane, S. E., Walker, S., & Hildebrand, M. M. (2019). Serial homicide perpetrators' self-reported psychopathy and criminal thinking. *Journal of Police and Criminal Psychology*, *34*, 1–13. doi:10.1007/s11896-017-9245-x

Custers, K., & Van den Bulck, J. (2012). The relationship between news exposure to a serial killer case and altruistic fear: An exploratory study. *Studies in Communication and Media*, *1*, 167–192. doi:10.5771/2192-4007-2012-2-167

DeHart, D. D., & Mahoney, J. M. (1994). The serial murderer's motivations: An interdisciplinary review. *Omega: Journal of Death and Dying*, *29*(1), 29–45. doi:10.2190/75BM-PM83-1XEE-2VBP

Donnelly, A. M. (2012). The new American hero: Dexter, serial killer for the masses. *Journal of Popular Culture*, *45*(1), 15–26. doi:10.1111/j.1540-5931.2011.00908.x

Felton, D. (2021). *Monsters and monarchs: Serial killers in classical myth and history*. University of Texas Press.

Fridel, E. E., & Fox, J. A. (2019). The quantitative study of serial murder: Regression is not transgression. *Aggression and Violent Behavior*, *44*, 24–26. doi:10.1016/j.avb.2018.11.008

Gill, P., Silver, J., Horgan, J., & Corner, E. (2017). Shooting alone: The pre-attack experiences and behaviors of U.S. solo mass murderers. *Journal of Forensic Sciences*, *62*(3), 710–714. doi:10.1111/1556-4029.13330

Gudjonsson, G. (1999). The making of a serial false confessor: The confessions of Henry Lee Lucas. *Journal of Forensic Psychiatry*, *10*(2), 416–426. doi:10.1080/09585189908403693

Gunn, L., & Caissie, L. T. (2006). Serial murder as an act of deviant leisure. *Leisure*, *30*(1), 27–53. doi:10.1080/14927713.2006.9651340

Harrison, M. A., Murphy, E. A., Ho, L. Y., Bowers, T. G., & Flaherty, C. V. (2015). Female serial killers in the United States: Means, motives, and makings. *Journal of Forensic Psychiatry & Psychology*, *26*, 383–406. doi:10.1080/14789949.2015.1007516

Henson, J. R., & Olson, L. N. (2010). The monster within: How male serial killers discursively manage their stigmatized identities. *Communication Quarterly*, *58*(3), 341–364. doi:10.1080/01463373.2010.503176

Hickey, E. W. (2016). *Serial murderers and their victims*. Cengage Learning.

Hodgkinson, S., Prins, H., & Stuart-Bennett, J. (2017). Monsters, madmen . . . and myths: A critical review of the serial killing literature. *Aggression and Violent Behavior*, *34*, 282–289. doi:10.1016/j.avb.2016.11.006

Holmes, R. M., & Holmes, S. T. (1998). *Serial murder* (2nd ed.). Sage Publications.

Interview with Dr. Scott Bonn (n.d.). All-about-Psychology.com. https://www.all-about-psychology.com/scott-bonn.html

James, V., & Gossett, J. (2018). Of monsters and men: Exploring serial murderers' discourses of neutralization. *Deviant Behavior*, *39*(9), 1120–1139. doi:10.1080/01639625.2017.1409980

Kalof, L., Fitzgerald, A., & Baralt, L. (2004). Animals, women, and weapons: Blurred sexual boundaries in the discourse of sport hunting. *Society and Animals*, *12*(3), 237–251. doi:10.1163/1568530042880695

Knight, Z. (2007). Sexually motivated serial killers and the psychology of aggression and "evil" within a contemporary psychoanalytical perspective. *Journal of Sexual Aggression*, *13*(1), 21–35. doi:10.1080/13552600701365597

Kraemer, G. W., Lord, W. D., & Heilbrun, K. (2004). Comparing single and serial homicide offenses. *Behavioral Sciences and the Law*, *22*(3), 325–343. doi:10.1002/bsl.581

Kular, S. (2021). *Evil through and through: Lay prediction of "evil" individuals' everyday behaviours* [Unpublished honors thesis]. University of Waterloo.

Lee, M. R., & DeHart, E. (2007). The influence of a serial killer on changes in fear of crime and the use of protective measures: A survey-based case study of Baton Rouge. *Deviant Behavior*, *28*(1), 1–28. doi:10.1080/01639620600887246

Lester, D., & White, J. (2014). A study of African American serial killers. *Journal of Ethnicity in Criminal Justice*, *12*(4), 308–316. doi:10.1080/15377938.2014.894485

Leyton, E. (2001). *Hunting humans: The rise of the modern multiple murderers*. Carroll & Graf Publishers.

McCarthy, R. (2000, March 17). Killer's sentence: Cut into 100 pieces. https://www.theguardian.com/world/2000/mar/17/rorymccarthy

Merritt, A. C., Effron, D. A., & Monin, B. (2010). Moral self-licensing: When being good frees us to be bad. *Social and Personality Psychology Compass*, *4*(5), 344–357. doi:10.1111/j.1751-9004.2010.00263.x

Miller, L. (2014a). Serial killers: I. Subtypes, patterns, and motives. *Aggression and Violent Behavior*, *19*(1), 1–11. doi:10.1016/j.avb.2013.11.002

Miller, L. (2014b). Serial killers: II. Development, dynamics, and forensics. *Aggression and Violent Behavior*, *19*(1), 12–22. doi:10.1016/j.avb.2013.11.003

Murray, J. L. (2017). The role of sexual, sadistic, and misogynistic fantasy in mass and serial killing. *Deviant Behavior*, *38*(7), 735–743. doi:10.1080/01639625.2016.1197669

Myers, W. C., Husted, D. S., Safarik, M. E., & O'Toole, M. E. (2006). The motivation behind serial sexual homicide: Is it sex, power, and control, or anger? *Journal of Forensic Sciences*, *51*(4), 900–907. doi:10.1111/j.1556-4029.2006.00168.x

Patterson, G. (1999). The killing fields. http://www.garethpatterson.com/articles

Pettigrew, M. (2020). Confessions of a serial killer: A neutralization analysis. *Homicide Studies*, *24*(1), 69–84. doi:10.1177/1088767918793674

R v. Wettlaufer. (2017a). OSCJ Court file 05/17 (Agreed statement of facts on guilty plea). Exhibit 1 at Long-term Care Homes Public Inquiry. https://longtermcareinquiry.ca/en/exhibits

R v. Wettlaufer. (2017b). OSCJ Court file 05/17 (Appendix D to the agreed statement of fact—Centre for Addiction and Mental Health [CAMH]—Discharge data). Exhibit 1 at Long-term Care Homes Public Inquiry. https://longtermcareinquiry.ca/en/exhibits

Reid, S. (2017a). Compulsive criminal homicide: A new nosology for serial murder. *Aggression and Violent Behavior*, *34*, 290–301. doi:10.1016/j.avb.2016.11.005

Reid, S. (2017b). Developmental pathways to serial homicide: A critical review of the biological literature. *Aggression and Violent Behavior*, *35*, 52–61. doi:10.1016/j.avb.2017.06.003

Reid, S., Katan, A., Ellithy, A., Della Stua, R., & Denisov, E. V. (2019). The perfect storm: Mapping the life course trajectories of serial killers. *International Journal of Offender Therapy and Comparative Criminology*, *63*, 1621–1662. doi:10.1177/0306624X19838683

Schlesinger, L. B. (2001). The contract murderer: Patterns, characteristics, and dynamics. *Journal of Forensic Sciences*, *46*(5), 1119–1123.

Schmid, D. (2005). *Natural born celebrities: Serial killers in American culture*. University of Chicago Press.

Skrapec, C. A. (2001a). Motives of the serial killer. In A. Raine & J. Sanmartín (Eds.), *Violence and psychopathy* (pp. 105–122). Springer Science + Business Media.

Skrapec, C. A. (2001b). Phenomenology and serial murder: Asking different questions. *Homicide Studies*, *5*(1), 46–63. doi:10.1177/1088767901005001004

Soothill, K. (1993). The serial killer industry. *Journal of Forensic Psychiatry*, *4*(2), 341–54. doi:10.1080/09585189308407983

Tang, F. (2020). *A qualitative exploration into the subjective experiences of healthcare serial killers* [Unpublished master's thesis]. Wilfrid Laurier University.

White, M. S. (2014). *A façade of normalcy: An exploration into the serial murderer's duplicitous lifestyle* [Unpublished doctoral dissertation]. Old Dominion University.

Wiest, J. B. (2016). Casting cultural monsters: Representations of serial killers in U.S. and U.K. news media. *Howard Journal of Communications*, *27*(4), 327–346. doi:10.1080/10646175.2016.1202876

Williams, A. (2020). Shockingly evil: The cruel invasive appropriation and exploitation of victims' rights of publicity in the true crime genre. *Journal of Intellectual Property Law*, *27*, 303–328.

Williams, D. J. (2017a). Entering the minds of serial murderers: The application of forensic leisure science to homicide research. *Leisure Sciences*, *39*(4), 376–383. doi:10.1080/01490400.2016.1234953

Williams, D. J. (2017b). Mephitic projects: S forensic leisure science analysis of the BTK serial murders. *Journal of Forensic Psychiatry & Psychology*, *28*(1), 24–37. doi:10.1080/14789949.2016.1247187

Williams, D. J., Thomas, J. N., & Arntfield, M. (2020). An empirical exploration of leisure-related themes and potential constraints across descriptions of serial homicide cases. *Leisure Sciences*, *42*(1), 69–84. doi:10.1080/01490400.2017.1384941

Winter, D. A. (2006). Destruction as a constructive choice. In T. Mason (Ed.), *Forensic psychiatry: Influences of evil* (pp. 153–178). Humana Press.

Yaksic, E. (2015) Addressing the challenges and limitations of utilizing data to study serial homicide. *Crime Psychology Review*, *1*(1), 108–134. doi:10.1080/23744006.2016.1168597

Yaksic, E. (2018). The folly of counting bodies: Using regression to transgress the state of serial murder classification systems. *Aggression and Violent Behavior*, *43*, 26–32. doi:10.1016/j.avb.2018.08.007

Yaksic, E., Allely, C., De Silva, R., Smith-Inglis, M., Konikoff, D., Ryan, K., Gordon, D., Denisov, E., & Keatley, D. A. (2019). Detecting a decline in serial homicide: Have we banished the devil from the details? *Cogent Social Sciences*, *5*(1), 1678450. doi:10.1080/23311886.2019.1678450

Yorker, B. C., Kizer, K. W., Lampe, P., Forrest, A. R., Lannan, J. M., & Russell, D. A. (2006). Serial murder by healthcare professionals. *Journal of Forensic Sciences*, *51*(6), 1362–1371. doi:10.1111/j.1556-4029.2006.00273.x

8
Organized Evil

Have you ever been a part of a group that did something "evil"?

Before you say "no"—perhaps with a dismissive sneer directed at me for asking yet another intrusive and potentially offensive question—think about the *groups* that you belong to. Most people may think of groups as collectives composed of individuals who choose to affiliate based on shared interests, goals, or ideologies. Nevertheless, groups also include those into which a person is born, such as one's nation, ethnicity, faith tradition, or family.

With that in mind, let's return to the original question, rephrased: Have any of your groups or their members ever willfully engaged in a course of action that harmed others? If your answer is "yes," you can pretty safely assume by this point in the book that the key players tried to justify this course of action to themselves. It's a safe bet that they also tried to conceal the harm, minimize their responsibility for it, and/or justify it to outsiders as needed. Maybe you were one of those key players. Alternatively, perhaps you were a passive bystander—that is, you knew what was happening, but chose not to intervene to change your fellow group members' course of action.

Or maybe you only learned about what your group did after the fact. Maybe you were on the other side of the world or hadn't even been born when and where the events in question came to pass. Herein lies one of the unique quandaries of belonging to a group. For sure, there are not only practical (survival-related) benefits of being connected to others, but also psychological benefits—as when the successes of fellow group members build us up because they're "our" successes. Nevertheless, the same mechanisms that allow us to experience collective self-esteem following group members' successes can also push us to experience collective guilt and shame in response to their failures (e.g., Lickel et al., 2011 [Canada/USA]). And the moral failures of "our" groups seem to be particularly evocative. For example, Ferguson and Branscombe (2014 [USA]) reviewed research suggesting that individuals are especially likely to experience collective guilt when they perceive their group as *being responsible for illegitimate harm*. This should be quite familiar

Evil in Mind. Christopher T. Burris, Oxford University Press. © Oxford University Press 2022.
DOI: 10.1093/oso/9780197637180.003.0008

to you by now, as it clearly parallels the three prototypic features of behavior deemed "evil" (see Chapter 1).

Thus, regardless of whether someone was directly involved in harmful acts perpetrated by a group, a key question is whether that person accepts the justification(s) offered for the group's course of action, as well as any ensuing coverups. Barring such acceptance, one can perhaps choose to castigate key players and passive bystanders. For example, one might question whether those actors should be seen as representative of—or, indeed, whether they even *truly belong* to—one's group. A different approach is to *distance oneself* from the group in question. Of course, this is much easier when that group is *not* the kind into which one is born, and one's practical well-being (like a paycheck or a place to sleep) doesn't hinge on staying connected to it.

These issues should serve to remind you of the obvious point that *groups are made up of individuals* like you and me. Consequently, the big principles that have framed our consideration of evil at the interpersonal level still apply. That is, we're still chasing feelings ("If I do A, then B will happen. If B happens, then I'll feel more of C and/or less of D"). In so doing, we set certain priorities, sometimes at the expense of others' well-being (MioMa: "I don't mind, and you don't matter [enough];" see Chapter 4). And as we pursue our individual goals, we seem to be reflexively mindful of the ever-present risk of condemnation by others (the Mark of Cain; see Chapter 3)—so *of course* we often feel compelled to justify our choices to ourselves and others. Belonging to groups doesn't nullify any of these principles.

The "G Force": How Groups Amplify Evil

The question, then, is whether groups add anything extra to the mix. Let's explore this question by using the three prototypic features of evil behavior as an organizing framework.

Harm

Prototypic evil involves inflicting harm on others—or, at bare minimum, intending to inflict it. Can groups increase the severity of harm? The answer is "yes" in many instances, for two different reasons. First, if a greater number of individuals engage in the same kind of harmful behavior, net harm severity increases by simple addition. Irreparable damage to protected natural areas by "overeager tourists on the hunt for the perfect photo" (Marcus, 2016 [USA]) illustrates this. Second, if the "group" designation implies more than simple category membership—that is, organization and coordination—then a group's capacity for inflicting harm may increase exponentially, much as an assembly line increases manufacturing productivity. Indeed, despite the fact that corporate crime is often not framed as "real" crime (see Whyte, 2016 [UK]), Ashforth and Anand (2003 [USA], p. 2) noted that the "U.S. Department of Justice estimates that the economic costs of corporate crime are seven to 25 times greater than that of street crime." More broadly, and based in part on his own study of Dutch police services, Kolthoff (2016) has argued that human rights tend to be violated where organizational corruption is tolerated.

Intentionality

In many interpersonal contexts, drawing a connection between a harmful outcome and an individual actor's intentions can be straightforward. In contrast, when harm results from the policies and actions of groups such as corporations or regimes, it is seldom possible to make a one-to-one connection with the intentions of a single individual. After all, "assembly-line" or "mass-produced" harm is an explicitly interdependent undertaking. That is, it requires the active participation of a critical mass of group members coupled with everyone else's unwillingness to obstruct the process. Under these circumstances, who in the group should be held accountable for the harm? Leaders? A few "bad apples"? Everyone? No one?

Such judgments are further complicated by the fact that groups often embody a sort of "fuzzy personhood." That is, when perceived as discrete entities rather than collectives composed of individuals, groups can be regarded as vaguely godlike—almost, but not quite, human. For example, although some research suggests that corporations are seen as being equally capable of intentional actions compared to individuals, they are also seen as being less capable of feeling (see Gray & Wegner, 2010 [USA]; Knobe & Prinz, 2008 [USA]). Moreover, people tend to see a contract as less indicative of a promise when "signed" by a corporation versus an individual (Haran, 2013 [Israel]).

Justifications

As I noted in Chapter 3, invoking justifications is often the fail-safe strategy for attempting to deflect the Mark of Cain when one enacts behavior that is unambiguously intentional and harmful. Because the menu of justifications I presented there was intentionally broad, it can be applied to group situations with minimal modification. For example, "I am good" easily translates to "we are good," such that the harm inflicted by a group serves an allegedly higher purpose. "Good enough" reasons can be invoked as well. For example, one's own group is sometimes portrayed as being under duress or otherwise disadvantaged, so one inflicts harm on its behalf. Alternatively, one may go along with a group's harmful agenda out of fear of suffering consequences if one chooses not to do so (see the discussion of "crimes of obedience" in Hamilton & Sanders, 1999 [USA]). The individual might also feel put upon by the world in general, and group membership provides practical and social empowerment for lashing out (recall the analysis of sadistic motivation in Chapter 6).

Drawing on a cross-section of research, my main goal is to show you how elements of this analysis play out in three group settings. The first two settings may strike many of you as obvious candidates for inclusion in a book about evil. Although the third may come to mind less readily, I hope you'll quickly see how it fits as well. More about that later.

Group Setting #1: Corporate and Bureaucratic Corruption

In Chapter 4's consideration of the process of becoming "evil," I suggested that harmful consequences can result from an individual's attempts to feed an appetite for "more." This is especially likely when that individual experiences the appetite for more as ultimately insatiable and relies on the MioMa principle as a decision guide. Paralleling this analysis, Ashforth and Anand (2003, p. 5) suggested that motives centered on "resource procurement and financial success" prompt decision-making in organizational contexts that is often amoral or immoral. In MioMa terms, corporate/bureaucratic organizations can choose to prioritize their own well-being at the expense of: (1) perceived competitors; (2) personnel, constituents, or customers; and (3) the rest of the world (e.g., the general public, the environment).

Decision-making that produces harmful outcomes can sometimes become an organization's standard operating procedure. This "normalization of corruption," according to Ashforth and Anand (2003, p. 3), is built on the "three pillars" of *institutionalization*, *rationalization*, and *socialization*. Let's take a look at each.

Institutionalization

Institutionalization can be gauged based on the extent to which harm-producing behaviors are experienced as routine and commonplace, and are consequently enacted without much conscious deliberation. Repetition creates a sense of routine: As Ashforth and Anand (2003, p. 14) put it, "an organization is corrupt today because it was corrupt yesterday."

Leadership plays an important role in this process: Even if not directly engaged in corrupt behavior themselves, leaders authorize organizational corruption by "rewarding, condoning, ignoring, or otherwise facilitating" it (Ashforth & Anand, 2003, p. 7). In particular, DeCelles and Pfarrer (2004 [USA], p. 74) noted that the "special ability for charismatic leaders to manage external façades allows for greater opportunity to engage in corrupt behaviors internally because they can effectively hide it from external stakeholders and the public eye."

The institutionalization of harm-producing behavior is further enhanced by: (1) *(selective) organizational memory*, rooted in the questionable assumption that (surely!) somebody has previously concluded that their organization's practices are ethical and productive enough to adopt and maintain; and (2) the *removal of decision points*—that is, breaking down tasks into an assembly line of micro-tasks. The latter effectively eliminates the need for individual pondering and makes the "big picture," including the moral implications of organizational undertakings, more difficult to perceive.

Rationalization

Ashforth and Anand (2003, p. 36) asserted that "[t]he most difficult act of corruption is often one's first act." Through the power of institutionalization, the first act is often followed by a second. And a third. And a fiftieth.

Nevertheless, people are seldom *completely* unreflective or completely detached from decision points. Consequently, it makes sense that individuals embedded in harm-producing organizations will latch onto strategies that make their own participation seem "okay enough" to continue. Ashforth and Anand's discussion of such rationalization processes veers into classic Mark of Cain territory (see Chapter 3)—for example, "*corrupt individuals tend not to view themselves as corrupt*" (p. 15, italics in original) because they have a "need to believe in their own goodness" (p. 24). Importantly, Ashforth and Anand suggest that corporate/bureaucratic organizations oftentimes offer *rationalizing ideologies* to their personnel rather than leaving individuals to fend for themselves.

In all, Ashforth and Anand (2003) described eight possible elements of rationalizing ideologies that appear in various combinations across groups. Some are marshaled in advance of questionable acts and may therefore often seem relatively plausible. Others are more likely invoked after the fact and may therefore appear more far-fetched and desperate, at least to outsiders. The eight elements, accompanied by stylized quotes intended to capture the spirit of Ashforth and Anand's depictions, are:

(1) *denial of injury*—"This isn't really a big deal." "Others do much worse."
(2) *denial of victim*—"They deserved it." "They started it." "They wanted it." "They don't really feel anything."
(3) *denial of responsibility*—"I don't really have a choice." "Everybody else is doing it, too."
(4) *legality*—"If it's not against the law, then it's not a problem."
(5) *metaphor of the ledger*—"I/we do a lot of good, so that should count for something."
(6) *social weighting*—"They are in no position to judge me."
(7) *appeal to higher loyalties*—"Me and mine first." "The end justifies the means."
(8) *refocusing attention*—"The pay is unbeatable." "I enjoy a challenge."

None of the themes underlying these elements should strike you as unexpected or novel by now. For example, (1) and (2) include attempts to minimize *harm*, and (3) tosses in some minimization of *intent*—two key elements of prototypic "evil" behavior. The span of responses spurred by aversion to the Mark of Cain described in Chapter 3 appear across (1) through (6). And (7) and (8) embody the MioMa principle. Depending on where the individual sits in the hierarchy, certain tweaks are possible. For example, higher-ups might tend toward plausible deniability of their involvement in harm-producing behavior: They may assert that they didn't do it, certainly didn't order it, and may not have even known about it. In contrast, subordinates are more likely to stress that leadership mandated it, modeled it, and seemed more than okay with it.

Socialization

The vast majority of members of corporate/bureaucratic organizations begin their tenure as subordinates, so there's always a learning curve. That is, subordinates must learn *what to do* and—if their assigned role contributes to harmful outcomes—*how to justify* what they're doing. Ashforth and Anand (2003) suggested that organizations accomplish this by creating a sort of moral microcosm wherein specific harm-producing behaviors are encouraged and rewarded without undermining the individual's self-image as "basically a good person." Thus, newbies may be offered concrete rewards and praised for their loyalty and initiative, and they may be punished and chastised for their hesitance and misgivings. Because the drift toward corrupt behavior is often so gradual, "it may be very difficult to halt the behavior and extricate oneself from the strong situation without suffering stiff psychological, social, financial, and legal costs from guilt, shame, job loss, and so on" (p. 31) should a full-bodied realization of the moral import of one's behavior occur.

Of course, socialization into corruption is smoother when there is less variation in attitudes within the group to begin with (see Gorsira et al., 2018 [Netherlands]). In fact, personal agendas may lead some individuals to seek out groups with a penchant for creating harmful outcomes, and it makes sense that these same groups are on the lookout for recruits who do not seem fazed by the organization's mission and methods. Morally troubled recruits who do not "get with the program" are often forced out of the organization. Consequently, Ashforth and Anand (2003, p. 33) asserted that a "corrupt group is likely to be even more homogeneous than a typical group."

Not surprisingly, then, organizational shifts toward less corrupt practices seldom emerge spontaneously from within the organizations themselves. Indeed, Ashforth and Anand (2003) speculated that misguided assumptions concerning personal and collective invulnerability can sometimes result in organizations becoming "suicidally corrupt"—that is, that it's mostly a matter of time until such organizations suffer negative consequences for the harm that they create. Note that I wrote *mostly* a matter of time: An organization's practices must be exposed to scrutiny by outsiders who have the power to punish—as when a business's products and services are boycotted via social or mass media campaigns, for example. Internal whistleblowers who expose organizational corruption are typically regarded as heroes by outsiders, but they're often seen as traitors who deserve to be martyred by organizational insiders (e.g., Pohjanoksa et al., 2019 [Finland]). Thus, Mark of Cain dynamics—the pull and push of inclusion versus exclusion—play out differently depending on who is doing the judging.

Let's consider some corruption examples, starting with Whyte (2016), who examined three cases involving major automakers in the 2007–2015 period. First, in response to numerous incidents of Jeep gas tanks exploding on impact and causing severe burns or death, Fiat Chrysler initially resisted a U.S. government push for recall and repair, attacked regulators' testing methodology, and repeatedly insisted that Jeeps were safe—or, at least, that "the rate of collisions experienced by Jeeps is not out of line for similar vehicles in that class" (p. 171). Fiat Chrysler was eventually fined and coerced into buying back over one million vehicles, including those that had been recommended for recall. Second, prompted by their vehicles' occasionally fatal "sudden acceleration" issues, Toyota issued consumer safety advisories and large-scale recalls involving "pedal entrapment" attributed to unsecured floor mats and, eventually, to "sticky pedals." Although this sounded proactive and responsible on the surface, the real cause appeared to be a defective throttle system. Toyota knew about this early on but did not admit knowledge until forced to do so. They paid a fine to avoid prosecution. Finally, Volkswagen installed "cheat" software on millions of vehicles in order to pass emissions tests while exceeding emission standards (often wildly) during normal operation. No one in senior management had admitted that this was a deliberate, calculated decision by the time Whyte's article had gone to press. Instead, it was initially framed as a technical problem, and then as the outcome of a series of "mistakes." Throughout, Volkswagen asserted that it was a good corporate citizen and was cooperating fully with authorities. Moreover, Volkswagen (like Toyota) was quick to tout the good that the company does (job creation, customer satisfaction, green initiatives, etc.).

Shifting the focus onto other industries, Talbot and Boiral (2015) identified six themes in their interviews with representatives from large Canadian greenhouse gas emitters. Some interviewees focused on their companies' recognized efforts to be proactive with respect to emissions reductions. Most encouraged adoption of a mindset wherein greenhouse emissions associated with production were only one part of a bigger picture that included socioeconomic contributions and the benefits of manufactured products (e.g., reusability and weight-fuel savings associated with aluminum). A few attempted to frame their emissions as small compared to other producers, and that the net impact on climate was trivial, anyway. Over two-thirds claimed that their companies were unfairly caricaturized as large emitters by a media and general public who don't understand industry complexities and guiltlessly consume what the industries produce. Many claimed that their companies were already doing the best that they could, and that increasingly stringent emission reduction targets would put them at an economic disadvantage internationally. Finally, a number attempted to deflect attention to other sectors wherein greenhouse emissions volume was *really* a problem. Talbot and Boiral also pointed to research documenting more underhanded persuasive attempts known as "astroturfing," wherein a corporation sets up and funds a fake grassroots organization intended to nudge public attitudes in a pro-industry direction—in this case, by sowing doubt concerning the legitimacy of climate change science (see Cho et al., 2011 [Canada/France]).

Three themes emerged when Sachet-Milliat et al. (2017) examined justification strategies employed by French alcohol and tobacco marketers. First, some positioned themselves as representatives of basically moral companies: Their products are not harmful if enjoyed in moderation, and the companies participate in efforts to safeguard consumers from excesses. Second, some argued that their industry is so highly regulated that they cannot really act unethically; alternatively, governments are so concerned with tax revenue, and consumers with personal pleasure, that neither wants the industry to restrain itself too much. Finally, some emphasized the material and professional rewards that their marketing jobs provided, along with the bubble that their companies created to insulate marketers from branding as "merchants of death" by outsiders.

According to the mostly German interviewees contacted by Campbell and Göritz (2014), "[c]orrupt organizations perceive themselves to fight in a kind of war" (p. 298), and "the enemy" is any entity that poses a threat to the survival of the organization. The war narrative fosters a sort of anything-goes-survivalism wherein "the underlying assumption 'the end justifies the means' is the key characteristic of a corrupt organizational culture" (p. 305).

This includes attempts to curtail and punish insiders who challenge the corruption status quo, because such challenges are perceived as threatening the well-being of the (already-embattled) organization and, by extension, the well-being of individual organization members.

Group Setting #2: Genocidal Campaigns

Although there are good reasons why a one-size-fits-all understanding of corporations as evil is unlikely to materialize (see Litowitz, 2003–2004 [USA]), labeling genocidal campaigns as "evil" is a much easier sell for many people. After all, the harm inflicted is unambiguous and nearly incalculable, and the enormity of planning necessary even to attempt to destroy a target group leaves no question about perpetrators' intentions. Moreover, most people cannot even begin to wrap their heads around a package of justifications that would be "good enough" for such a course of action. Thus, consistent with the three-feature model described in Chapter 1, genocide is often "perceived as being synonymous with extraordinary evil" (Hollows & Fritzon, 2012 [Australia], p. 458).

Nevertheless, genocides persist. Thus, it is clear that some people are able to summon for themselves "good enough" reasons to undertake such campaigns. As might be expected, each historical case has its nuances, as documented by the emerging field of *genocide studies* (see Üngör, 2016 [international]).

Staub (2012, 2014 [USA]) suggested that the convergence of a number of factors substantially increases the likelihood that wholesale violence directed toward specific groups will manifest, however. In simplest form, leaders must identify a target group and then convince the remaining citizenry that life would be better if the target group were wiped out—that is, that doing so would decisively settle historical grievances and eliminate any possible future threat to well-being or way of life that the target group could pose (for analysis of the Rwandan government's use of media, especially radio, during the 1994 genocide, see: Baisley, 2014 [Canada]; Fujii, 2004 [Canada]; Kellow & Steeves, 1998 [USA]; and Li, 2004 [USA]). Citizenry are most likely to be receptive to this message when the prevailing cultural norm is not to question authority, when they themselves feel personally wounded or disadvantaged by the target group in question, and when they perceive that their leaders are giving them permission (and often the means) to strike out against the target group. A strong "we-feeling" between followers and leaders coupled with weak opposition from inside and outside the group often seals the deal: "No one is telling 'us' why genocide in this specific instance would be wrong, and no one is even attempting to stand in 'our' way." It is at this point that genocide proper often begins.

Genocide is a mass-produced form of harm. Thus, just as corporate wrongdoing often involves coordination between supervisors and underlings (see Campbell & Göritz, 2014), division of labor makes genocide easier. Fujii (2004, p. 107) bluntly put it this way: "Motivating non-killers to kill and to kill repeatedly takes practice. People must not only be emotionally charged and psychologically prepared, they must also be logistically trained in the rudiments of mass murder: when to start, when to stop, who to target, and who to spare."

In an attempt to map out the roles likely to manifest within genocidal campaigns, Hollows and Fritzon (2012) analyzed court documents linked to 80 perpetrators of genocide-related crimes sentenced by the International Criminal Tribunal for the former Yugoslavia convened after the Bosnian conflict in the early 1990s. Although the authors made a case for four distinct types of genocidal perpetrators, they admitted that there was a fair bit of overlap between especially their "sadist" and "avenger" categories. Close inspection suggests overlap between their "instigator" and "dutiful leader" categories as well. Consequently, I'd suggest that the perpetrators can be differentiated most clearly along a dimension that runs from "logistic" to "sadistic." The logistic end is populated by comparatively high-power, stable individuals such as politicians and career military who appeared to frame genocide in predominantly practical terms, and who were capable of motivating and efficiently mobilizing those on the ground to carry out the various subtasks required. Those at the sadistic end tended to be less efficient and more process-oriented, as indicated by their use of humiliation, non-lethal weapons, sexual violation, and torture. These individuals had less education and were more likely to be single; they were also more likely to have a history of psychological disorder, substance abuse, and criminality. Thus, sadistic perpetrators appeared to be comparatively marginalized and unstable. This is broadly consistent with the model of sadistic motivation set forth in Chapter 6.

Although not labeled as such, sadism also figures centrally in Rauxloh's (2016 [UK]) analysis of participation in massacres—which can perhaps be loosely referred to as "necessary but not *efficient*" components of a genocidal campaign. She argued that people typically do not engage spontaneously in the sort of wanton, collective violence characteristic of massacres simply based on their animosity toward a target group. Rather, a "physiological confrontational barrier" must first be overcome (p. 1020; cf. Baumeister, 1997 [USA]). Drawing on work by Collins (2013 [USA]), Rauxloh suggested that attaining "emotional energy dominance" over the target group is critical to this process. Key to this presumed state is to perceive the target group as weak and thus, by contrast, to experience oneself *and one's group* as powerful. Directing extreme violence toward the target group dramatically affirms this realization, often resulting in a rush of self-congratulatory emotions, and even giddiness. In other words, there is a positive emotional payoff when self is elevated at the expense of the other—which is the heartless heart of sadism.

According to Rauxloh (2016), perpetrating groups often don't launch immediately into massacres. Instead, they start with smaller, more impersonal attacks such as destruction of the target group's property. Experiencing such attacks as "successes" (manifest, in part, by target group resistance that is absent or ineffectual) can help empower perpetrators' move toward a massacre proper. And it is here that sadistic dynamics seem impossible to overlook.

For example, Rauxloh (2016) observed that perpetrators occasionally use racial epithets toward members of the target group even when a massacre is not based on race. Eventual victims also may be coerced to say denigrating things about themselves. Others are forced either to engage in or to observe humiliating or desecrating behaviors such as sex acts between family members before being slaughtered. In addition, "killing games" involving gauntlets or victims futilely bargaining for their lives are sometimes incorporated, as well as mutilation of victims' corpses. Such unconscionable actions seem gratuitous at best if the goal is efficient killing. If, however, such deeds serve to amplify and sustain a "triumphant atmosphere" (p. 1027) among perpetrating groups—congruent with the positive emotional payoff associated with sadistic motivation—then they make more sense (cf. the analysis of serial killers' motives and experiences in Chapter 7).

Of course, nothing can quash such a triumphant atmosphere more effectively than being held accountable for one's role in mass atrocities. So how do people talk about themselves and their actions when facing judgment, especially in a formal legal context? Bryant et al. (2018 [USA]) attempted to answer this question by analyzing transcripts from 27 International Criminal Tribunal for Rwanda (ICTR) defendants accused of genocidal participation (1995–2015).

Broadly speaking, defendants' strategies were not really that different from the ones people use in less extreme contexts. Although none of the defendants attempted to deny that large-scale harm had occurred, those who acknowledged the broader harm often referred to it as "war" rather than genocide (cf. use of the war metaphor by corrupt organizations in Campbell & Göritz, 2014). Given the trial context, it made little sense for defendants to confess their role in the perpetration of mass suffering. Consequently, mitigating justifications—claiming necessity, following orders, pointing to a higher purpose, blaming victims and denying their humanity, or asserting one's goodness in other contexts as a counterbalance—were seldom used.

Instead, defendants focused on distancing themselves from the gravest accusations. For example, some denied the occurrence of *specific* harmful episodes—predictably, the ones that would implicate them. Some asserted that they were never in a powerful enough position to start or stop specific genocidal events despite the fact that the ICTR's selection process focused on defendants believed to have occupied power positions, and who therefore had the wherewithal to mobilize others. Indeed, a few attempted to portray themselves and their ingroup as victims. Most commonly, however, defendants claimed that they were simply not capable, from a character standpoint, of doing what they were accused of. They often adopted a conspiratorial tone by "denouncing both the accusations against them and those levying the allegations . . . [such as] the international community, genocide survivors and their families, and the Rwandan Patriotic Front [that constituted most of the Rwandan government when the ICTR trials were being conducted]" (Bryant et al., 2018, p. 590, brackets inserted).

By now, you should have certainly expected that the accused would say whatever they thought might offer them the best chance of avoiding a conviction. Over and above this pragmatism, however, Bryant et al. (2018, p. 585) suggested that defendants were also attempting to "assert a positive, socially accepted sense of self in light of identities deeply tarnished by ICTR accusations." In other words, people accused of genocidal acts were concerned about being seen as "bad"—or "evil"—people. So we're right back in Mark of Cain territory.

Some evidence suggests that Mark of Cain dynamics can extend beyond perpetrators proper. For example, based on their review of the available cross-cultural research, Leach et al. (2013 [Bosnia/USA], p. 47) concluded that "explicit and strong self-criticism for past generations' genocide, or other mass violence, is a rarity . . . [and instead that people] tended to *disagree* with self-critical sentiment when they were given the opportunity to do so." In other words, descendants of perpetrator groups tended *not* to experience feelings of collective guilt or feel a strong sense that their group should attempt to make amends for the past. Based on research reviewed by Vollhardt and Bilewicz (2013 [Poland/USA]), descendants are likely to point to specific situational pressures that forced the hands of their genocidal ancestors. Or else the victimized group is seen as deserving its fate. Or else "bad things happened, for sure, but they were done a long time ago by people that aren't really connected to *me*" (see the beginning of this chapter). Descendants of bystanders sometimes wrestle with feelings of inherited accountability as well.

Group Setting #3: Abusive Family Systems

Corrupt corporations and genocidal regimes offer easy examples of "big bad groups." In both cases, sheer size and bureaucratic structure allow for the mass production of harmful outcomes. But smaller groups are not inherently more virtuous. For example, family systems are capable of inflicting damage that is both profound and lasting. On rare but significant occasions, this can be traced to a family's connection to larger groups. For example, Fogel (2006 [USA]) observed that "countries with more extensive family control over their large corporate sectors tend to have worse social economic outcomes" (p. 617) such as greater income inequality, inadequate health care, and greater likelihood of bureaucratic corruption. Likewise, many of the financiers of RTLM, the radio station that played a key role in the Rwandan genocide, had family ties to the president and his wife (Kellow & Steeves, 1998).

Much more commonly, however, the greatest harm inflicted by a family is on its own members. Predictably, those who suffer the most are those who, by virtue of their practical or emotional dependence on the family, are the most vulnerable. Two examples here—focused on the young and the old, respectively—should suffice.

Child sexual abuse (CSA) and the family

Many would consider sexual violation of a child by a family member to be the ultimate betrayal. Social support, especially from non-abusing family members, has been identified as a key factor that helps to minimize the adverse impact of CSA on victims, especially younger ones (see Domhardt et al., 2015 [Germany]). Nevertheless, reactions to CSA within a specific family system are often varied and complex (e.g., Cyr et al., 2013 [Canada]; Elliott & Carnes, 2001 [USA]). For example, although non-victimized siblings often respond empathically when learning of a child's victimization, some experience a variety of negative reactions such as confusion (concerning whether the accused really did it, or why the victim was targeted and they were not; see Schreier et al., 2017 [USA]).

Consider also a study by Bux et al. (2016) based on a small sample of Black South African interviewees (mostly mothers) who had reported suspected sexual abuse of a child to a social service agency. When the abuse was alleged to have occurred within the family system, caregivers described the predominant family reaction as "alienating and unsupportive, especially when caregivers attempted to seek medico-legal assistance" (p. 96).

Malloy et al. (2007) reviewed over 400 CSA cases filed in a large city in the southwestern United States wherein the alleged perpetrator was a parent figure or relative about 90% of the time. What's especially noteworthy is that nearly one in four children in these cases eventually recanted their allegations. According to Malloy et al., the recantation rate was only slightly lower (by about 3%) when focusing specifically on cases in which there was compelling evidence of the truthfulness of the child's original accusation (e.g., medical findings, perpetrator confession). Thus, although it is possible that a small proportion of the original allegations were false, *the great majority of children who recanted were taking back demonstrably true accusations of abuse.* And the two best predictors of whether a child recanted were: (1) The perpetrator was a parent figure; and (2) the non-offending caregiver (usually the biological mother) failed to support the victim. That is, the non-offending caregiver "initially expressed disbelief or skepticism about the allegation(s), exerted direct verbal pressure on the child to recant, blamed the child, remained romantically or interpersonally involved with the perpetrator after CSA discovery (e.g., the perpetrator continued to live with the caregiver), or behaved in an unsupportive manner (e.g., forced the child to leave home)" (p. 164; for experimental evidence of the impact of parental disapproval on children taking back allegations of adult wrongdoing, see Malloy & Mugno, 2016 [USA]).

Unfortunately, it gets worse. Reid et al. (2015) reviewed the cases of 92 girls/young women in the southeastern United States receiving support services from an agency that specializes in victims of sex trafficking. For nearly one-third of the cases, the trafficker was a relative, most often the victim's mother or maternal figure. Reid et al. (p. 370) noted that even in "cases when the mother was not the trafficker or directly involved in selling her daughter, the mothers were often aware of the sexual exploitation of their daughters." Money was the most often cited motive, often to finance the trafficker's chemical dependency. These results are apparently not atypical. In fact, a family member was the trafficker in nearly two-thirds of social service workers' recent cases (boys as well as girls), based on survey results in a south-central U.S. state reported by Cole (2018).

Abuse of the aged in families

Elderly individuals can be targets of abuse within families just as children can. Although physical and psychological forms tend to predominate (see Dong, 2015 [USA]), sexual abuse occurs as well. In instances of the latter, the old and the young often face similar disclosure barriers, such as the threat of being taken out of one's home and placed in an unfamiliar environment (see Shamaskin-Garroway et al., 2017 [USA]).

Elderly individuals must also face the prospect of *financial abuse* (that is, the misappropriation of money or assets), which—owing to its increasing frequency—has been regarded by many as the "Crime of the 21st Century" (Roberto, 2016 [USA]). Pertinent to present considerations, a broad-based survey study in the northeastern United States (Peterson et al., 2014) found that family members were the perpetrators nearly 60% of the time. The rate may be comparable in less prosperous areas of the world, although relevant data are nearly nonexistent (see Lloyd-Sherlock et al., 2018 [South Africa/UK]).

What drives financial abuse of elderly family members? Based on the responses of 160 Australian service providers who work with the elderly and their families, the most frequently endorsed risk factor was a "family member with a strong sense of entitlement to an older person's property/possessions" (Bagshaw et al., 2013, p. 96). Strikingly, family entitlement even outranked other risk factors such as the elderly individual's diminished capacity or family members with substance abuse or gambling issues.

And what does "a strong sense of entitlement" look like? Dalley et al. (2017) reviewed 34 UK Court of Protection cases involving familial execution of power of attorney (PoA) duties on behalf of mostly seniors. In one, despite payments for an elderly woman's care being £29,000 delinquent, her PoA son had paid himself well over £100,000 out of her estate for alleged out-of-pocket expenses, including a £400-a-day charge for visiting his mother as her "attorney." When attempting to convince the court not to strip him of PoA over his mother's affairs, he stated: "I am the sole heir and because of my mother's dementia and current poor health, there is no need to protect the estate's financial interests *which are effectively mine*" (Dalley et al., p. 6, emphasis added).

"Better Together?" Not Always

Early in this chapter I argued that groups sometimes amplify "evil"—that is, that they can often dramatically increase the expanse and severity of intentional, unjustifiable harm. We subsequently explored what enhanced harm can look like in three different group contexts: corporate/bureaucratic corruption, genocidal campaigns, and familial abuse. At first glance, these phenomena may seem quite different save for the fact that multiple individuals are involved in each. I'd suggest that a closer look reveals substantial similarities, however. For example, although I specifically discussed the MioMa principle only in the context of corporate corruption, genocidal campaigns and familial abuse also illustrate the dogged pursuit of (positive) feelings—based on acquisition of assets, a sense of personal or group supremacy, or use of another person's body—irrespective of the suffering that may result. Thus, the MioMa principle applies across the board.

Likewise, the Mark of Cain was explicitly mentioned in the context of examining people's justifications for participating in corrupt organizations or genocidal massacres. Mark of Cain dynamics are evident in cases of familial abuse as well, however, even though the bulk of harm occurs *within the group* rather than being directed toward an external target such as an unwitting consumer or a marginalized outgroup.

That seemed obvious in the cases of financial abuse targeting elderly family members reviewed by Dalley et al. (2017), who noted that "[c]ase reports often included statements by respondents expressed in tones ranging from contrition, faux surprise, apparent amazement, brazen self-justification to argumentative contestation of the judge's view" (p. 3). Consider also work by Tener (2018), whose 20 Israeli female interviewees spoke of pressure that functioned to discourage focus on the incidents of within-family CSA that they had survived. Tener concluded that this pressure within the victims' families manifested at three different "levels." In the first, all but the victim conspire to maintain an appearance of normality while treating the victim as essentially an outsider. In the second, the victim opts not to disclose in order to maintain a semblance of connection to other family members, including the abuser. In the third,

> when the family is presented as normal, the survivors clearly see through the lie, but it is often valuable for them as well since it raises their own status as family members. In this case, disclosure would shatter the family's normative identity as well as that of the survivor. Some of the women described this normal family appearance as a source of strength enabling them to survive the abuse. As one interviewee put it, "Other than that, we were a normal loving family." (p. 14)

Clearly, this is Mark of Cain territory: Whenever inclusion-versus-exclusion is on the line, most people want to assert their goodness and deny their badness. The simplest tactic is to deny or conceal any perceived wrongdoing. Should such deeds be exposed, people will try to justify themselves. *Of course* they will. The "something extra" here is that the vested interest implied by group membership can move people to deny, conceal, or justify *others*' harmful deeds as well.

Their capacity for *division of labor* in the production of harmful outcomes also distinguishes groups from lone individuals. Thus, within any specific instance of "mass-produced evil" there can be initiators, minions, do-nothings, and know-nothings. In such settings, carrying out formally assigned responsibilities—even trivial ones—can nudge a person in a pro-group direction. For example, Folkes and Whang (2003) showed across multiple studies that American students assigned to a "spin doctor" role—that is, who generated justifications, excuses, or apologies for a problematic corporate practice (i.e., overseas child labor)—were subsequently more likely to condone that practice. Group influence is often much more informal and subtle, however. For example, in a Dutch study involving several hundred public officials and private-sector employees, willingness to offer or accept a bribe was better predicted by what respondents thought that their close colleagues would do compared to what they themselves thought of the practice (Gorsira et al., 2016).

Not everyone is corrupt or complicit. Whistleblowers sometimes speak out despite the risks to their well-being. So do abuse survivors. And protectors and rescuers can stymie the genocidal mission to "get 'em all." This could make for a lovely good-versus-evil narrative were it not for the fact that people's allegiances—and, therefore, the motives driving their behavior—are not always "switched on" and stable over time. So, for example, we must come to terms with stories of Rwandan "killer rescuers," such as the "man who admitted to participating in more than seven murders, yet warned a fleeing Tutsi boy to avoid a path that would have led him straight to the *interahamwe* [Hutu militia]," or the "man from Ngali who participated in the killing of a stranger while hiding four of his Tutsi neighbours in his home" (Greene, 2012 [USA], p. 107; see also Fujii, 2011 [Canada]).

To whom do we feel most connected? Who are our "neighbors"—really? What do we fear losing most if we become disconnected or excluded? Our moment-by-moment answers to these questions have an unsettling impact on our capacity to inflict—or to alleviate—suffering as part of a group.

References

Ashforth, B. E., & Anand, V. (2003). The normalization of corruption in organizations. *Research in Organizational Behavior, 25*, 1–52. doi:10.1016/S0191-3085(03)25001-2

Bagshaw, D., Wendt, S., Zannettino, L., & Adams, V. (2013). Financial abuse of older people by family members: Views and experiences of older Australians and their family members. *Australian Social Work, 66*(1), 86–103. doi:10.1080/0312407x.2012.708762

Baisley, E. (2014). Genocide and constructions of Hutu and Tutsi in radio propaganda. *Race & Class, 55*(3), 38–59. doi:10.1177/0306396813509194

Baumeister, R. F. (1997). *Evil: Inside human cruelty and violence*. W. H. Freeman.

Bryant, E., Schimke, E. B., Brehm, H. N., & Uggen, C. (2018). Techniques of neutralization and identity work among accused genocide perpetrators. *Social Problems, 65*(4), 584–602. doi:10.1093/socpro/spx026

Bux, W., Cartwright, D. J., & Collings, S. J. (2016). The experience of non-offending caregivers following the disclosure of child sexual abuse: Understanding the aftermath. *South African Journal of Psychology, 46*(1), 88–100. doi:10.1177/0081246315595038

Campbell, J., & Göritz, A. S. (2014). Culture corrupts! A qualitative study of organizational culture in corrupt organizations. *Journal of Business Ethics, 120*, 291–311. doi:10.1007/s10551-013-1665-7

Cho, C., Martens, M., Kim, H., & Rodrigue, M. (2011). Astroturfing global warming: It isn't always greener on the other side of the fence. *Journal of Business Ethics, 104*, 571–587. doi:10.1007/s10551-011-0950-6

Cole, J. (2018). Service providers' perspectives on sex trafficking of male minors: Comparing background and trafficking situations of male and female victims. *Child and Adolescent Social Work Journal, 35*(4), 423–433. doi:10.1007/s10560-018-0530-z

Collins, R. (2013). Entering and leaving the tunnel of violence: Micro-sociological dynamics of emotional entrainment in violent interactions. *Current Sociology, 61*(2), 132–151. doi:10.1177/0011392112456500

Cyr, M., McDuff, P., & Hébert, M. (2013). Support and profiles of nonoffending mothers of sexually abused children. *Journal of Child Sexual Abuse, 22*(2), 209–230. doi:10.1080/10538712.2013.737444

Dalley, G., Gilhooly, M., Gilhooly, K., & Levi, M. (2017). Exploring financial abuse as a feature of family life: An analysis of Court of Protection cases. *Elder Law Journal, 7*(1), 28–37.

DeCelles, K. A., & Pfarrer, M. D. (2004). Heroes or villains? Corruption and the charismatic leader. *Journal of Leadership & Organizational Studies, 11*(1), 67–77. doi:10.1177/107179190401100108

Domhardt, M., Münzer, A., Fegert, J. M., & Goldbeck, L. (2015). Resilience in survivors of child sexual abuse: A systematic review of the literature. *Trauma, Violence, and Abuse, 16*(4), 476–493. doi:10.1177/1524838014557288

Dong, X. Q. (2015). Elder abuse: Systematic review and implications for practice. *Journal of the American Geriatrics Society, 63*(6), 1214–1238. doi:10.1111/jgs.13454

Elliott, A. N., & Carnes, C. N. (2001). Reactions of non-offending parents to the sexual abuse of their children: A review of the literature. *Child Maltreatment, 6*(4), 314–331. doi:10.1177/1077559501006004005

Ferguson, M. A., & Branscombe, N. R. (2014). The social psychology of collective guilt. In C. von Scheve & M. Salmela (Eds.), *Collective emotions: Perspectives from psychology, philosophy, and sociology* (pp. 251–265). Oxford University Press. doi:10.1093/acprof:oso/9780199659180.003.0017

Fogel, K. (2006). Oligarchic family control, social economic outcomes, and the quality of government. *Journal of International Business Studies, 37*(5), 603–622. doi:10.1057/palgrave.jibs.8400213

Folkes, V. S., & Whang, Y.-O. (2003). Account-giving for a corporate transgression influences moral judgment: When those who "spin" condone harm-doing. *Journal of Applied Psychology, 88*(1), 79–86. doi:10.1037/0021-9010.88.1.79

Fujii, L. A. (2004). Transforming the moral landscape: The diffusion of a genocidal norm in Rwanda. *Journal of Genocide Research, 6*(1), 99–114. doi:10.1080/1462352042000194737

Fujii, L. A. (2011). Rescuers and killer-rescuers during the Rwanda genocide: Rethinking standard categories of analysis. In J. Semelin, C. Andrieu, & S. Gensburger (Eds.), *Resisting genocide: The multiple forms of rescue* (pp. 145–157). Columbia University Press. doi:10.1093/acprof:oso/9780199333493.003.0010

Gorsira, M., Denkers, A., & Huisman, W. (2016). Both sides of the coin: Motives for corruption among public officials and business employees. *Journal of Business Ethics, 151*, 179–194. doi:10.1007/s10551-016-3219-2

Gorsira, M., Steg, L., Denkers, A., & Huisman, W. (2018). Corruption in organizations: Ethical climate and individual motives. *Administrative Sciences, 8*(1), 1–19. doi:10.3390/admsci8010004

Gray, K., & Wegner, D. M. (2010). Blaming God for our pain: Human suffering and the divine mind. *Personality and Social Psychology Review, 14*(1), 7–16. doi: 10.1177/1088868309350299

Greene, A. L. (2012). Resisting genocide: The multiple forms of rescue [book review]. *Journal of Genocide Research, 14*(1), 105–109. doi:10.1080/14623528.2012.656904

Hamilton, V. L., & Sanders, J. (1999). The second face of evil: Wrongdoing in and by the corporation. *Personality and Social Psychology Review, 3*(3), 222–233. doi:10.1207/s15327957pspr0303_5

Haran, U. (2013). A person–organization discontinuity in contract perception: Why corporations can get away with breaking contracts but individuals cannot. *Management Science, 59*(12), 2837–2853. doi:10.1287/mnsc.2013.1745

Hollows, K., & Fritzon, K. (2012). "Ordinary men" or "evil monsters"?: An action systems model of genocidal actions and characteristics of perpetrators. *Law and Human Behavior, 36*(5), 458–467. doi:10.1037/h0093987

Kellow, C. L., & Steeves, H. L. (1998). The role of radio in the Rwandan genocide. *Journal of Communication, 48*(3), 107–128. doi:10.1111/j.1460-2466.1998.tb02762.x

Knobe, J., & Prinz, J. (2008). Intuitions about consciousness: Experimental studies. *Phenomenology and the Cognitive Sciences, 7*, 67–83. doi:10.1007/s11097-007-9066-y

Kolthoff, E. (2016). Integrity violations, white-collar crime, and violations of human rights: Revealing the connection. *Public Integrity, 18*(4), 396–418. doi:10.1080/10999922.2016.1172933

Leach, C. W., Zeineddine, F. B., & Čehajić-Clancy, S. (2013). Moral immemorial: The rarity of self-criticism for previous generations' genocide or mass violence. *Journal of Social Issues, 69*(1), 34–53. doi:10.1111/josi.12002

Li, D. (2004). Echoes of violence: Considerations on radio and genocide in Rwanda. *Journal of Genocide Research, 6*(1), 9–27. doi:10.1080/1462352042000194683

Lickel, B., Steele, R. R., & Schmader, T. (2011). Group-based shame and guilt: Emerging directions in research. *Social and Personality Psychology Compass, 5*(3), 153–163. doi:10.1111/j.1751-9004.2010.00340.x

Litowitz, D. (2003–2004). Are corporations evil? *University of Miami Law Review, 58*, 811–841.

Lloyd-Sherlock, P., Penhale, B., & Ayiga, N. (2018). Financial abuse of older people in low- and middle-income countries: The case of South Africa. *Journal of Elder Abuse & Neglect, 30*(3), 236–246. doi:10.1080/08946566.2018.1452656

Malloy, L. C., Lyon, T. D., & Quas, J. A. (2007). Filial dependency and recantation of child sexual abuse allegations. *Journal of the American Academy of Child & Adolescent Psychiatry, 46*(2), 162–170. doi:10.1097/01.chi.0000246067.77953.f7

Malloy, L. C., & Mugno, A. P. (2016). Children's recantation of adult wrongdoing: An experimental investigation. *Journal of Experimental Child Psychology, 145*, 11–21. doi:10.1016/j.jecp.2015.12.003

Marcus, L. (2016, September 6). Vandals destroy "Duckbill" rock formation at Oregon National Park. www.cntraveler.com/story/vandals-destroy-duckbill-rock-formation-at-oregon-national-park

Peterson, J. C., Burnes, D. P. R., Caccamise, P. L., Mason, A., Henderson, C. R., Jr., Wells, M. T., Berman, J., Cook, A. M., Shukoff, D., Brownell, P., Powell, M., Salamone, A., Pillemer, K. A., & Lachs, M. S. (2014). Financial exploitation of older adults: A population-based prevalence study. *Journal of General Internal Medicine, 29*, 1615–1623. doi:10.1007/s11606-014-2946-2

Pohjanoksa, J., Stolt, M., Suhonen, R., Löyttyniemi, E., & Leino-Kilpi, H. (2019). Whistle-blowing process in healthcare: From suspicion to action. *Nursing Ethics, 26*(2), 526–540. doi:10.1177/0969733017705005

Rauxloh, R. E. (2016). Group offending in mass atrocities: Proposing a group violence strategies model for international crimes. *Oñati Socio-legal Series, 6*(4), 1016–1031.

Reid, J. A., Huard, J., & Haskell, R. A. (2015). Family-facilitated juvenile sex trafficking. *Journal of Crime and Justice*, *38*(3), 361–376. doi:10.1080/0735648X.2014.967965

Roberto, K. A. (2016). The complexities of elder abuse. *American Psychologist*, *71*(4), 302–311. doi:10.1037/a0040259

Sachet-Milliat, A., Baïada-Hirèche, L., & Bourcier-Béquaert, B. (2017). The clear conscience of the controversial sector marketer: A neutralization theory approach. *Recherche et Applications en Marketing* (English Edition), *32*(3), 28–48. doi:10.1177/2051570717706828

Schreier, A., Pogue, J. K., & Hansen, D. J. (2017). Impact of child sexual abuse on non-abused siblings: A review with implications for research and practice. *Aggression and Violent Behavior*, *34*, 254–262. doi:10.1016/j.avb.2016.11.011

Shamaskin-Garroway, A. M., Giordano, N., & Blakley, L. (2017). Addressing elder sexual abuse: The critical role for integrated care. *Translational Issues in Psychological Science*, *3*(4), 410–422. doi:10.1037/tps0000145

Staub, E. (2012). The origins and inhibiting influences in genocide, mass killing, and other collective violence. In M. Breen-Smith (Ed.), *The Ashgate research companion to political violence* (pp. 205–223). Routledge.

Staub, E. (2014). Obeying, joining, following, resisting, and other processes in the Milgram studies, and in the Holocaust and other genocides: Situations, personality, and bystanders. *Journal of Social Issues*, *70*(3), 501–514. doi:10.1111/josi.12074

Talbot, D., & Boiral, O. (2015). Strategies for climate change and impression management: A case study among Canada's large industrial emitters. *Journal of Business Ethics*, *132*, 329–346. doi:10.1007/s10551-014-2322-5

Tener, D. (2018). The secret of intrafamilial child sexual abuse: Who keeps it and how? *Journal of Child Sexual Abuse*, *27*(1), 1–21. doi:10.1080/10538712.2017.1397015

Üngör, U. Ü. (Ed.) (2016). *Genocide: New perspectives on its causes, courses, and consequences*. Amsterdam University Press. doi:10.1515/9789048518654

Vollhardt, J. R., & Bilewicz, M. (2013). After the genocide: Psychological perspectives on victim, bystander, and perpetrator groups. *Journal of Social Issues*, *69*(1), 1–15. doi:10.1111/josi.12000

Whyte, D. (2016). It's common sense, stupid! Corporate crime and techniques of neutralization in the automobile industry. *Crime, Law and Social Change*, *66*, 165–181. doi:10.1007/s10611-016-9616-8

PART 3
EPILOGUE

9

"EVIL" Spelled Backwards Is . . .?

You will have probably noticed that each of the previous eight chapters has begun with a question for you to consider. Some may have left you feeling a bit ambushed, so let's let this chapter's title serve as a "softball question." We'll return to it later, but I want to focus first on the answers to questions about evil that this book has tried to offer you. I also want to address some other questions that may have occurred to you in response to those very answers.

The Basic Principles of "Evil"

Part 1 of this book—the first four chapters—was theoretical, but grounded wherever possible in relevant research. As a set, these chapters introduced key principles intended to help you better understand evil in its various forms.

For example, Chapter 1 offered an answer to the question "What is 'evil'?" from a psychological perspective. The answer? "Evil" is a label that people are most likely to apply when the behavior in question is seen as (1) *intentionally* producing (2) *harm* that is (3) judged to be *unjustifiable*. All three of these prototypic features of "evil" are important, but the third is especially so. After all, whereas harm and intent can be easy to establish, there is often an impressive lack of consensus concerning the justifiability of specific actions. Predictably, differences of opinion are most likely to emerge between the doer and everyone else. Although this may sound like a common-sense observation, it is not a trivial one: It reflects the fact that *most people don't want to see themselves—or be seen by others—as "evil."*

Chapters 2 and 3 delved into why this is so, making use of an ancient story as an object lesson: After murdering his own brother Abel and subsequently being marked and shunned by God, Cain's reaction was a mix of shame and desperation. It's a reaction consistent with research suggesting that people have a hard-wired need to feel accepted by and connected to *at least* some other people—so much so that the experience of being rejected can be physically painful. Being labeled "evil," then, is the psychological equivalent of

Evil in Mind. Christopher T. Burris, Oxford University Press. © Oxford University Press 2022.
DOI: 10.1093/oso/9780197637180.003.0009

being branded with *the Mark of Cain*. It is the ultimate signifier of social exclusion.

People may be especially averse to being accused of "evil" because there's a natural pull toward explaining "evil" behavior in terms of evil characteristics. That is, by definition, "evil" behavior can't be excused based on circumstances. Rather, "evil" behavior comes from "evil" people. And what are evildoers like? Their stereotypic characteristics are neatly summarized in the myth of pure evil (MOPE): Among other things, evildoers are assumed to be evil through-and-through and essentially unchangeable. Thus, given their supposedly unrelenting capacity to inflict unjustifiable harm, evildoers pose the ultimate threat—which can, in turn, be embraced as the ultimate justification for attempting to resist, punish, or destroy them. Moreover, as our exploration of certain understandings of demonic possession and exorcism revealed, evildoers don't have to be human, or even visible.

So the Mark of Cain is a big deal, for being labeled "evil" can have consequences that most of us would rather not face. People will therefore often go to great lengths to avoid either seeing themselves or being seen by others as "evil," and they rely on a rather broad menu of strategies in their attempts to ensure this.

For example, people may attempt to conceal or deny their questionable behavior. When the audience is other people, this can include simple lying as well as more elaborate cover-ups involving scapegoats. When the audience is oneself, this can include such seemingly exotic mechanisms as motivated forgetting, whereby an individual may be able to claim—*honestly*—that "I don't remember [doing that harmful thing]."

If a person cannot deny or cover up their involvement in a harmful outcome, there are other options. For example, one can attempt to deflect attention away from, or reduce the significance of, the harm itself. Alternatively, one can attempt to decrease the perceived intentionality of the behavior. This can include proactive measures to reduce one's sense of agency (such as ingesting chemicals) so that one might be able to assert to oneself and others that "I was not myself [or in control of my behavior] when I did that harmful thing."

On many occasions, attempts to minimize perceived harm or intentions may be so transparent that they appear ridiculous. In such instances, justifying harmful intentions and outcomes is the fallback. Broadly speaking, justifications can be of the "I am good" variety or the "I am not bad" variety.

The key to "I am good" messaging is to frame the harmful act as not being the product of self-interest, but instead as in the service of a greater good that transcends the wants and needs of both oneself and the target: "This is bigger than you and me, and it's the right thing to do." In contrast, "I am not bad" justifications take a few steps down from the moral high ground. There's no attempt to deny self-interest. Indeed, when justifying harmful behavior, the focus is squarely on *what has happened* or *what could happen* to oneself. For example, seeing oneself as having been harmed by others can evoke the motive to strike back—that is, revenge. Alternatively, it can create a sense of being "hard done by" and a felt need for compensation that can stoke the motive to *strike forward*—that is, to treat innocent others in an abusive or exploitative fashion. Or else, even if nothing bad has happened, *it could unless the "real" evildoers are dealt with* beforehand. In each of these instances, the goal is to offer a "good enough" reason for causing harm—good enough to avoid condemnation by either conscience or outside observers.

Although these strategies focus on dismantling the three features of prototypic "evil" behavior (harm, intent, inadequate justification), there are other approaches. For example, the framing of so-called moral licensing is: "Sure, I did this bad thing, but the good I've done elsewhere should more than make up for it." Or else the behavior is acknowledged as harmful, but it's also normalized in the sense of being "no worse than what other people do." Or else nastiness is touted to support a claim that one is unfazed by others' judgments and fully capable of unleashing even more mayhem on them.

However different these various approaches may appear at first glance, they can all be seen as *attempts to deflect or neutralize the Mark of Cain*. That is, the core message from the wrongdoer to an audience is: "You shouldn't reject or exclude me." Some add: ". . . because you risk being seen as small-minded, heartless, and hypocritical if you do." Others add: ". . . but if you do, know that I could *really* make your lives miserable." The importance of Mark of Cain dynamics when attempting to understand evil simply cannot be overstated.

The other key idea, introduced in Chapter 4, was the MioMa principle. That is, people choose to engage in "evil" behavior when the expected net benefits to themselves or their ingroup outweigh any perceived costs to the victim(s): "I don't mind, and you don't matter (enough)." And what is the nature of "net benefits"? At the most basic level, I suggested that *people are chasing feelings*: Thus, like other behavior, "evil" action (or inaction) fits the formula: "If I do A, then B will happen. If B happens, then I will feel more of

C [positive feelings such as excitement or satisfaction] and/or less of D [negative feelings such as fear, disgust, or shame]."

Without a doubt, there is a measure of rationality in this decision-making process—but only a measure, for chasing feelings often creates a kind of tunnel vision wherein "the costliness of the costs" that could befall self and others are overlooked or minimized relative to the glittering prizes that await. Before-the-fact justifications can be used to deal with whatever other points of resistance may remain. Moreover, moving through the world with an *insatiable appetite for positive feelings* and an *intolerance of negative feelings* can amp up MioMa dynamics even further.

Recognizing the Basic Principles Among Some of Evil's "Usual Suspects"

In the four chapters were featured in Part 2, we explored a number of phenomena that would likely appear way up on many people's list of contenders for the "evil" label. My intent was to show you that even the most extreme instances of evil can be better understood by making use of the core principles laid out in Part 1.

For example, if understood as "wanting a target to experience harm," *hate* encompasses two of the three features of prototypic evil: intentionality and harm (see Chapter 5). Thus, to avoid the dreaded Mark of Cain—being seen as "evil"—haters should be especially motivated to disguise or justify their harmful intentions, with some going so far as to call hate "love." And whether a hater is willing to hurt someone else in the hopes of getting a sense of sweet revenge or temporarily quashing the fear of being abandoned, for example, hate clearly follows the MioMa principle.

Whenever a person intends to make another being suffer—or wants to learn about someone else doing the same—as a means of experiencing pleasure, excitement, or satisfaction, *sadism* is present (see Chapter 6). Given its brazen self-focus—hurting someone because it's fun or arousing, for example—sadistic motivation is arguably the ultimate incarnation of the MioMa principle. As an unnervingly unjustifiable form of hate, it's no surprise that people intending to stay in an intimate relationship seem particularly reluctant to explain a partner's harm-causing behavior in sadistic terms. It also shouldn't be surprising that sadistic tendencies are part of the evildoer stereotype (that is, the MOPE). Moreover, research (e.g., Burris & Hood, 2020

[Canada]; Burris & Leitch, 2018 [Canada]) has demonstrated a link between sadistic motivation and Mark of Cain dynamics, in that the pursuit of positive feelings via harming others appears to be fueled by a deeper motivation to elevate the self in response to an indignant sense of being disrespected.

Despite their sensationalistic portrayal as a modern face of the MOPE, *serial killers'* motives appear rather mundane. Indeed, I made the case that sadism appears central for the vast majority (see Chapter 7). Moreover, despite displaying a black hole of disregard for their victims' well-being, serial killers will often go to great lengths to justify their own actions and highlight their positive qualities. Thus, the MioMa principle/chasing feelings and Mark of Cain dynamics once again appear to be indisputably relevant.

This was also the case when we shifted our focus from individuals to *groups* and specifically examined corporate corruption, genocidal campaigns, and abusive family systems (see Chapter 8). The main difference between such groups versus individuals operating independently is groups' capacity to make use of collaborative division of labor to mass-produce harm and devise and execute Mark of Cain deflection strategies. The motives are basically the same: People want to feel a certain way, and they're sometimes willing to hurt someone else in the process, and they don't want to be seen—by self or others—as (too) bad if that happens.

Some Things That Might Be Bothering You

You may be thinking: *"What I just read sounds simplistic. It doesn't really tell me why [insert bad thing] happened."* Let me make a couple of comments in response to this. First, it wasn't my intent in this book to map out ALL of the possible influences that might lead a *specific* individual, in a *specific* time and place, to choose a course of action that causes harm. Indeed, if I could do that, I would probably have the full attention of everyone from intelligence agencies to suspicious partners. Instead, my goal was to show you where to look (cf. Deepak & Ramdoss, 2021 [India]).

So, for example, when I wrote that people who engage in evil behavior are "chasing feelings," I wasn't trying to sound pointlessly vague. Instead, I was aiming for flexible and comprehensive: Although a perpetrator's behavior may crush, horrify, or infuriate you, it must have seemed like a "good (enough) idea at the time" to them. In other words, the hoped-for good feelings outweighed any anticipated bad feelings. Like it or not, you and I and "that monstrous evildoer over there" have this in common. Were this not so, evil would have to remain forever mysterious. But the very fact that I wrote this book should tell you that I don't believe that that's the way it has to be.

Second, some readers might recall American figure skater Nancy Kerrigan's anguished "Why, why, WHY?!" following "The Whack Heard 'Round the World" in 1994. The straightforward answer to Kerrigan's question is that individuals linked to a rival skater conspired to injure Kerrigan with the goal of eliminating her as a competitive threat (Brennan, 2014). But we must come to terms with the fact that, on many occasions, people who ask "Why?" are not expressing idle curiosity or simply thirsting for intellectual fulfillment. Instead, "Why?" is punchy shorthand for "This horrible thing *shouldn't have happened* (to me)." In those moments, explanations centering on the MioMa principle and the Mark of Cain may feel hollow and unsatisfying at best—and insulting at worst.

Indeed, *feeling* arguably plays at least as big a role in the labeling of "evil" as it does in the actual *doing* of it. Very simply, if something doesn't make us feel bad—whether it's the moans of the suffering or a creepy basement—we probably won't label it "evil." That very feeling can hamper our ability to appreciate a fact-based answer to the "Why?" question, however, and this can make "they did it because they're evil" seem like a much more satisfying explanation.

"[THAT thing you talked about] isn't really evil. You should have talked about [THIS thing]." I'd suggest that a reaction like this reinforces the importance of focusing on the core principles, because it's actually a beautiful illustration of the usefulness of the three-feature model of prototypic "evil" behavior that I laid out in Chapter 1. That is, if you *truly* think that a specific behavior or course of action ISN'T "evil," then my guess is that you perceive it as: (1) not harmful enough; (2) not intentional/controllable; and/or (3) ultimately justifiable, on whatever grounds that may seem relevant to you. And, chances are, you don't feel angry, or afraid, or disgusted, or humiliated (enough) when you think about it. Of course, there's another reason why we may be reluctant to label someone else's problematic behavior as "evil": We do it, too. Thus, if we label others, we ought to label ourselves. And so we're right back in Mark of Cain territory, scrambling to explain why it isn't really a big deal, why it's different in our case, etc.

"The 21st-century world is an online world. You didn't talk much about that." That's true, on both counts, although I briefly mentioned some research relevant to online pranking and trolling, as well as cyberbullying and

cyberstalking, in Chapters 4 and 6. Rather than attempting a standalone (and probably quickly outdated) overview of relevant research, I think it's more prudent to focus your attention on principles. Specifically, there are a number of features of online environments that can magnify the applicability and impact of the core principles of evil that I've presented in this book. Let's consider a few of these.

First, recall work by Rauxloh (2016 [UK]) and Collins (2013 [USA]) in Chapter 8 concerning the internal resistance that perpetrators oftentimes must overcome in order to harm others during face-to-face confrontations. Online environments can render such resistance irrelevant by allowing for *anonymity*. Thus, it's possible for "randomusernameA" to attack "randomusernameB" without any of the messiness associated with face-to-face confrontation. The MioMa principle can reign supreme while the threat of the Mark of Cain can no longer evoke much dread—for perpetrators, at least.

For victims, it's a very different story. Besides affording perpetrators the option of remaining anonymous, online environments can endow attacks with unprecedented levels of *speed*, *breadth*, and *longevity*. The era in which a person could relocate, leave the past behind, and get a fresh start has largely passed. Instead, despite the promises of for-profit "Internet scrubbers," online words and images that could harm an individual can spread worldwide quickly—and then stay there (see Roos, 2016 [USA]). Consequently, attacks need not be face-to-face to inflict catastrophic damage on vulnerable individuals, as evidenced by the clear link between various forms of cyberbullying and suicide risk among children, adolescents, and adults (see Stevens et al., 2021 [UK] and van Geel et al., 2014 [Netherlands]).

To give you a better understanding of how even minor online rejection cues can trigger Mark of Cain dynamics, consider the "Cyberball" studies by Williams et al. (2000 [Australia]). Participants learned that Cyberball is an online game in which they themselves and two other players can toss a virtual ball back and forth to one another. Some participants received a fair number of throws from the other two players, whereas others were not thrown to at all. Unbeknownst to participants, the two other players were not real—instead, their "throws" were, in fact, pre-programmed and intended to create a sense of either inclusion or exclusion among actual study participants. And how effective was this? Williams et al. remarked that it was "rather astounding that despite the fact that [their] participants did not know, could not see, could not communicate with, and were not anticipating future interaction with 'virtual others,' they felt ostracized when these others neglected to throw them a virtual disc or ball" (p. 759).

And why is this? The inclusion–exclusion concerns that make the Mark of Cain sting likely stem from our historical need to rely on others of our own species in order to survive (see Baumeister & Leary, 1995 [USA]). The more closely a psychological process is linked to basic survival needs, the more likely it is monitored and regulated by "stupid" (that is, unsophisticated) parts of the brain. Stupid parts of the brain often respond to *approximations* of stimuli, so when a pair of invisible, computer-generated playmates seemingly don't want to play with us . . . well, that's close enough to being rejected by real, face-to-face others to generate a negative reaction in us.

" 'EVIL' spelled backwards is 'LIVE.' So what?" Although it's a coincidental artifact of my writing in English, the EVIL ←→ LIVE reversal is a useful reminder that a central feature of the evil prototype—harm—manifests, at the extreme, as the destruction of vitality. Indeed, remember in the old story that the Mark of Cain emerged from the unjustifiable taking of life. The EVIL ←→ LIVE reversal is also reminiscent of the centrality of inversion (typically of "the sacred") within some variants of satanic philosophy and practice (see Shakespeare & Scott, 2015 [UK]). More practically, as long as you or I LIVE, it's pretty much guaranteed that dark-mirrored EVIL will be a part of our existence. It's there any time we are confronted with other people's behavior that we think matches evil's three prototypic features. And, just as importantly, it's there any time other people perceive the same match in *our* behavior.

That last point probably made you feel uncomfortable. Again. I can't really fault you for that. It makes me uncomfortable, too.

So let's make the optimistic assumption, you and I, that we'd both like to be a little less evil. Do we have a chance in hell (so to speak) of doing this? Let's work it through, again based on the core principles.

It's unrealistic to think that we can just stop chasing feelings because *the consequences of chasing feelings make us* feel *bad.* Hopefully you got the irony there: It's a loop from which we cannot escape. Likewise, it's unrealistic to think that we can simply eliminate the impact that the Mark of Cain has on us, for it appears to be so hard-wired (see Burris et al., 2020 [Canada]) that even those who assert that they're not bothered seem to do so *because* they're bothered (see Chapter 3).

Instead, I think that we need to be a bit more self-reflective and creative. So if we *know* that we chase feelings, then: (1) We're in a better position to map how our intermediate goals relate to our feeling goals; and (2) we can seek out alternate (non-MioMa) means of pursuing those goals. To illustrate, let's look at sadism. In Chapter 6, I made the case that sadism seems to be driven, at least in part, by simmering anger and a sense that one has been disrespected. Thus, for some, engineering or witnessing another's pain or humiliation can feel good because it affords them the opportunity to lift themselves up by feeling cleverer and more in control than the victims, for example. Armed with this understanding, people can choose to deal with their anger issues directly and develop strategies for feeling more respected that do not hinge on others' suffering.

Likewise, if we *know* that we feel pushed to deflect the Mark of Cain, we're in a better position to ask ourselves hard questions about our own past or future behavior. The three-feature model of "evil" behavior even gives us a sort of worksheet to guide our questions (see Chapter 3). Consider *harm*, for example: When contemplating a course of action, have you *really* thought through the possible negative consequences—for you and for others, both long-term and short-term? Or has "tunnel vision" and a sense of invulnerability clouded your judgment? With respect to *intention*, are you lucid enough in the moment to be deciding and acting? Could you even be deliberately sabotaging your capacity to have a sense of control over your behavior? Regarding *justifications*, we have an amazing capacity for coming up with all sorts of "good" reasons for why we do things. But "good" reasons are often not the *real* reasons. What would your Hidden Observer say (see Chapter 5)?

You've Reached the End, But We Haven't

I'd love to be able to offer you something really inspirational here—you know, words that generate a nod, a tear, and maybe a slow clap before we rush back out onto the playing field of the world to defeat evil with our goodness.

I can't do that.

The world through which we walk is not so much a playing field as a *minefield* of moral dilemmas. Choosing "the greater good" can sometimes seem like an unimaginable luxury amidst an array of barely distinguishable "bads." And there's always at least one audience—the one inside our own heads.

But evil is not really all that mysterious. You and I and the world's greatest evildoers are pushed and pulled by the same basic motives, and we make use of the same bag of tricks when giving account of our choices.

Once that realization really soaks in, I think that we're—maybe, possibly, perhaps—in a better position to choose less evil as we move through the world.

At least, we can try.

I hope this book has helped.

References

Baumeister, R. F., & Leary, M. R. (1995). The need to belong: Desire for interpersonal attachments as a fundamental human motivation. *Psychological Bulletin, 117*, 497–529. doi:10.1037/0033-2909.117.3.497

Brennan, C. (2014, January 2). Tonya, Nancy reflect on "The Whack Heard 'Round the World." https://www.usatoday.com/story/sports/olympics/2014/01/02/christine-brennan-tonya-harding-nancy-kerrigan/4294753/

Burris, C. T., & Hood, T. W. (2020, June). *Bitter taste in YOUR mouth: Aversive flavour experiences assigned by ostensible others evoke sadistic aggression*. Poster to be presented at Conference of the Consortium of European Research on Emotion (CERE), Granada, Spain. (Postponed due to COVID-19 pandemic)

Burris, C. T., & Leitch, R. (2018). Harmful fun: Pranks and sadistic motivation. *Motivation and Emotion, 42*(7), 90–102. doi:10.1007/s11031-017-9651-5

Burris, C. T., Rempel, J. K., & Viscontas, T. (2020). Sins of the flesh: Subliminal approval by God or people decreases endorsement of hedonistic sex. *Psychology of Religion and Spirituality, 12*(2), 223–230. doi:10.1037/rel0000267

Collins, R. (2013). Entering and leaving the tunnel of violence: Micro-sociological dynamics of emotional entrainment in violent interactions. *Current Sociology, 61*(2), 132-151. doi:10.1177/0011392112456500

Deepak, S. A., & Ramdoss, S. (2021). The life-course theory of serial killing: A motivation model. *International Journal of Offender Therapy and Comparative Criminology, 65*(13–14), 1446–1472. doi:10.1177/0306624X20981030

Rauxloh, R. E. (2016). Group offending in mass atrocities: Proposing a group violence strategies model for international crimes. *Oñati Socio-legal Series, 6*(4), 1016–1031.

Roos, D. (2016, April 21). Can you scrub bad press from the Internet? https://computer.howstuffworks.com/internet/social-networking/networks/can-you-scrub-bad-press-the-internet.htm

Shakespeare, S., & Scott, N. (2015). The swarming logic of inversion and the elevation of Satan. *Helvete: A Journal of Black Metal Theory, 2*, 1–11.

Stevens, F., Nurse, J. R. C., & Arief, B. (2021). Cyber stalking, cyber harassment, and adult mental health: A systematic review. *Cyberpsychology, Behavior, and Social Networking, 24*(6), 367–376. doi:10.1089/cyber.2020.0253

van Geel, M., Vedder, P., & Tanilon, J. (2014). Relationship between peer victimization, cyberbullying, and suicide in children and adolescents: A meta-analysis. *JAMA Pediatrics, 168*(5), 435–442. doi:10.1001/jamapediatrics.2013.4143

Williams, K. D., Cheung, C. K., & Choi, W. (2000). Cyberostracism: Effects of being ignored over the Internet. *Journal of Personality and Social Psychology, 79*(5), 748–762. doi:10.1037/0022-3514.79.5.748

Index

For the benefit of digital users, indexed terms that span two pages (e.g., 52–53) may, on occasion, appear on only one of those pages.